The Bots
>p. 29

Abuse
Standards
Violations
>p. 49

Hannah
Uncut
>p. 113

Personal
Photographs
>p. 87

Portraits
>p. 101

Eva & Franco Mattes
Dear Imaginary Audience,

fotomuseum winterthur
Spector Books

Dear Imaginary Audience,

Doris Gassert

If anything could have prepared us for the reality of a global pandemic that has us glued to our screens day in, day out, we might be tempted to point to the artistic works of Eva & Franco Mattes.

Since the mid-1990s, the artist duo have been investigating the networked condition that many of us have been experiencing more consciously and incessantly in these past months, as our social lives have been for the most part reduced to, and at the same time enabled by, the internet.

In fact, almost a year into the "new normal" and with the exhibition opening postponed to an uncertain future date, I am scared to think that even the title that Eva & Franco Mattes suggested for their show at Fotomuseum Winterthur might prove to have taken on an all too literal meaning.

Dear Imaginary Audience, points to the pervasive presence and dominant status of photography in the twenty-first century.

Circulating through digital channels and online platforms, the **networked image** [>p. 136] presents a radical shift in photographic practices – an expansion, subversion and complete reconfiguration that can be traced through the works of Eva & Franco Mattes.

Positioning the spectator in a physical relationship with the screen and at the centre of their explorations, the artist duo meticulously dissect the internet's effects on our daily lives, behaviours and practices, while demonstrating that the networked image brings with it not only the reconfiguration of the subject qua spectator online but also the gradual restructuring of the visible and imaginary in the age of **social media** [>p. 138] as well as new exploitative forms of labour in a globalised (image) economy.

In *Dear Imaginary Audience,* Eva & Franco Mattes leave no doubt that today's (image) world is predominantly an economic endeavour, one in which the circulation of networked images and the attention they constantly demand from us are entangled in different value systems.

For one thing, there is the reality of social media and the effects of an online audience whose imaginary gaze is deeply ingrained not only in today's habitual photographic practices but in how we perceive ourselves and the world.

As the artist, curator and writer Aria Dean points out, "every single networked human being now exists under this condition of ... living, watching, being watched, watching yourself watch others" – a state in which "we are each the constant voyeuristic subject and object, both surveilled and surveyor".[1]

Trapped in this networked condition, the **imaginary audience**[>p. 135] is no longer a figment in our minds invented by the ego, as the original psychological term implied.

Instead, the omnipresent acknowledgment and social crediting through clicks, likes and **shares**[>p. 137] online increasingly makes our self-image, self-definition and self-worth dependent on the gaze – and judgement – of others.

This forms the backdrop to the thousands of photographs displayed in *Hannah Uncut* (2021), a new work commissioned by Fotomuseum Winterthur.

As much as photography has always been a performative space of negotiation of our self-images and a site of projection of our cultural imaginaries, Hannah's photographs show that the creation and curation of our networked self has significantly infiltrated our day-to-day performances for the camera.

The gaze she directs on herself is often self-examinatory and at times self-mocking, and we might eventually find an authentic portrait of Hannah in the many forgotten or neglected images of her extensive archive.

Yet there are many cases in which online representation results in the standardisation of (exchangeable) appearances, sacrificing individuality for the sake of instantaneous attention through sexualised and seductive visual triggers.

This is reflected not only in the Instagram feeds of today's influencers but also in Eva & Franco Mattes's avatar *Portraits* (2006–2007) and the beauty standards that are re-enacted by **users**[>p. 138] online.

With increased standardisation and mass circulation online comes a decline in the value and relevance of content. Summarised as "images without viewers"[2] by the political theorist Jodi Dean, who is also a contributor to this book[>p. 34], this becomes evident in Eva & Franco Mattes's site-specific installation *Personal Photographs* (2019–).

The intertwined network of cable trays leaves the viewers with no images, not even their visible traces, exposing the abstractness of data circulation.

1 Aria Dean, "Closing the Loop", *The New Inquiry Magazine* 50 (March 2016), https://thenewinquiry.com/closing-the-loop
   (all URLs accessed on 30 December 2020).
2 Jodi Dean, "Images without Viewers", *Still Searching …* (blog), Fotomuseum Winterthur, 6 January 2016,
   https://www.fotomuseum.ch/en/explore/still-searching/articles/26418_images_without_viewers.

We might even say that highlighting this
infrastructure, which has become an integral yet
hidden part of today's architecture, materialises
Dean's claim that the "message is simply part of
a circulating data stream.
Its particular content is irrelevant.
Who sent it is irrelevant.
Who receives it is irrelevant.
That it need be responded to is irrelevant.
The only thing that is relevant is circulation,
the addition to the pool."[3]
In what Dean calls "communicative capitalism", the
exchange value, not the use value, is the
determining factor: "A contribution need not be
understood; it need only be repeated, reproduced,
forwarded."[4]

Circulation can be understood as the primary mode of both the
image and capital, as media theorist Jonathan Beller has
pointed out.[5]
Yet as the term infrastructure implies, the technology of
circulation exerts power beneath the visible surface
level, where it "imperceptibly shapes our emotions,
memories, fears and desires".[6]
Eva & Franco Mattes reverse the order by
materialising the network through a construction
of yellow cable trays that wind through the entire
exhibition venue of Fotomuseum Winterthur.
"In navigating real space and contending with
pre-existing structures, it mirrors the
assimilation of the internet's operations into
everyday life," Eva & Franco Mattes say.
Furthermore, "it 'reprograms the museum' by
changing the circulation of people within it."

It's not that in this infrastructure the viewer becomes
obsolete.
Rather, it is here that the spectator is reconfigured –
or "programmed" – as a labourer of today's
networked economy in which "human attention is
productive of value".[7]
It is not surprising that big online
corporations like Facebook or Google want more
and more of our **attention**[>p. 136] now that they
have capitalised our gaze.

Eva & Franco Mattes's investigations on the topic of
digital labour reveal that it is often either unconscious –
sourced from the clicks and scrolls of online users –
or hidden behind the surface of our image world, as is
the case with **content moderation**[>p. 133].

3 Jodi Dean, "Communicative Capitalism: Circulation and the Foreclosure of Politics", in *Cultural Politics: An International Journal* 1 (March 2005), p. 51–74, here: p. 58.
4 Jodi Dean, *Democracy and Other Neoliberal Fantasies: Communicative Capitalism and Left Politics* (Durham, NC: Duke University Press), p. 27.
5 Jonathan Beller, *The Cinematic Mode of Production: Attention Economy and the Society of the Spectacle* (Hanover, NH: Dartmouth College Press, 2006).
6 Eva & Franco Mattes, in conversation with José Freire, Team Gallery, Los Angeles.
7 Jonathan Beller, "Paying Attention: The Commodification of the Sensorium", in "Shadows", *Cabinet Magazine*, no. 24 (Winter 2006–2007).

Either way, it is based on exploitative structures governed by big online corporations that exert their power on the realm of perception through mechanisms that remain hidden from view.
The Bots (2020), *Dark Content* (2015) and *Abuse Standards Violations* (2016–) make us aware of the horrifying imagery – that goes beyond anything that we can imagine – and the psychological strain of content moderation, in which an invisible workforce bears responsibility for looking through and deleting discriminating, violent and objectionable content so that you and I don't have to.

In *BEFNOED* (2014–), our own voyeuristic drives, and thus our willingness to exploit and be exploited in the attention economy, are put on display as they literally force us to our knees.
By placing screens in such a way that to see their surface requires active physical engagement, we are meant to crawl, bend and stretch to engage with the content they show.
What we see, finally, are absurd performances that Eva & Franco Mattes **crowdsourced** [>p. 135] by contracting gig workers online, thereby employing the very structures of the **gig economy** [>p. 135] that they in turn subvert, dissect and criticise – a common artistic strategy they employ.
The capitalist sadism that thrives on the precarity of labour, often outsourced to developing and emerging countries, is ultimately exposed, just as the "imaginary audience" takes on yet another meaning: in accordance with the crowdsourcing platform's rules, the contractors qua performers receive no information about who has commissioned the videos or how they will be used.

How big is our desire and how far are we willing to go to find out what's on the screen?
And if our viewer engagement is hidden behind a simple click online, would anything change in terms of how we feel complicit or accountable?

Emily's Video (2012), finally, compiles the reactions of spectators who volunteered to watching "the worst video ever"[8] that the artists had sourced from the darknet.
The work exemplifies how spectatorship in the twenty-first century – this curious, often macabre mode of existence – reflects the many

8 Artists' description of the video in their open call.

facets of human behaviour that are triggered, spawned and accelerated by "the horrifying, funny, sick, banal and strange image cultures that find their home online", as curator and theorist Katrina Sluis points out in her contribution>p. 127 to this book.

With a darkly humorous edge, Eva & Franco Mattes transform the networked image condition into a unique spatial experience that is built on the premise of an audience that it envelops and mirrors.
Through carefully thought-out arrangements of screens, infrastructures and humans, their works break and reframe the spectators' habitual and often unconscious engagement with online content.
Forcing us into at times uncomfortable physical and moral positions, it is from here that our gaze is redirected to its modes and effects in the twenty-first century, and how it constitutes part of a network of exploitative structures and questionable forms of social behaviour in which we are all entangled.

Doris Gassert is Research Curator at Fotomuseum Winterthur and co-curator of the exhibition *Eva & Franco Mattes. Dear Imaginary Audience,*.

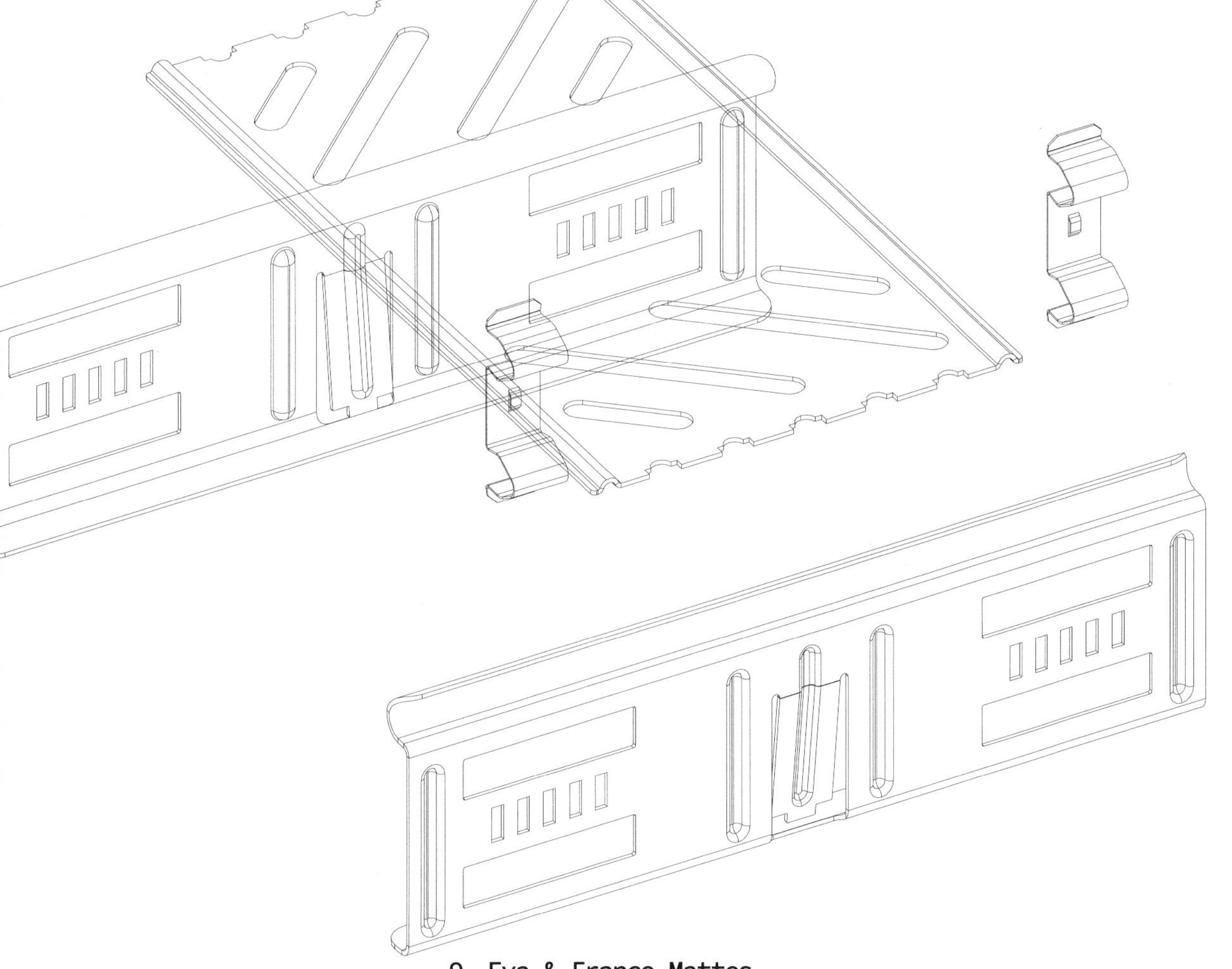

Half Cat, 2020
Ceiling Cat, 2016

No other images are shared and circulated online as often as those of cats, the fluffy favourites of the internet.
The taxidermic sculptures *Half Cat* and *Ceiling Cat* by Eva & Franco Mattes refer to so-called lolcat **memes**[>p. 136] – a social practice in which cat pictures with witty captions are shared millions of times on the internet.

High above the audience, the head of a tiny stuffed cat peeps out unobtrusively from a hole in the ceiling of the exhibition space.
The original meme which served as the inspiration for *Ceiling Cat* began circulating in the early 2000s, when it first appeared on the image-**sharing**[>p. 137] platform FunnyJunk.

In 2006, the sentence "Ceiling Cat is watching you masturbate" was added to the image: an insidious joke that evokes the dystopian figure of **Big Brother**[>p. 132] and turns the cat into a symbol of the omnipresent eye of the internet that monitors everything and of voyeuristic image consumption.

Half Cat is based on the image of a deformed cat with only two legs and no ears walking along a street.
It began circulating on the internet in 2010 with the caption "The longer you stare, the weirder it gets".
Since 2018 *Half Cat* has appeared online again with renewed intensity, increasingly under the Portuguese name Sinko Peso.

At first it was assumed that the strangely truncated image of the cat had been created by a technological error such as a Google Street View glitch or failed panorama shot, which is why the meme is often called *Panorama Fail Cat*.
Later, however, **users**[>pw. 138] of online forums were able to track down the original image of the four-legged cat with pointy ears, identifying its place of origin as Ottawa in Canada.
Half Cat's unusual form is thus the product of skilful photoshop editing.
Owing to the lack of clarity about its origins, *Half Cat* can be seen as a metaphor par excellence for the **networked image**[>p. 136] – for copies of images that are constantly on the move and constantly manipulated.

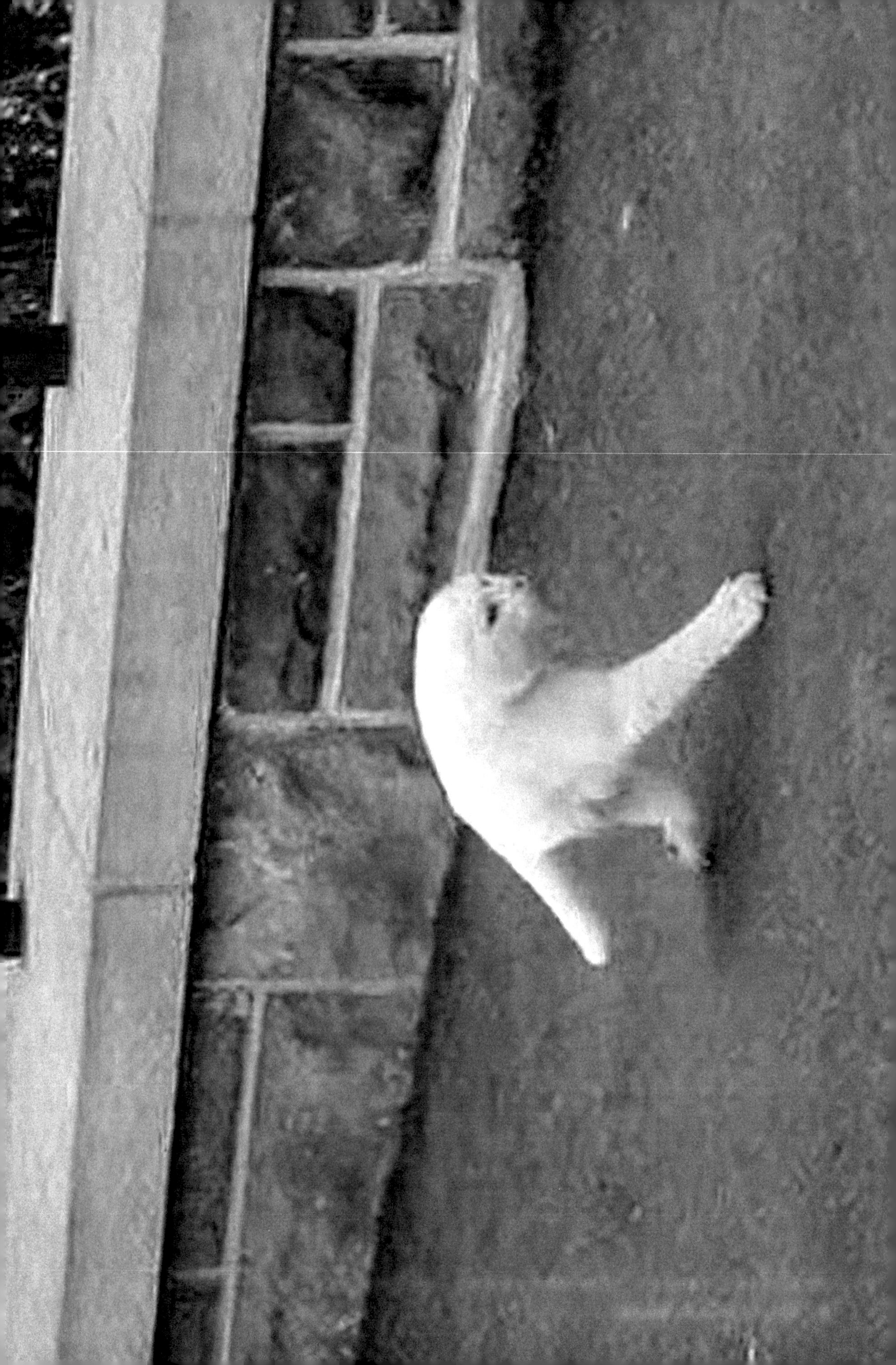

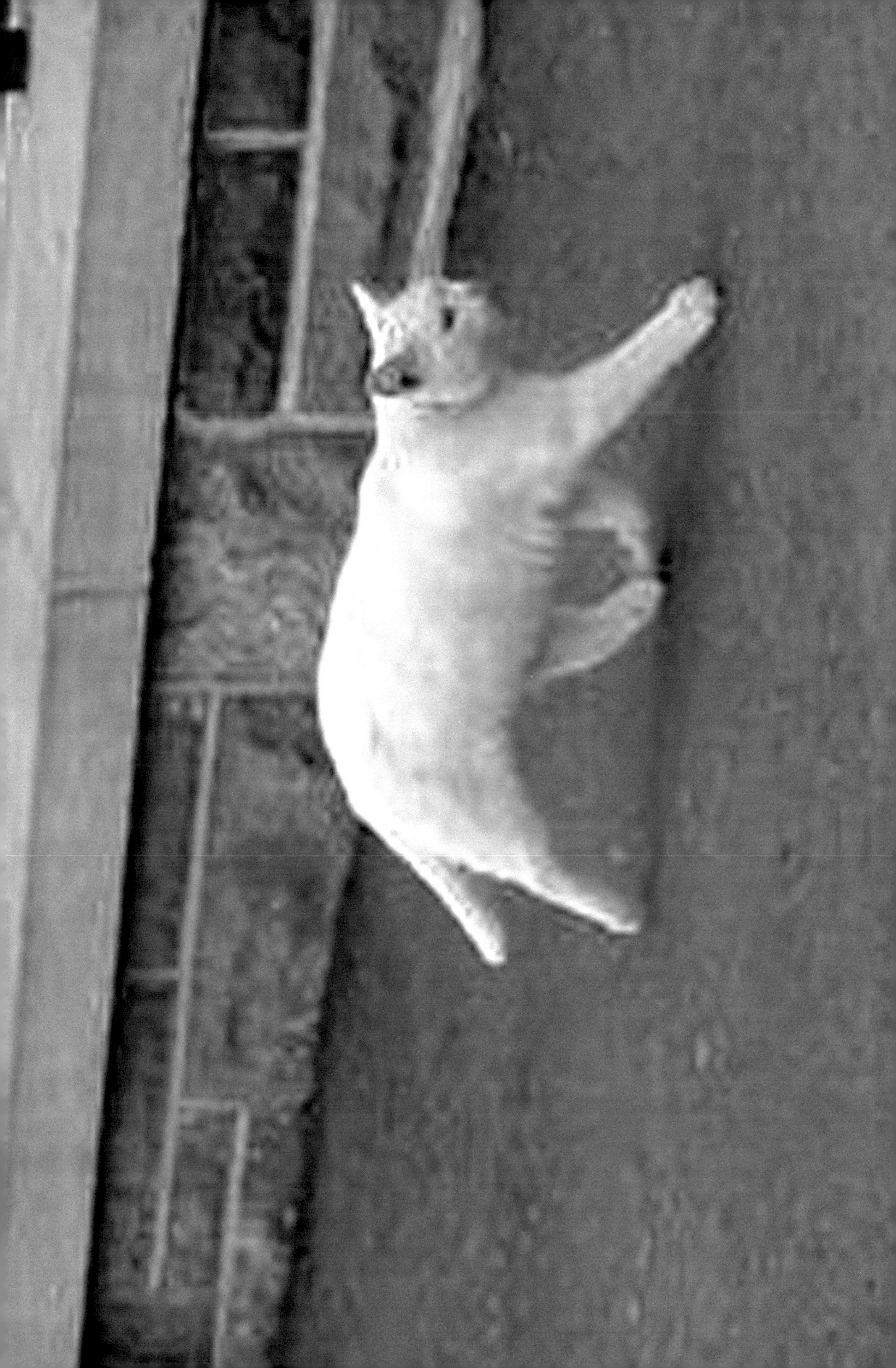

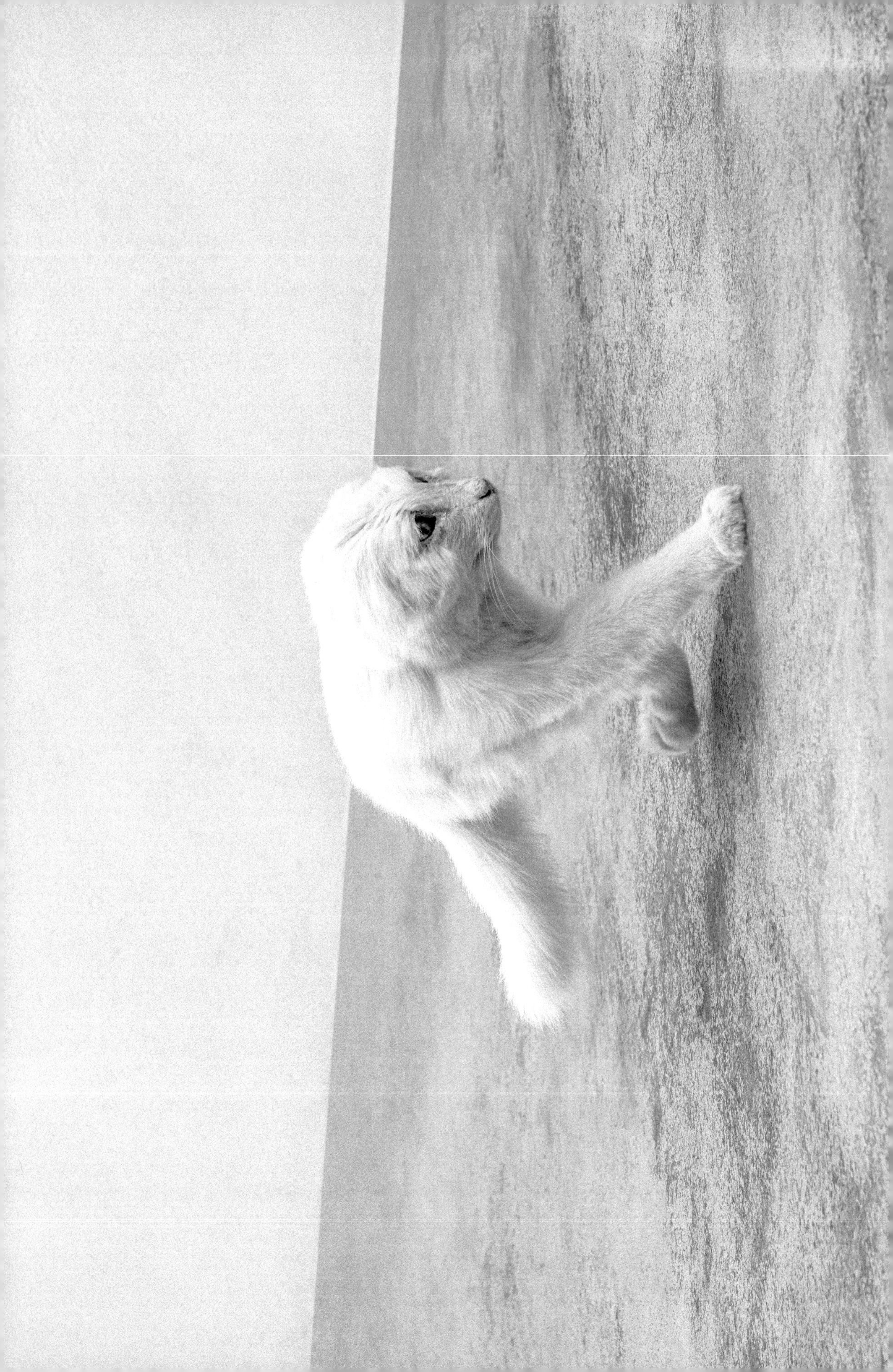

Catoptic according to Eva & Franco Mattes

Clément Chéroux

Rarely does a work of art have the power to startle. Yet this was the reaction provoked on countless occasions by Eva & Franco Mattes's *Ceiling Cat* when it was exhibited for more than four months at the Museum of Modern Art in San Francisco in 2019.[1]

One of the privileges of a curator is to be able to observe the effect that a work has on visitors. So whenever I had the opportunity, I would discreetly position myself in a corner of the room where the Mattes' cat was on display. Wide eyes, startled jumps, nervous little cries …: the discovery of *Ceiling Cat* – a tabby cat with big amber eyes, peeking through a hole in the ceiling – was usually marked by surprise. The sculpture is created from a real animal, an unfortunate road casualty, which a skilful taxidermist has preserved in this position. The hole is also an integral part of the work: next to the technical characteristics of the object – "Taxidermy cat, polyurethane resin" – the Mattes insist on adding the words "custom-made hole" in the work description. Within the museum space, this hole refers to the tradition of exploring the void established by artists such as Yves Klein, Robert Barry, Stanley Brouwn, Robert Irwin, Laurie Parsons and others.[2] *Ceiling Cat*, it should be pointed out, is inspired by a **meme** [>p. 136], one of the cultural tropes that circulate on the internet in the form of images accompanied by short texts with approximate spelling and which, by being appropriated, diverted and caricatured, end up signifying anything and everything.

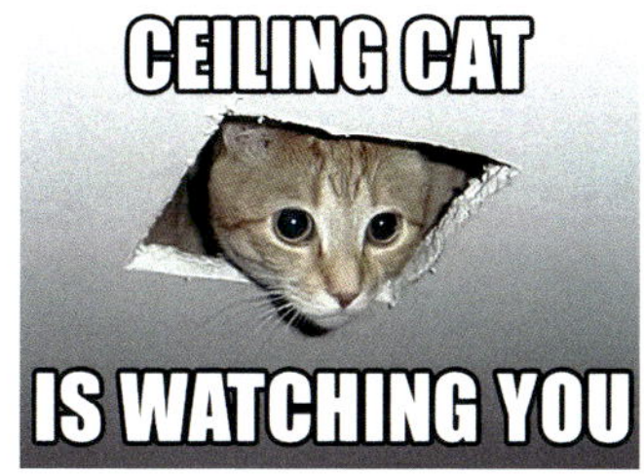

"Ceiling Cat" meme, anonymous.

1 "Meme-based sculpture" was the expression used by Eva & Franco Mattes during a Skype interview I conducted with them on 7 August 2020. The exhibition *snap+share: transmitting photographs from mail art to social networks* was held at SFMOMA from 30 March to 4 August 2019, curated by Clément Chéroux and assisted by Linde B. Lehtinen and Sally Martin Katz. At the end of the exhibition, the work was acquired by the museum and is now part of its collection.
2 See Laurent Le Bon et al., *Vides: Une rétrospective*, exh. cat. (Paris: Centre Pompidou, 2009).

Coined in 1976 by the biologist and evolutionary scientist Richard Dawkins, and modelled on the word "gene", it is a shortening of the Greek word *mimēma*, meaning "that which is imitated or simulated".

Since the time **social media**^{>p. 138} began to develop at the beginning of the twenty-first century, the meme has thrived.[3]

The author of the original photograph on which *Ceiling Cat* is based – first posted in 2003 on the comic image-**sharing**^{>p. 137} site FunnyJunk – is still unknown.[4]

The image went viral when it was published in combination with the text "Ceiling Cat is watching you" in 2006. Like many of the cats circulating on the internet, this one is both cute and disturbing at the same time.

This isn't the first time that Eva & Franco Mattes have employed the services of a taxidermist to transform a lolcat into a work of art.

In 2010, with *Catt*, a cat in a cage with a canary perched on top, they converted an image from the internet into a sculpture that they attribute to Maurizio Cattelan.

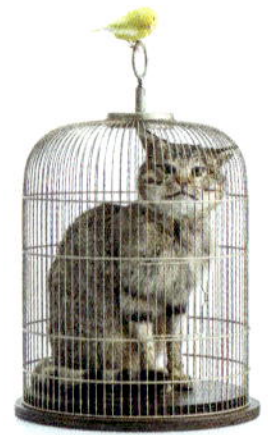
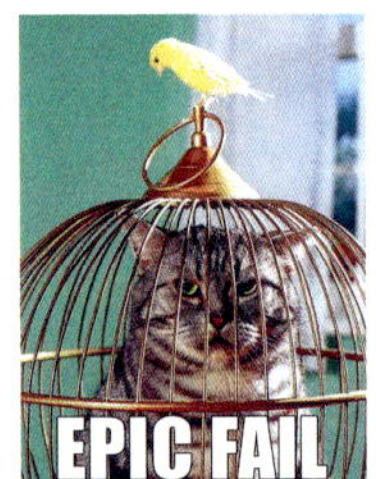

Eva & Franco Mattes, *Catt*, 2010.
"Epic fail" meme, anonymous.

Ceiling Cat dates from 2016.

The following year, their black cat sitting on a stack of three microwave ovens, in which hard disks are erased by radiation from the cooking process, refers to the persistence of the memory of traumatic internet images evoked in the meme "What has been seen cannot be unseen".

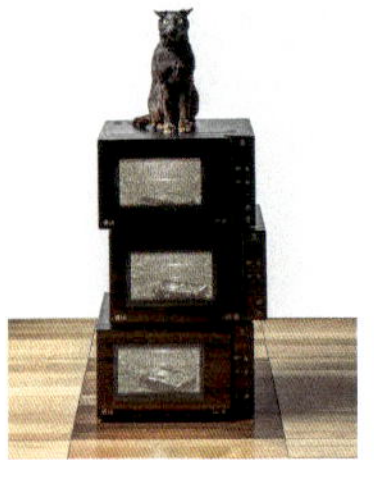
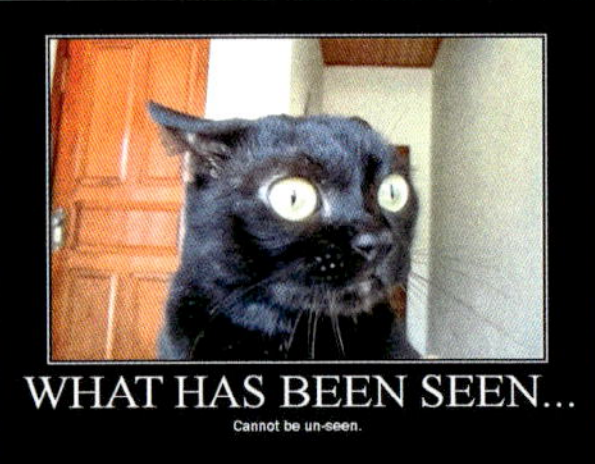

Eva & Franco Mattes, *What Has Been Seen*, 2017.
"What has been seen" meme, anonymous.

Finally, in 2020 with *Half Cat*, they exploit a digital image representing an anamorphic cat that has circulated widely on the internet with various captions.

3 See Richard Dawkins, *The Selfish Gene* (Oxford: Oxford University Press, 1989).
4 Information about the "Ceiling Cat" meme is taken from the website https://knowyourmeme.com/memes/ceiling-cat (accessed on 23 August 2020).

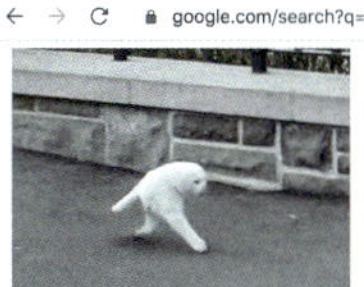
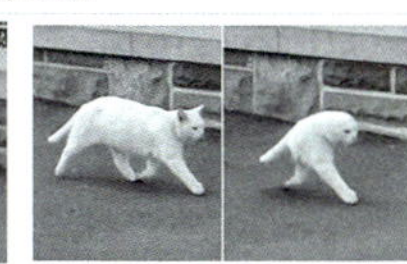
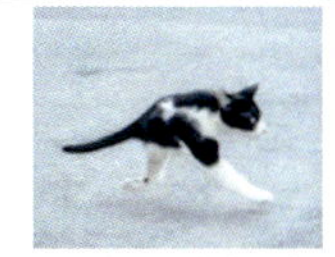
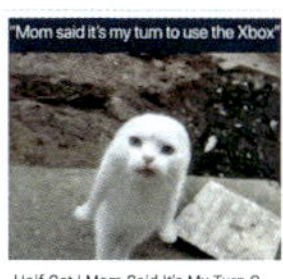

Revealed: The 'half-cat' not created by ...
independent.co.uk

Half-cat captured on Google Streetview ...
dailymail.co.uk

Weird and Warped World of the Half-...
catster.com

Half Cat | Mom Said It's My Turn O...
knowyourmeme.com

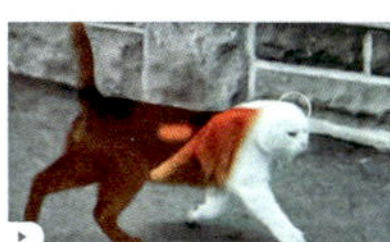
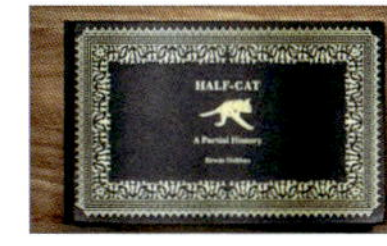
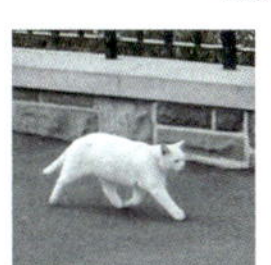
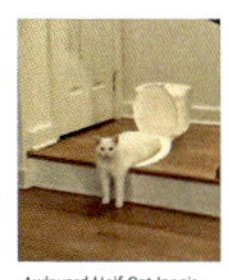

Half-Cat: The Documentary - Part 2 ...
youtube.com

HALF-CAT: A Partial History by Erwin ...
kickstarter.com

Half-cat captured on Google S...
dailymail.co.uk

Awkward Half-Cat Inspir...
boredpanda.com

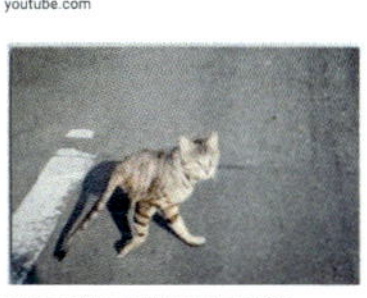
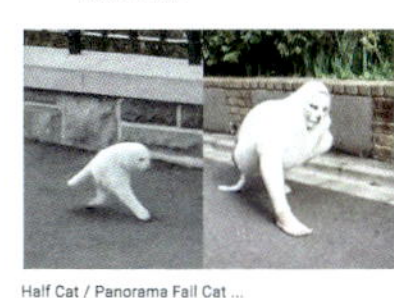
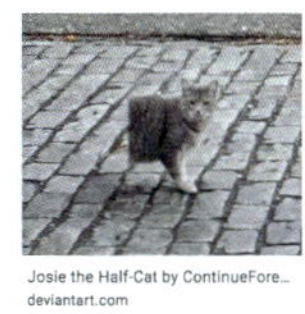
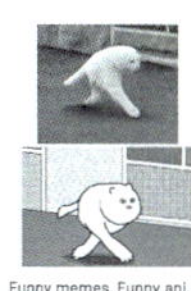

Weird and Warped World of the Half-Cat ...
catster.com

Half Cat / Panorama Fail Cat ...
knowyourmeme.com

Josie the Half-Cat by ContinueFore...
deviantart.com

Funny memes, Funny ani...
pinterest.com

It is important to note here that the Mattes do not have a cat at home.

When I asked them if they were cat lovers, they said that it was more about being obsessed with the internet,[5] where pictures of cats are among the most commonly shared images on social media.

Every year, one or two cats always top the charts. Some, like Attila Fluff or Happy Cat, have become real superstars of digital culture.

Others, like Lil Bub, Nala Cat or Grumpy Cat, to name but a few, each have millions of followers.[6]

In the last two decades, cats have not simply invaded our screens or been content to act as the mascots of this great globalised club that is the World Wide Web – they have become its true embodiment.

The face of the internet has pointy ears, a small pink furry nose and long tousled whiskers.

Far more than the cats themselves, what interests the Mattes is the insight they provide into the way we use social media.

Since 2010, they have been using different **avatar** [>p. 132] versions of the animal – especially the ones that circulate in a culturally crystallised form as memes – to *point out*, *question* or *criticise* what we project into this space of multiplied communication.

Their *Ceiling Cat* works according to the following syllogism: if the cat embodies the internet and if the cat is watching us, then the internet is watching us too.

Positioned on the ceiling, like a surveillance camera, their cat is the metaphor of the *digital panopticon* in which we now constantly live.

5 Clément Chéroux, Skype interview with Eva & Franco Mattes, 7 August 2020.
6 See Vincent Lavoie, *Trop mignon! Mythologies du cute* (Paris: PUF, 2020).

What distinguishes *Ceiling Cat* from the Mattes' other cats,
in that it looks down on us. If there is one word that is
essential here, it is "catoptic".[7]

In the scientific jargon of geometrical perspective
treatises from the sixteenth century onwards, the word
refers to vision from a high point: that is to say,
a view from above, a plunging or bird's-eye view.[8]
The "Catoptique", as Jean-François Niceron wrote in his
La perspective curieuse (Curious Perspective), is the
point of view "whereby we look down below us from above".[9]

The historian Jean-Marc Besse recalls that according
to the *Dictionnaire historique de la terminologie
optique des Grecs* (Historical Dictionary of Greek
Optical Terminology), the word "refers to the action
of observing attentively. Specifically, the *katoptes*
is the lookout, but also the god who registers an
action."[10]

Beyond the play on the English word "cat" in this
context of vision – which I can't resist here –
the Mattes' *Ceiling Cat* is fully in keeping with this
tradition of "cat-optic".

It recalls the eye of God emerging from the
clouds or the choirs of angels on the ceilings
of Catholic churches and Masonic temples.

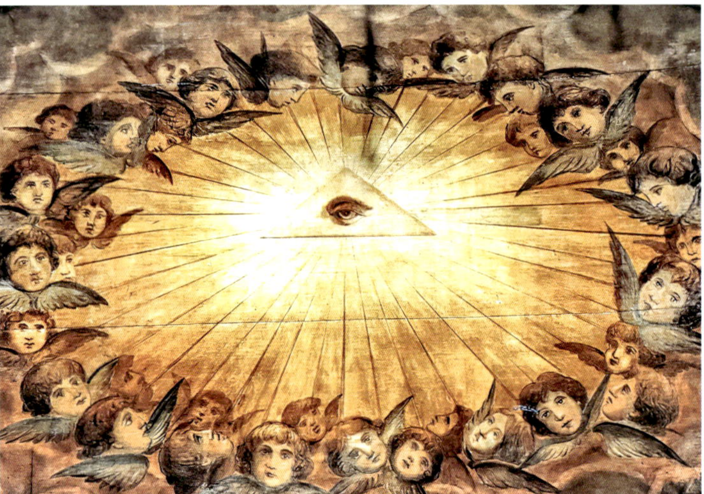

Anonymous photograph, *The Basilica of Saint Mary Major*,
Rome, undated.

It is also reminiscent of the popular magazines that praised
the merits of aerial observation in the first half of the
twentieth century, especially around World War I and II.

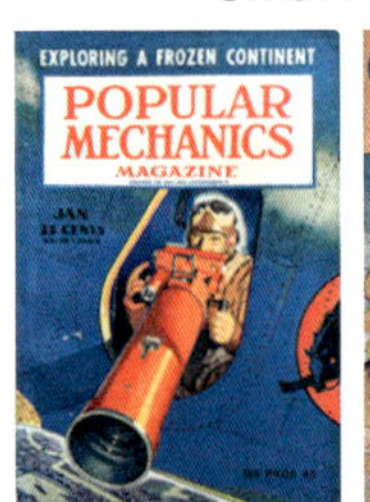
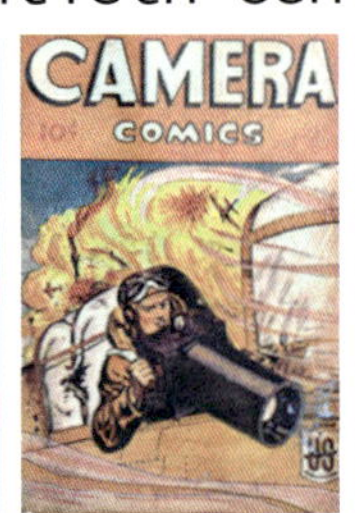
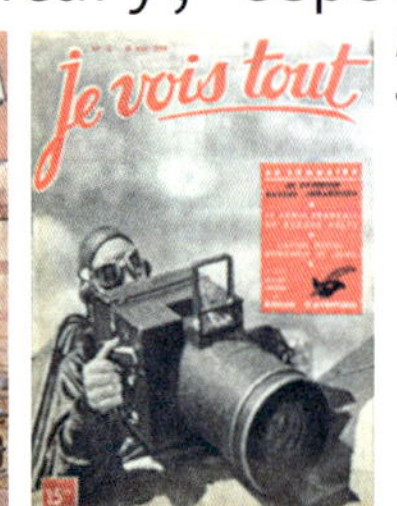

Popular Mechanics Magazine 1, January 1941 / *Camera Comics* 1, October 1944 /
Je vois tout 15, May 1946. Private collection, Paris.

7   See Jean-Marc Besse, "European Cities from a Bird's-Eye View: The Case of Alfred Guesdon", in Mark Dorrian and Frédéric Pousin (eds.),
    Seeing from Above: The Aerial View in Visual Culture (London: I. B. Tauris, 2013), p. 66–82.
8   The words "catoptique", "dioptique" and "peroptique" are used, for example, by Jean-Paul Marat, *Notions élémentaires d'optique*
    (Paris: Didot et Moutard, 1784), p. 12; "catoptique" and "anoptique" appear in Jean-François Niceron, *La perspective curieuse* (Paris: Jean Du Puis, 1663), p. 96.
    These notions are sometimes spelt slightly differently. René Descartes, in particular, in his *Dioptrique*, adds an "r".
9   Niceron, *La perspective curieuse*, p. 96.
10 Besse, "European Cities", p. 71.

The iconography was extended to the covers of science-fiction novels from the 1950s to the 1970s, where UFO-shaped eyes attack the earth or pursue its inhabitants.

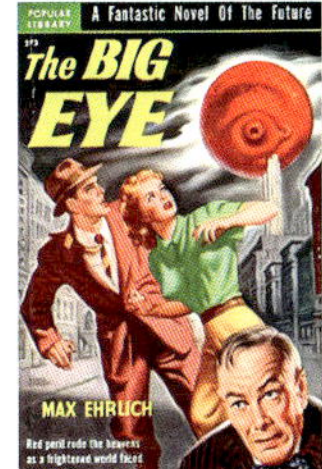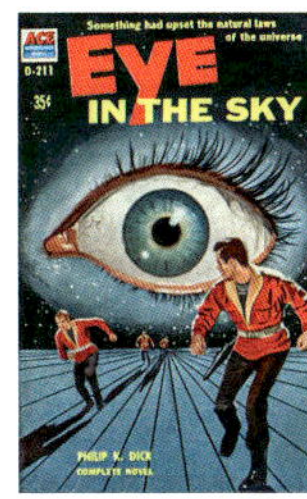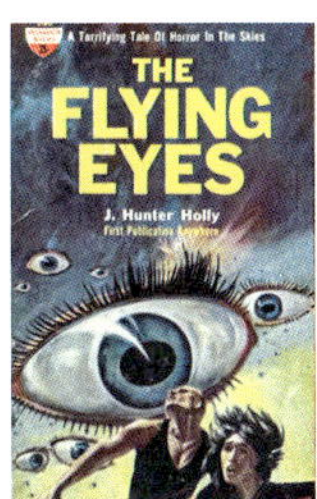

Max Ehrlich, *The Big Eye* (New York: Popular Library, 1950) / Philippe K. Dick, *Eye in the Sky* (New York: Ace Books, 1957) / J. Hunter Holly, *The Flying Eyes* (Derby, CT: Monarch Books, 1962).

Whatever the context, it is a question of evoking an inquisitorial or moralising higher power, which draws its omnipotence from its commanding position.
It is all-seeing and all-knowing.
It watches, assesses and punishes, when necessary.
The Mattes are quite familiar with all this.
"Ceiling Cat is watching you."
Their cat embodies a new age of catoptics governed by surveillance cameras, drones and satellites.
It is the contemporary, metaphorical representation of the absolute authority that we now place above us and on whom we confer the right to spy on and judge us.
Outside the realms of technology, psychoanalysis refers to this as the "superego".
It is worth recalling here that some of the iterations of the meme that inspired the Mattes are circulating with a more precise description of the supposed situation:
"Ceiling Cat is watching you *masturbate*."

Historians who work on the relationship between modern art and popular culture usually do so in one direction only.
Artists are readily compared to alchemists turning lead into gold.
They take minor forms such as graffiti, comics or advertising and turn them into masterpieces.
Reciprocity, i.e. the reappropriation of these noble forms by the general public, is rarely considered.
In the managerial vocabulary that describes the circulation of information within companies, this is called bottom-up interaction without top-down feedback.
Rosalind Krauss's criticism of the *High & Low* exhibition at the Museum of Modern Art in New York in 1990 was based on this very point.[11]
She criticised the exhibition's curators for defending this one-sided relationship, where the common man fades away before a demiurge artist, capable of sublimating the minor into the major.[12]

11 Kirk Varnedoe and Adam Gopnik, *High & Low: Modern Art and Popular Culture* (New York: The Museum of Modern Art, 1990).
12 Rosalind Krauss, "Introduction", *October* 56 (Spring 1991), p. 3–5.

Viewed in the context of this debate on cultural
hierarchy, the Mattes' *Ceiling Cat* is fascinating.
The artists became interested in the new form of
popular iconography represented by memes.
They took one of its best-known examples and converted it
into a genuine work of art.
But when their cat is exhibited in galleries or museums,
it is invariably photographed by visitors, posted
on social media, then reappropriated and transformed
back into a meme.

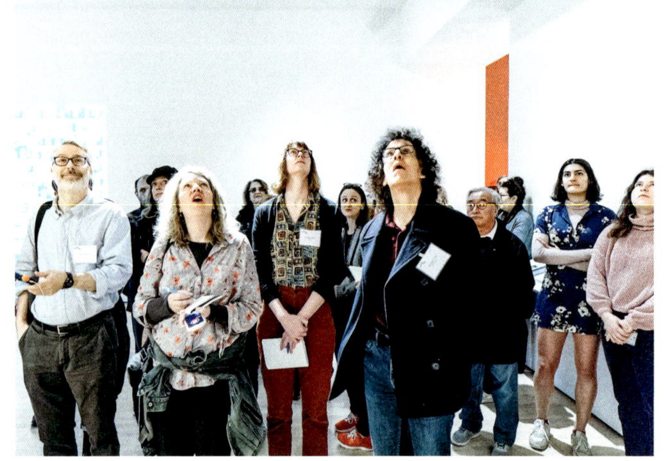

Ceiling Cat installed at SFMOMA. Photo: Jason Henry

Eva & Franco Mattes willingly encourage this *mise en abyme*
of the image of the image of the image ... For instance,
they have produced a life-size sticker of the cat's head
which, when glued to the ceiling, looks just like the
stuffed animal when photographed.
On social media, it is now impossible to tell whether
it's a photograph of the sculpture or a snapshot of
the sticker.
The image of the installation of the work at
SFMOMA, created for the *snap+share* exhibition by
Katherine Du Tiel, the museum's photographer,
is free of rights and has been placed in
the public domain so that it can circulate more
freely, indefinitely feeding the chain of
appropriations.
It can now be copied, modified and redistributed
permission-free.
The dissemination of the image in various forms is an
integral part of the work.
In fact, the work has several modes of
existence.
Today, in search engine results, the Mattes' sculpture
has ended up merging with the image of 2003 or its various
derivatives.
It has gone back to being a meme. The loop has gone
full circle.

Clément Chéroux is a French photography historian and Chief Curator
of Photography at the Museum of Modern Art, New York.

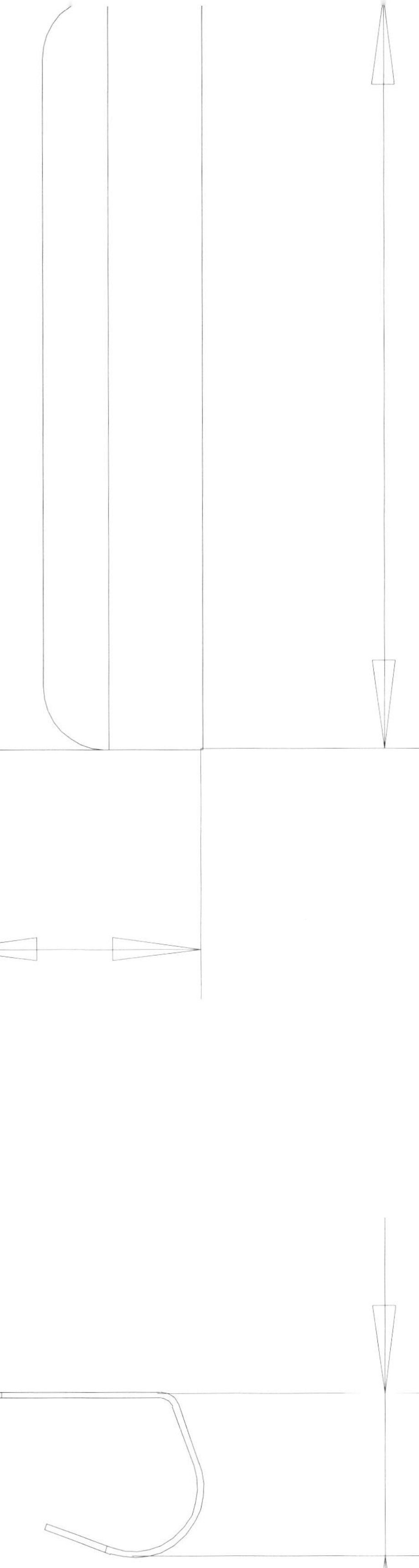

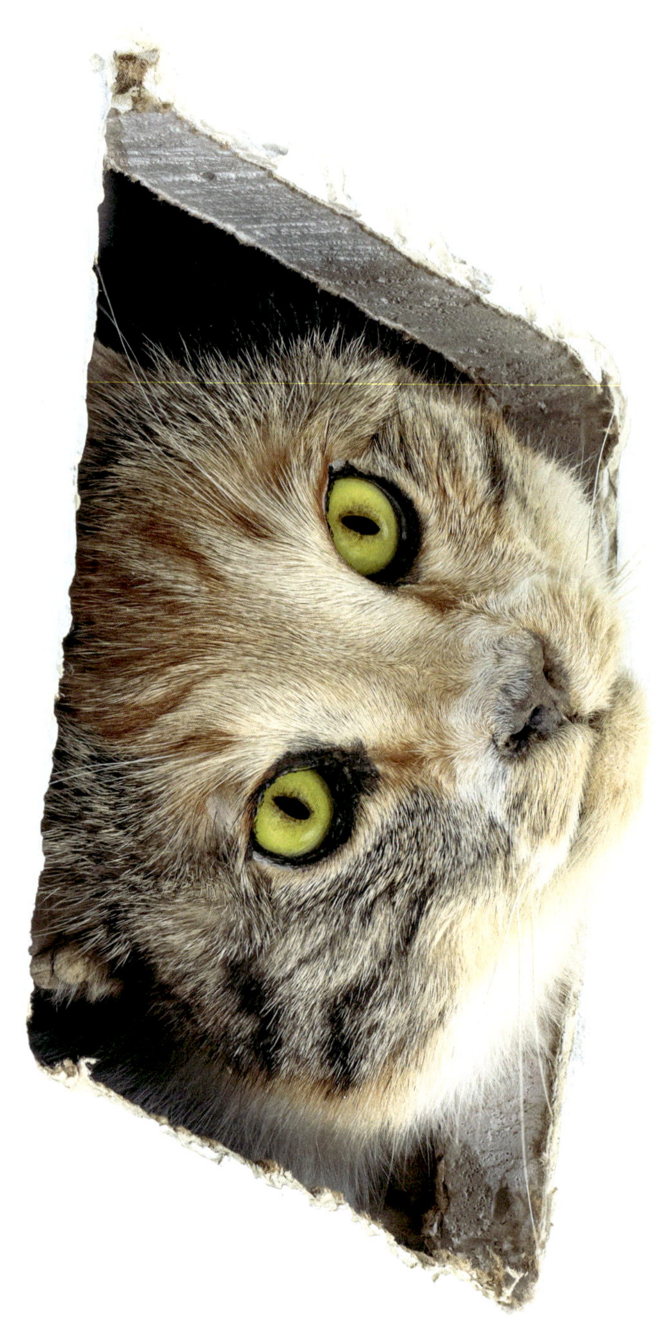

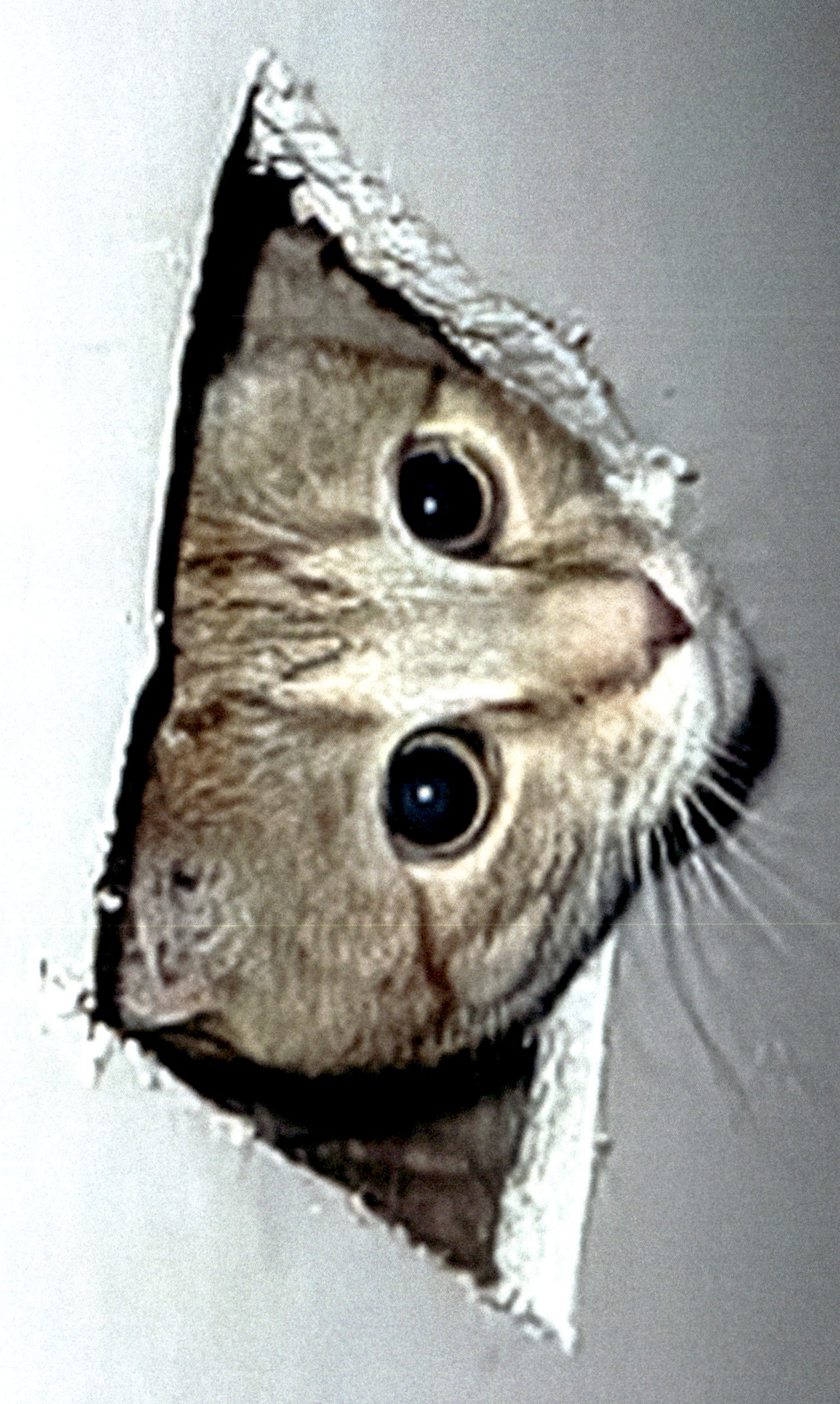

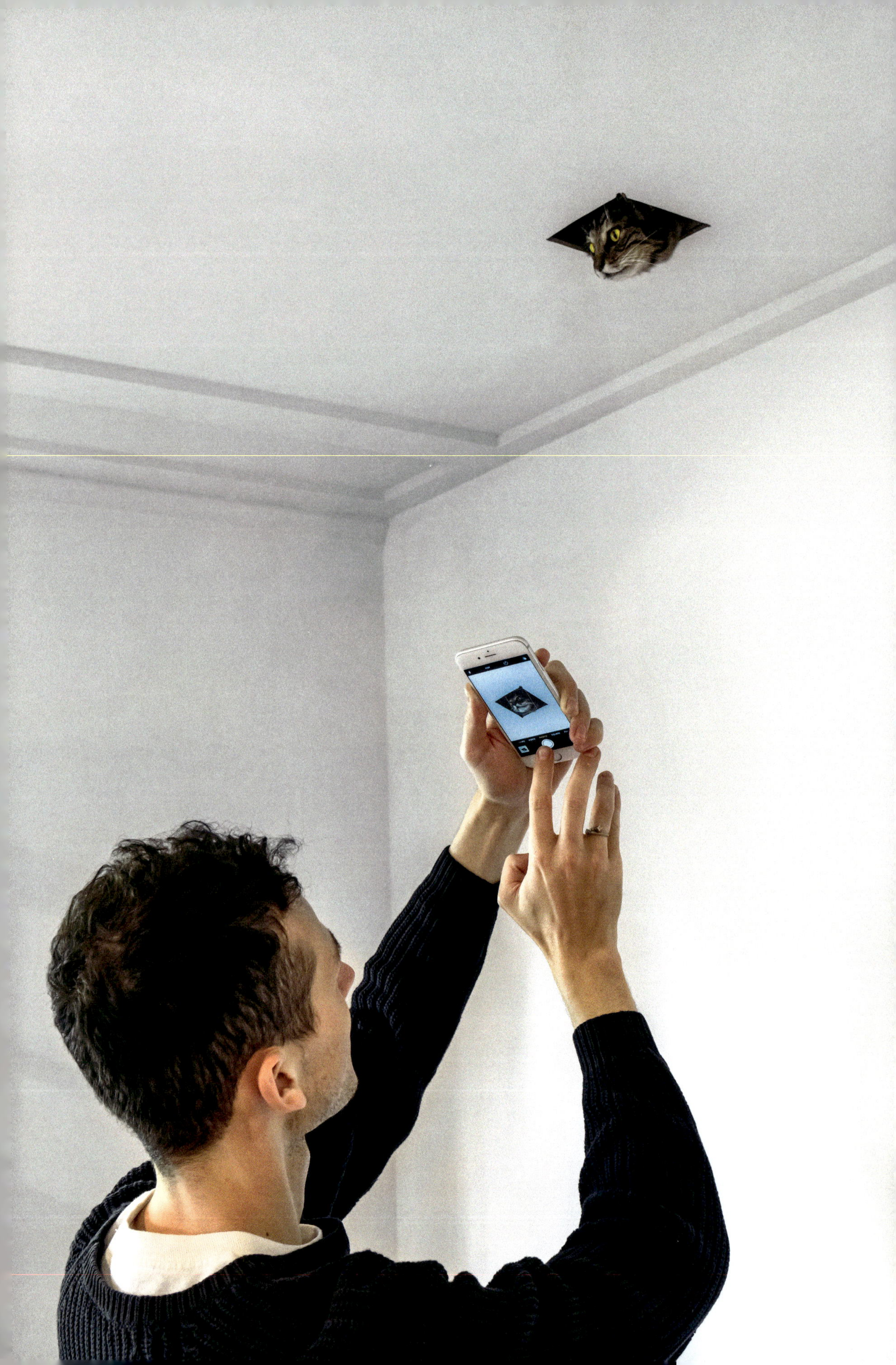

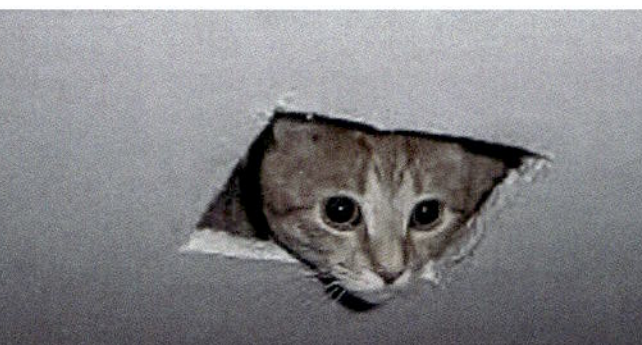
Ceiling Cat is Watching You

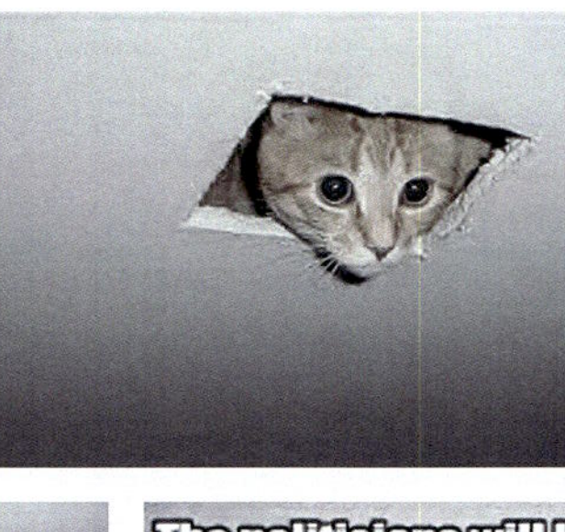

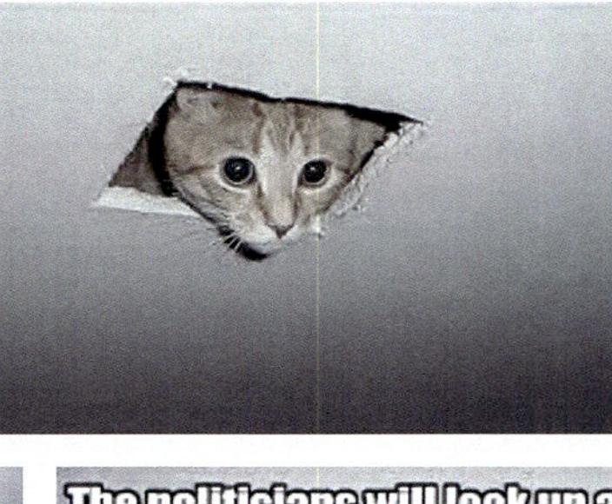
CEILING CAT
IS WATCHING YOU
MASTERBATE
memes.com

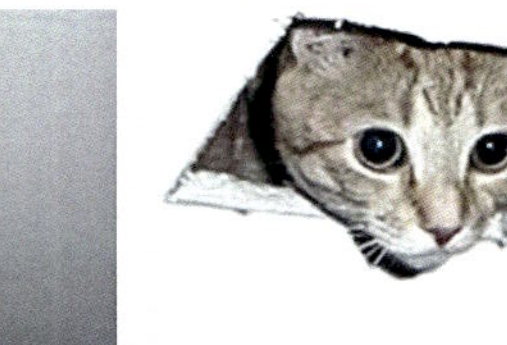

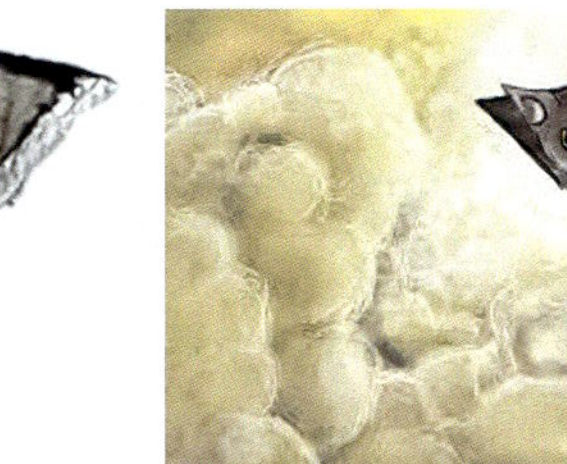
Den
cres
and
spea
eng
gud

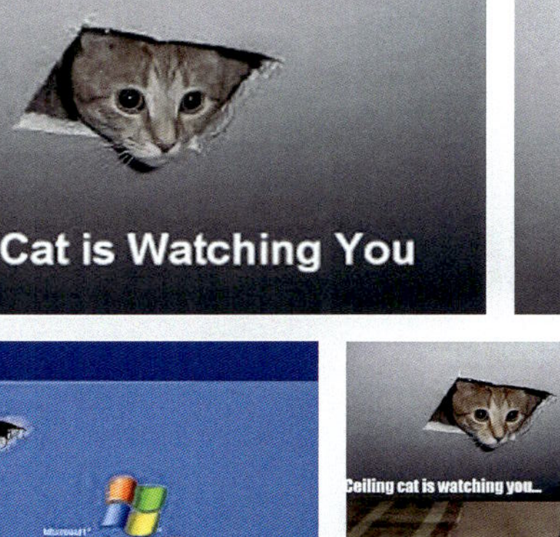
Windows XP
Preparing to hibernate…
Ceiling cat is watching you hibernate.

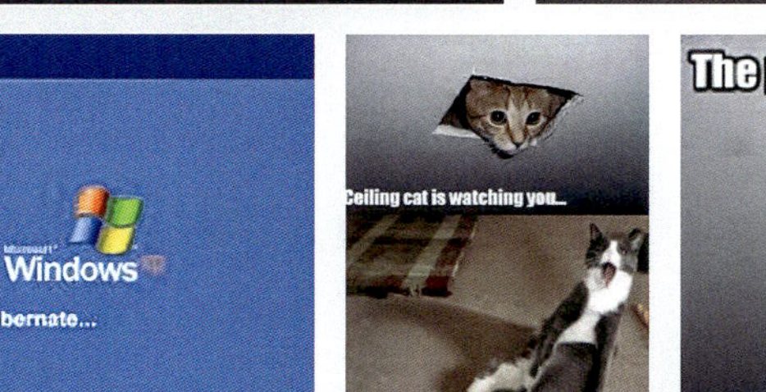
Ceiling cat is watching you…

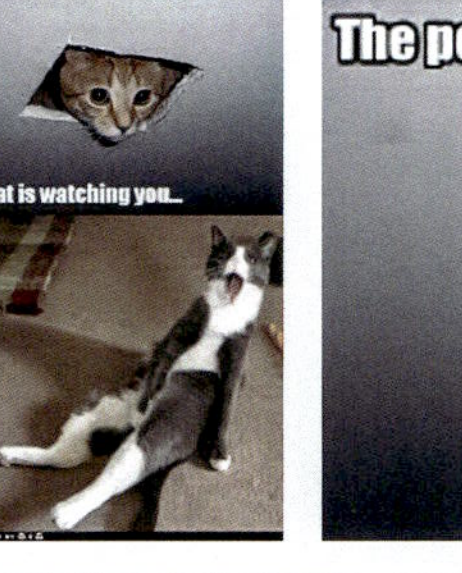
The politicians will look up and shout
SAVE US

…and I'll whisper,
LOL

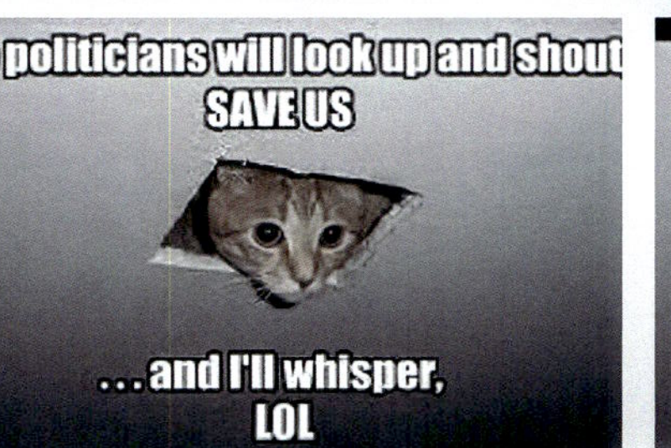

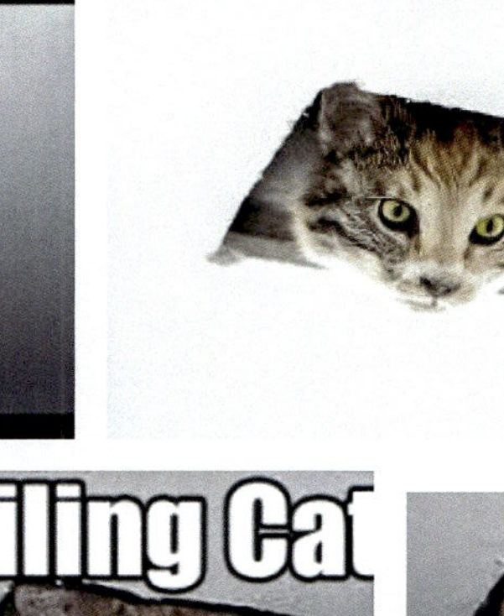

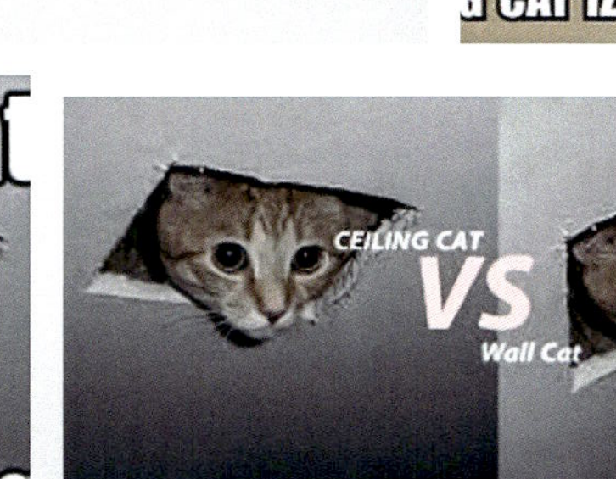
G CAT IZ PAF

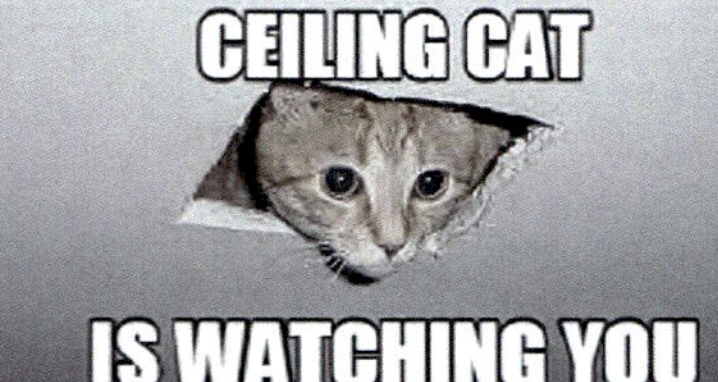
I SEE
YOU PEE
memegenerator.ne

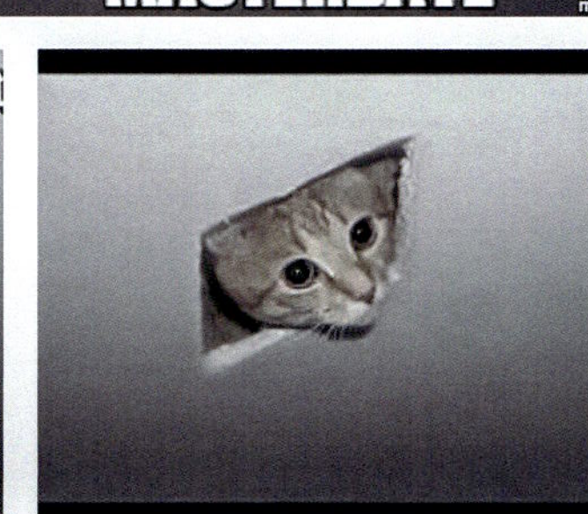
CEILING CAT
IS WATCHING YOU STARE AT THE
CEILING
memegenerator.net

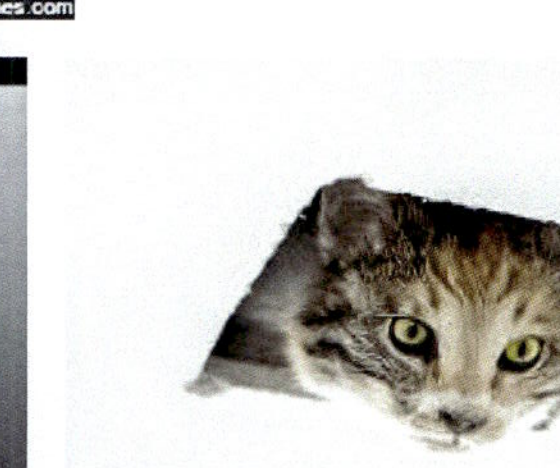
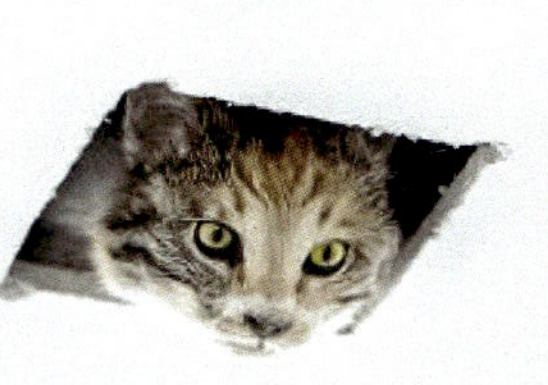
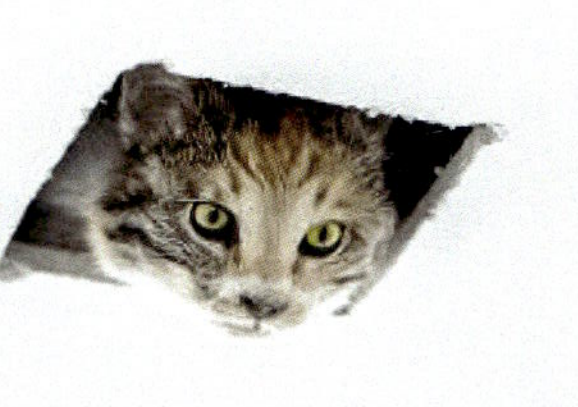
ceiling cat
creates man

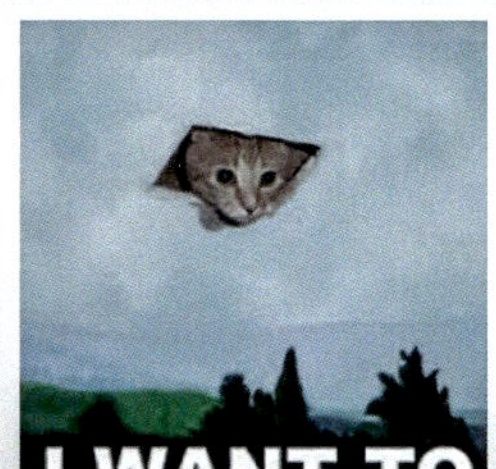
I WANT TO
BELIEVE

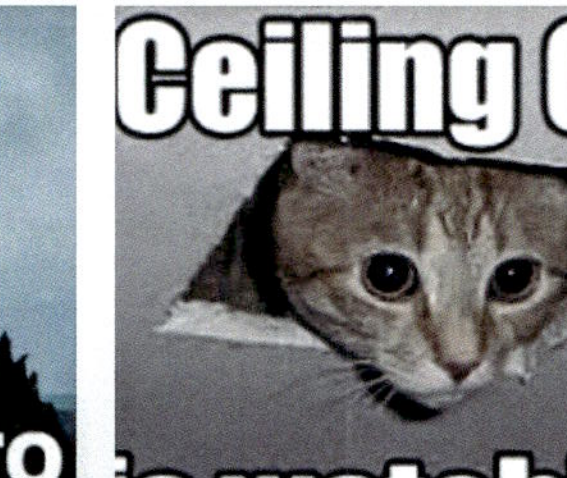
Ceiling Cat
is watching

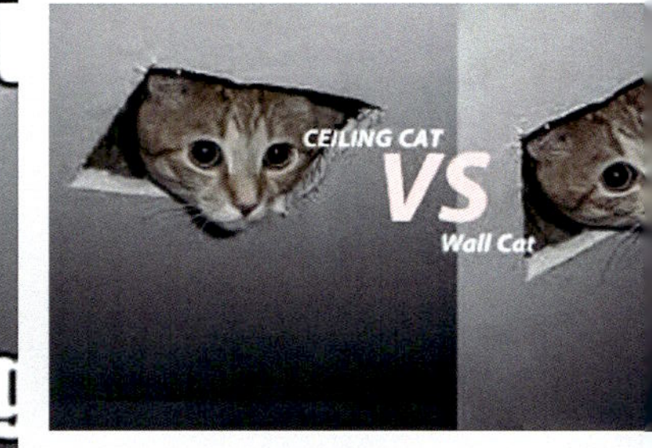
CEILING CAT
VS
Wall Cat

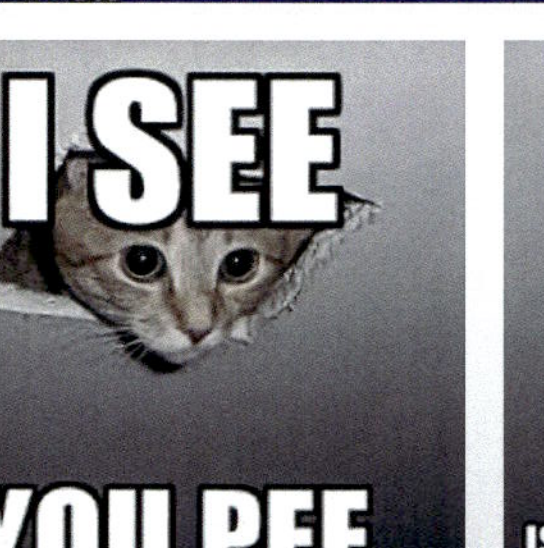

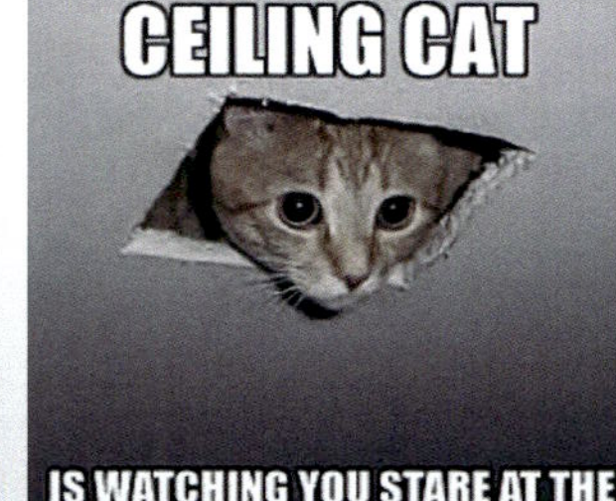

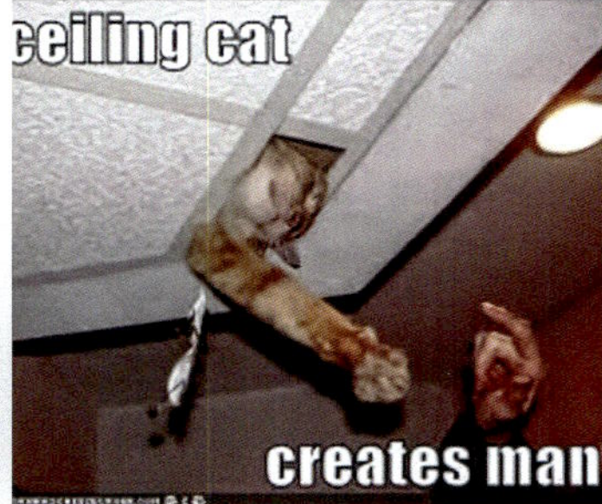
BASEMENT CAT

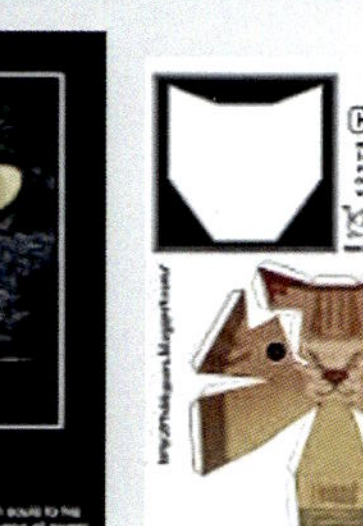
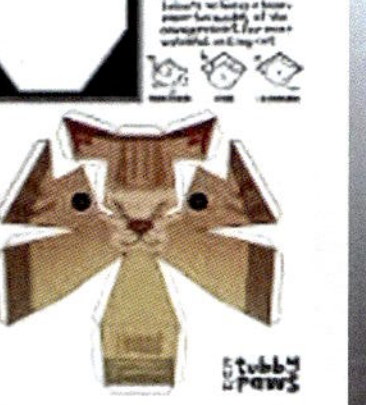
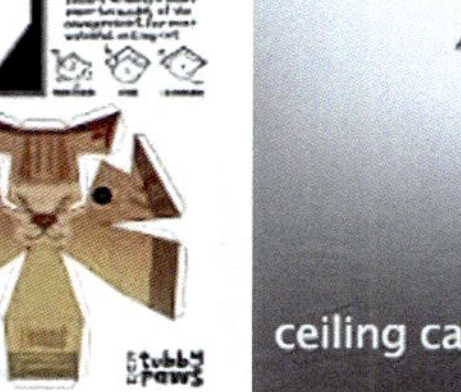
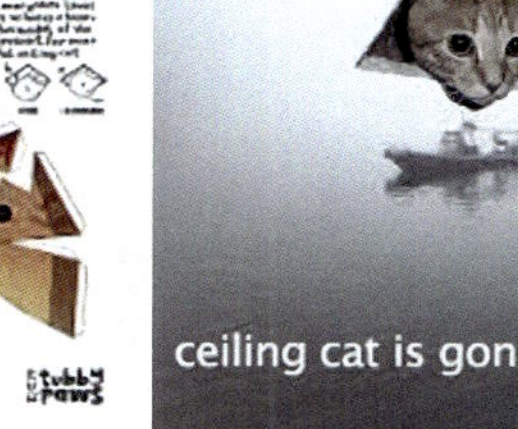
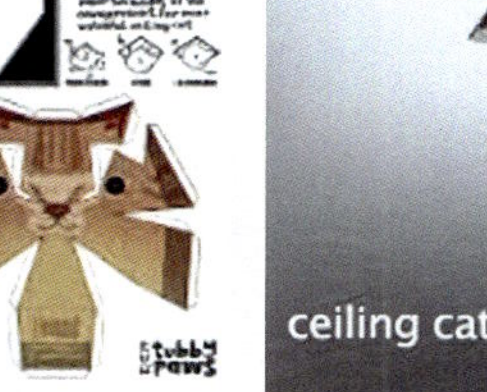
CEILING CAT

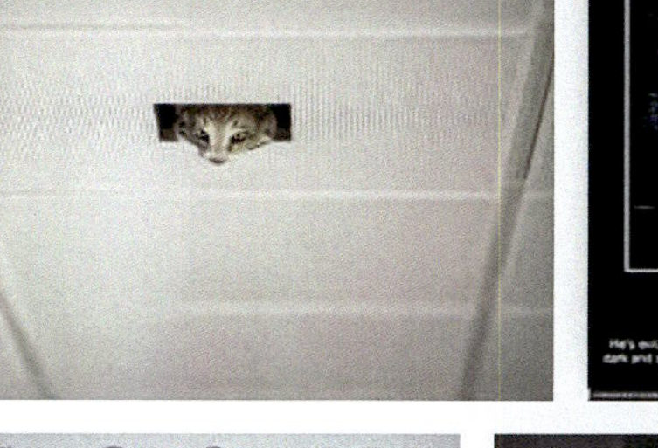
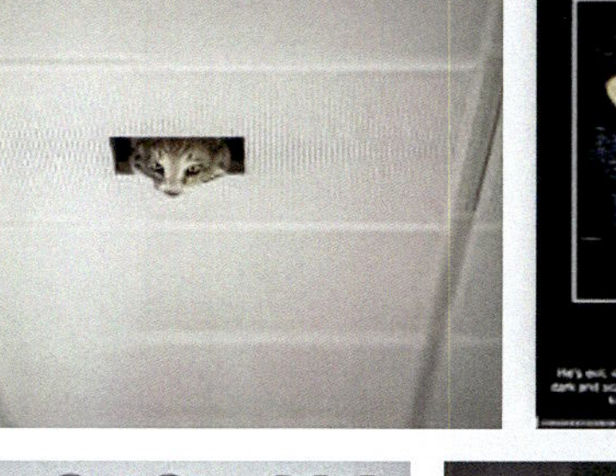
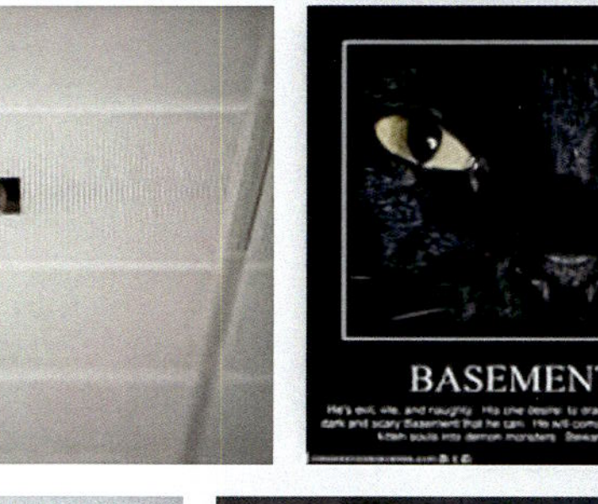
ceiling cat is gonna eat your boat

Basement cat ha
infiltrated heave

ling Cat Stealth Le

IV'E BEEN HERE

stairwell

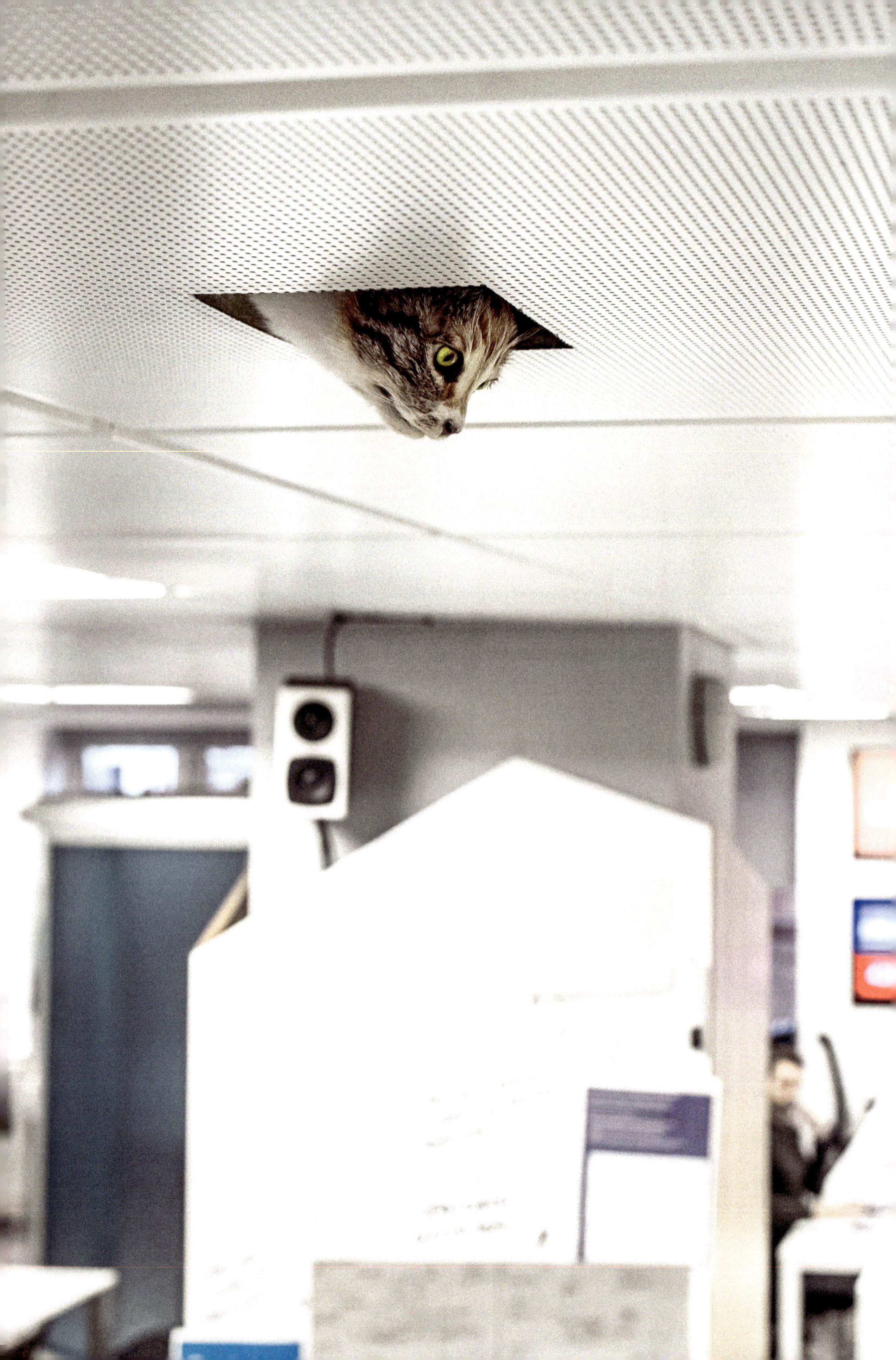

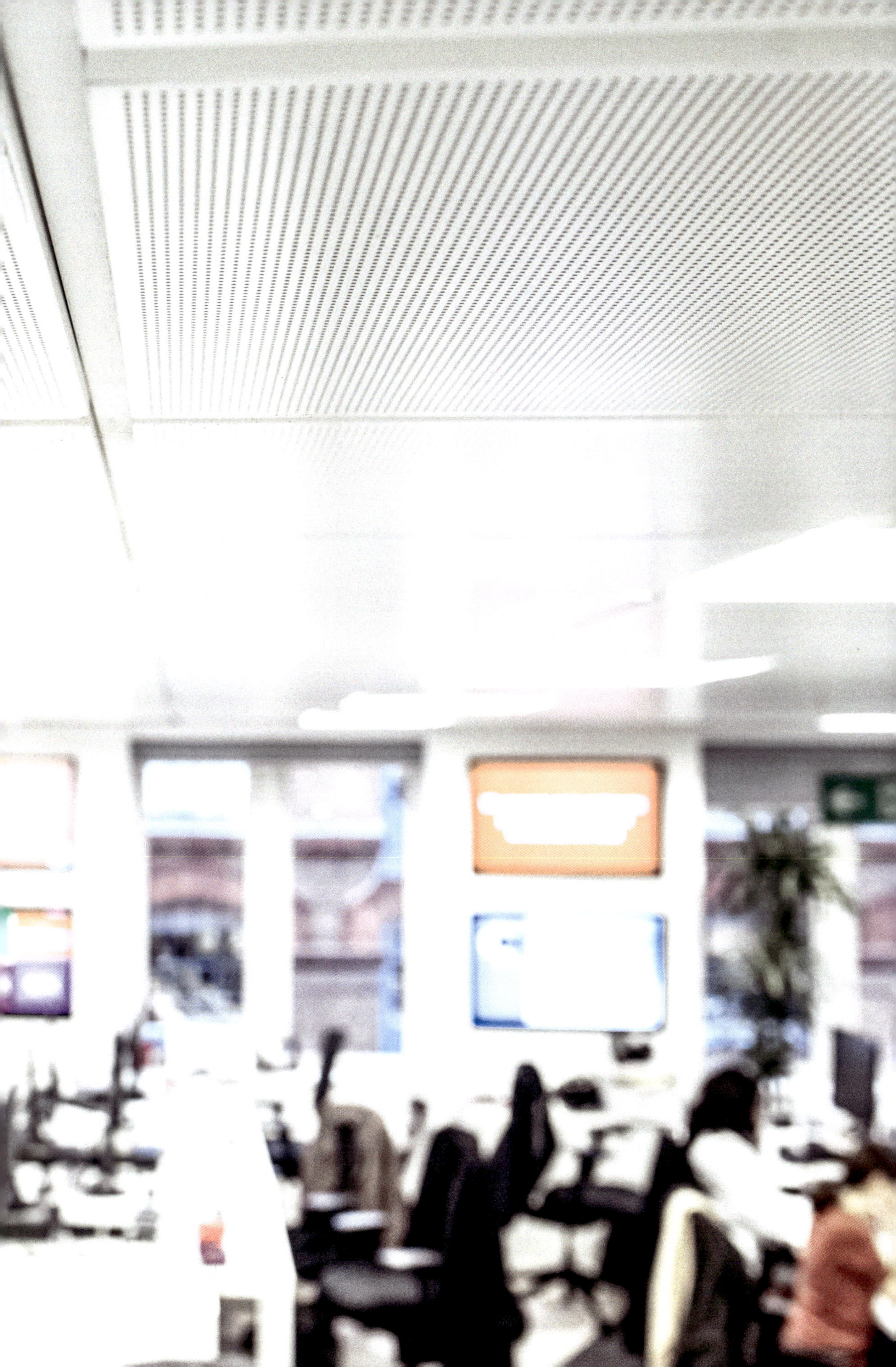

The Bots,
2020

Who keeps **social media**[>p. 138], internet forums and search engines clean of all the world's violence, hatred and horror?
Even if we might assume that **bots**[>p. 132], i.e. fully automated **software**[>p. 138] programs, are used to clean all the problematic content from online platforms like Facebook or Twitter, this work is actually done by human actors, so-called **content moderators**[>p. 133].

Eva & Franco Mattes's *Dark Content* (2015) was the artists' first foray into this shadowy business of private internet companies.
In *The Bots*, they continue their investigation through conversations with content moderators working for Facebook in Berlin.
Assigned to three different cultural sectors – the Greek, Italian and Arab "market" – the moderators share insights into their at times shocking everyday experiences, mirroring the social issues and concerns relevant to their specific location.

The conversations conducted in collaboration with investigative journalist Adrian Chen are re-enacted by actors Jake Levy, Ruby McCollister and Bobbi Salvör Menuez.
Filming themselves from home with their **smartphones**[>p. 137], they camouflage the sensitive information, disguising it as **make-up tutorials**[>p. 135] so as to bypass censorship.

Serious discourse around topics such as violence, sexual abuse, hate speech and terrorism is therefore constantly interrupted by make-up tips.
Installed in the back of the same customised desks used by workers at Facebook, the videos make the exploitation of labour visible as the flip side of the platforms' clean surface.

The videos were shot with support by DIS.

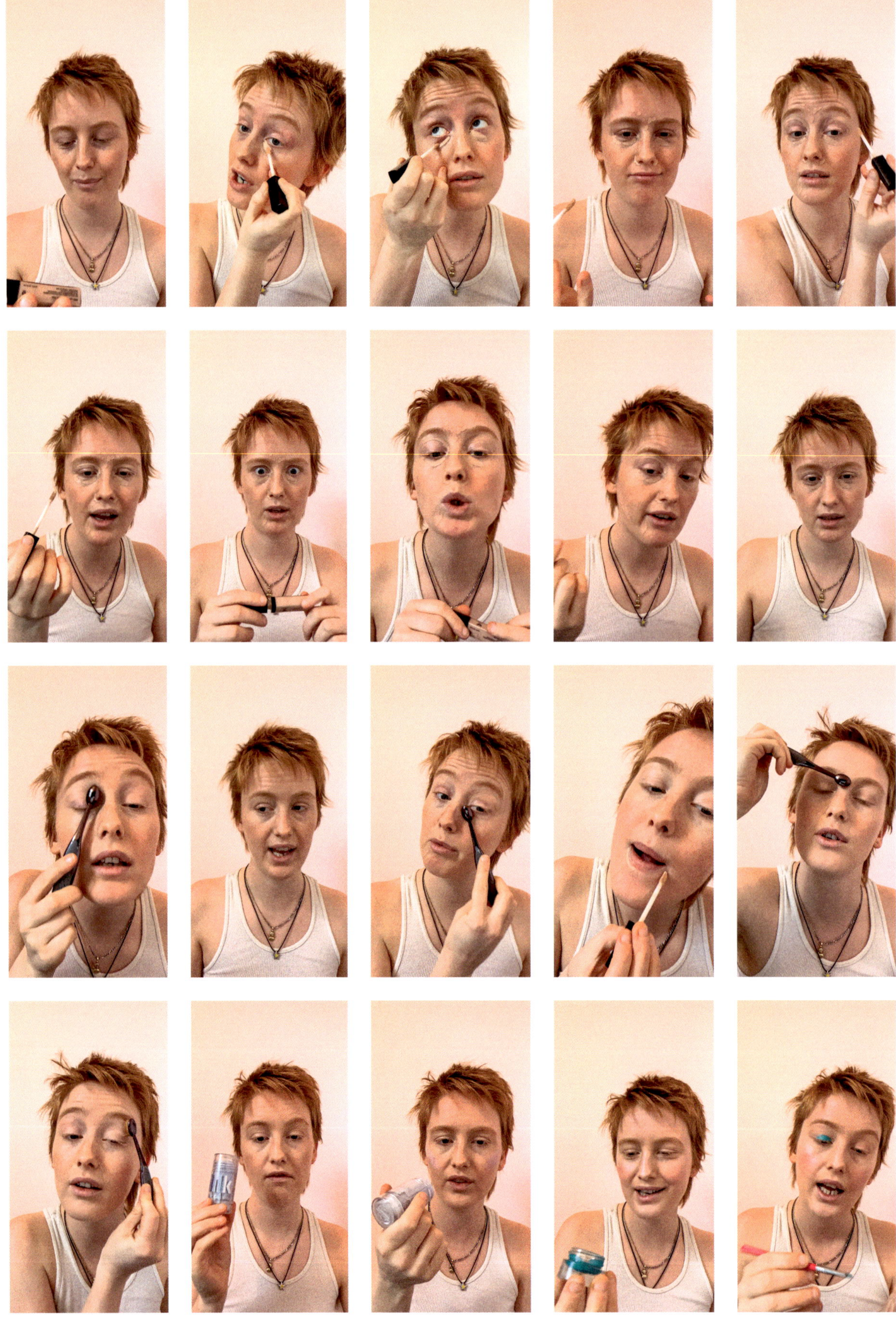

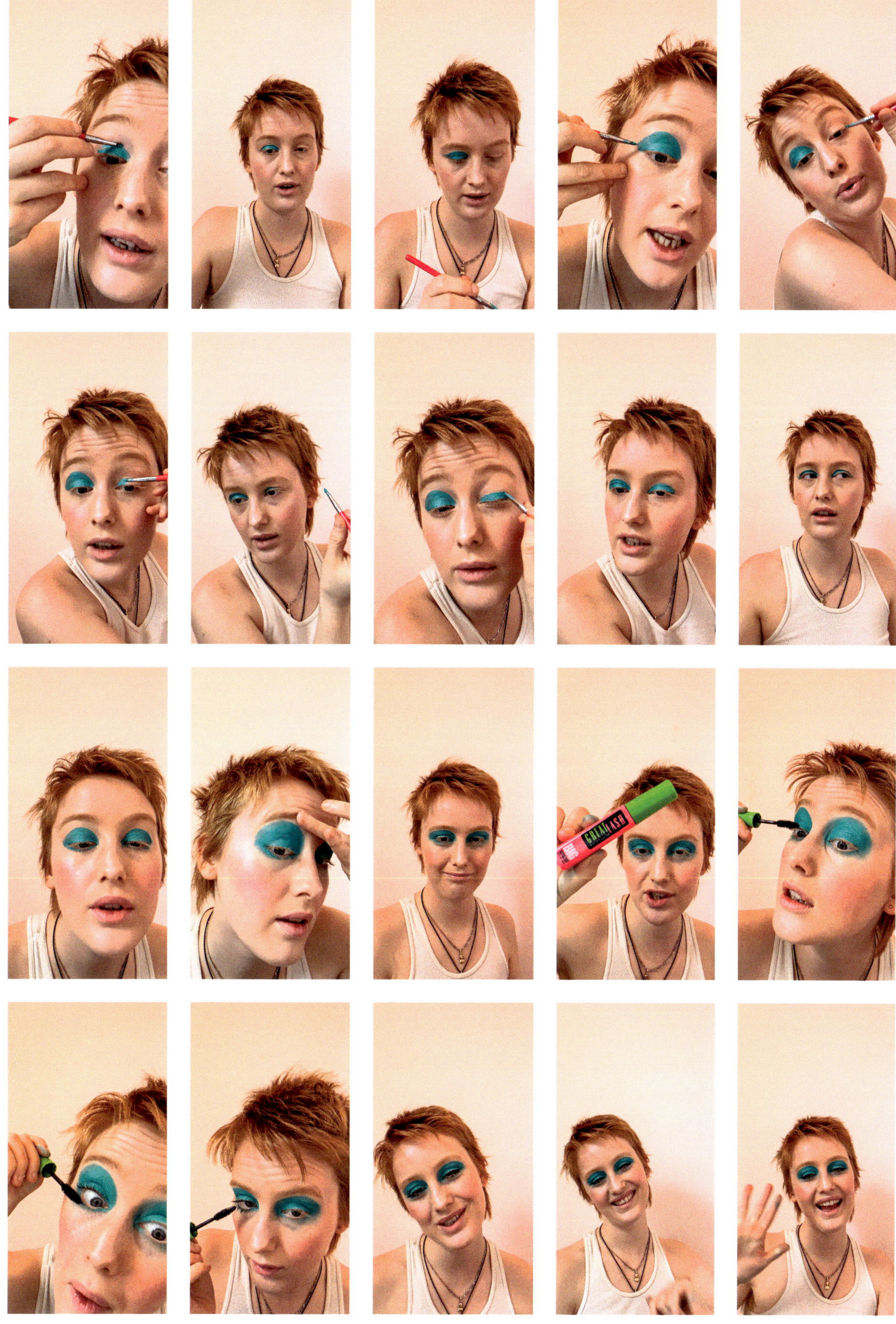

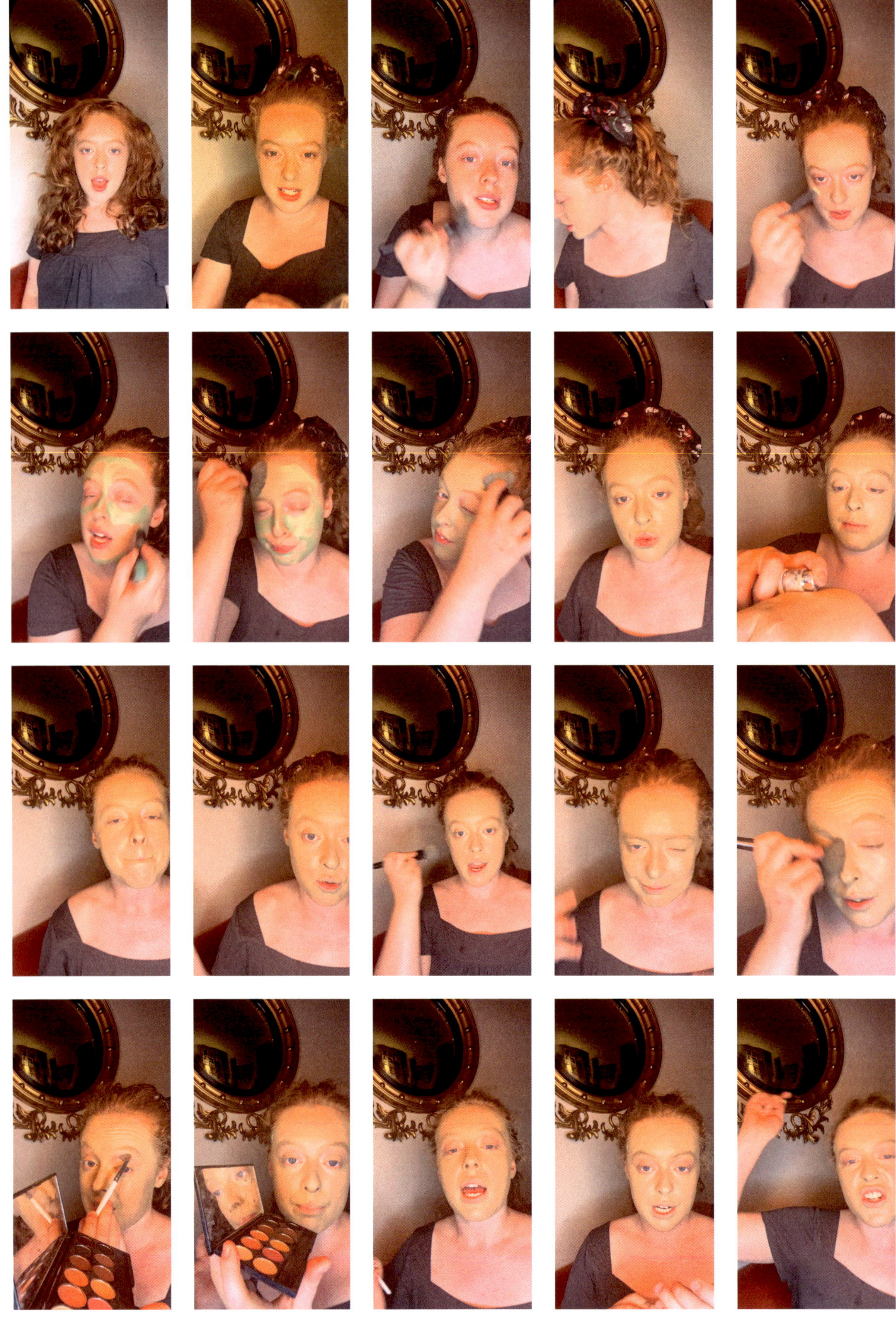

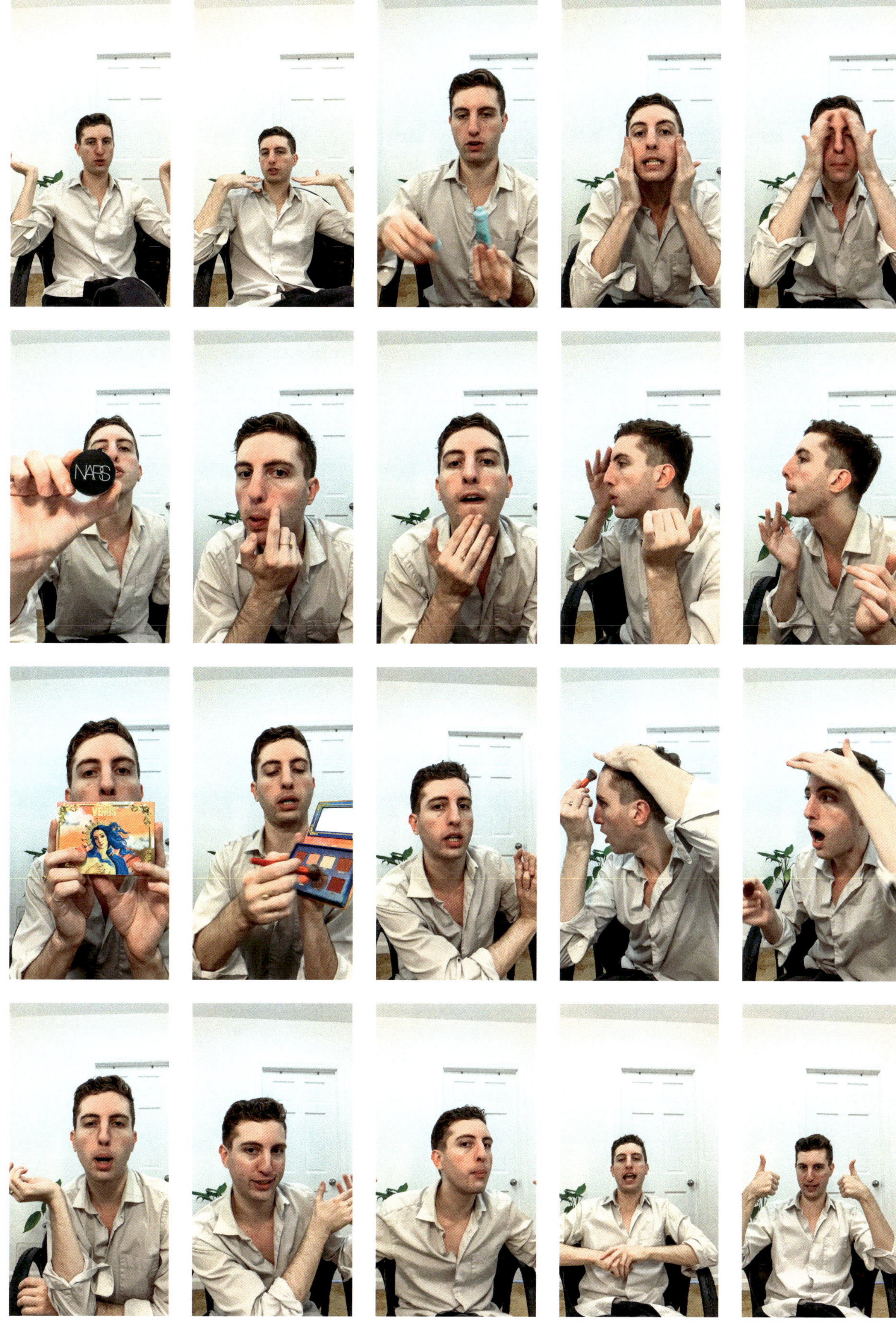

1   What we look for produces what we see.

When we enter queries into a search engine, we get
results.
    We type in words and phrases, click "enter", our
    screen refreshes and a list of words or images
    appears.
        The new page that we see was something created
        through our query.
We made it.

The "we" matters. Search engine **algorithms**[>p. 132] rely on
many searches, on search as a general practice, on
billions of searches happening every day.
    If you look for something, it's likely others have
    already looked for it.
        If no one else is looking for it, you probably
        won't find it.
You'll never even know it was out there.

Scrolling isn't searching.
    Our **social media**[>p. 138] feeds are the interrelated
    effects of our curation, others' inputs and
    algorithms in real time.
        We check our phones to see what's new, what's
        changed, who likes us.
When we scroll, we create what we are looking for but we
are not always looking for what we see.

Or maybe scrolling is searching without knowing for what.
    Finding it can be too jarring to bear.
        Better have someone else look for us.

2   Looking for work, love, sex?
For recognition, excitement?
Something new, something different?

The smooth pleasure of touchscreens provides distraction
and promises relief.
    Scrolling releases us from boredom, from the burden
    of being alone with our thoughts.
        We can be absorbed in the ephemeral.

Intruders disrupt our reveries, shattering the fantasy of
a frictionless elsewhere.
    The unwanted image – its pain, its violence – invades
    what feels like our space, stains what feels like
    our dreams. Unannounced and uninvited, it shocks us
    into responsibility.

But whose responsibility?

Who keeps us safe, and from what?

When we look for something new and it finds us, who is
to blame?

Tech giants, social media corporations, platform
capitalists: they have configured our lives and work in
their interest in capital accumulation.
        No wonder we blame them.
Let the lords of the internet solve the problems they
created.
        Security is their responsibility.
            Aren't they already surveilling us all the time,
            collecting our data and running it through their
            algorithms, finding patterns and making the
            future?

3   It's not algorithms all the way down.

The stack is built on people.
        Underneath it all is a human layer.

            In the 1990s, hacker-bros dreamed of leaving the
            meat, their cyber-visions erasing not just their
            own bodies but the work and workers who
            maintained them (even an uploaded
            consciousness requires someone to keep the
            electricity on).
The imaginary is one of immersion and limitlessness, the
end of frailty and dependence.
        It's the infantile fantasy of omnipotent oneness.

Communicative capitalism embeds this dream of de-embodiment
in the immediate satisfactions of one-click shopping.
        See, want, have – the technology always delivers.
            Algorithms show us what we want and then make
            sure we get it.
No need to speak with a person at all.
        The ultimate fetish, algorithms erase people altogether.

The ghost in the machine is actually embodied and alive.
        People make, shelve and deliver.
                People clean and fix.
People see, feel, breathe.

4   Content moderators are people.

(Spoiler alert) In the last scene of the 1973 eco-dystopia
Soylent Green, Charlton Heston raises a bloodied arm as he
is being carried away and shouts "Soylent Green is people!"

The fiction dominating the film is that the
population of a heavily polluted earth is being fed
with plankton.
   The oceans are dead and the climate is
   destroyed, but Soylent Industries is ostensibly
   able to stave off mass starvation by
   manufacturing and distributing the nutritious
   plankton-based Soylent Green.

Does the film require us to think that everyone believed –
against the overwhelming evidence of extinction and
environmental catastrophe – that the oceans were still
healthy enough, plankton was still plentiful enough
and climatic patterns were still stable enough to maintain
the human food supply?
   Do we have to presume that people couldn't see what
   was right before their eyes, especially given the
   police vehicles scooping rioters off the streets,
   dumping them into trucks and carting them off never
   to be seen again?
      No.
The final scene is climactic not because it changes what
people know.
   It's climactic because it changes what people can
   pretend not to know.

The myth of the algorithm is that technology does it for
us (the "it" could be anything, that's key to the
fantasy). Determining offence, discerning harm is a coding
problem.
   This myth lets us pretend that the criteria of
   ethical and epistemological validity are
   universally shared.
      All our online experiences to the contrary, all
      our knowledge of bullying, fake news,
      governmental cover-ups, corporate-funded
      science, scams, racism, obscenity and hate
      notwithstanding, the billionaire lords of the
      internet can eliminate harm from our social
      media platforms.

5   Contemporary sin eaters look for us.

Who and what is **content moderation**^{>p. 133} for?
   Who is the subject to be secured?

The children?
   The bumbling Boomers?
      The easily swayed masses?
The consumers, daydreamers and scrollers hoping for a
little peace as they look for love in all the wrong places?

An idealised vision of networked communication underpins
the demand for content moderation – an ideal of decency,

augmented by a modicum of respect, a repugnance for
suffering and a belief that capitalist corporations can
and will deliver truth.

Human content moderators exist outside this ideal as its
hidden guarantors.
        They encounter the shock so that we don't have to.
            They are communicative capitalism's sin
            eaters, absorbing the worst and absolving
            the rest of us.

And everyone still knows that every sort of cruelty,
intrusion, manipulation and lie will continue to bloom in
the welcoming networked environment.
        Everyone still knows that what drives big tech is
        profit not truth.
            Content moderation cannot guarantee otherwise,
            but it can let us pretend.
It secures the fantasy that the platforms operate for our
benefit, that the circulation of violence is a bug, not
a feature of the nets we can't escape.

Do we keep on, do we stay, because we pretend it's safe,
because we know it's not or because we no longer have
a choice?

6 Robots can't do everything.

The one who suffers in our place, the human sacrificed for
the sake of the rest of us, is a religious and literary
staple.
        Capitalism attempts a workaround by paying.
            One who gets paid can't be innocent, can't be
            a victim, no matter how much they hurt.
They can be exploited, but not violated.

In a famous case in US obscenity law, a Supreme Court
justice said, "I know it when I see it."
        One knows obscenity because of how it feels.
            The intensity associated with obscenity goes
            too far; the feeling violates.
Why?
        Because one knows that someone else enjoys it.
            Obscenity exposes us to the enjoyment
            (jouissance) of another person,
            confronting us not with an objective
            fact but with a pleasure-pain that is deeply
            subjective.

If they don't feel violated, content moderators can't do
their jobs.

7 When invisible labour appears as exploitation, it is still exploitation.

In the Marxist tradition, "exploitation" refers to the
fact that the worker generates more value than they accrue
in wages.
>The capitalist takes this extra, this surplus value,
>for their own.
>>It's why they went into business in the first
>>place.

In *Ghost Work*, Mary L. Gray and Siddharth Suri write:
>"The harsh irony is that ghost work platforms and
>individual requesters wash their hands of the pain
>they inflict on workers.
>>Companies, from MTurk to Uber – and this is
>>key – view workers as mere customers who are
>>selling their labor, as they might sell their
>>used record collection or rent a spare bedroom.
>In the eyes of ghost work companies, customers
>come to their sites strictly of their own volition.
>And, as customers, they can leave at any time."

Why are workers hard to see?

Jodi Dean is a US American political theorist. She is professor at the
Hobart and William Smith Colleges in New York.

"I was recruited based on my language skills, so I was assigned to the Arab world.   It's an outsourcing company that works for Facebook. I absolutely hated working as a moderator."

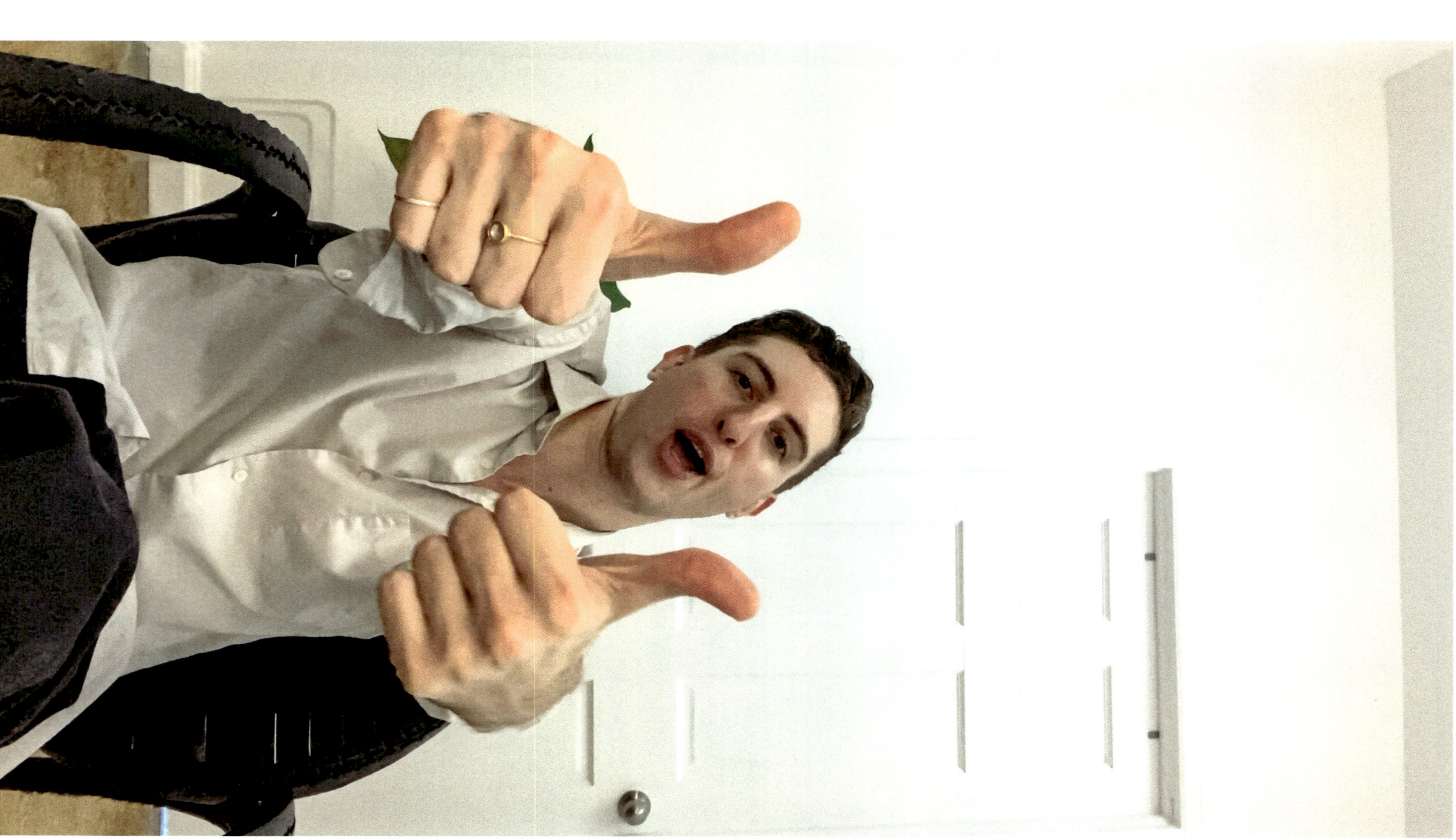

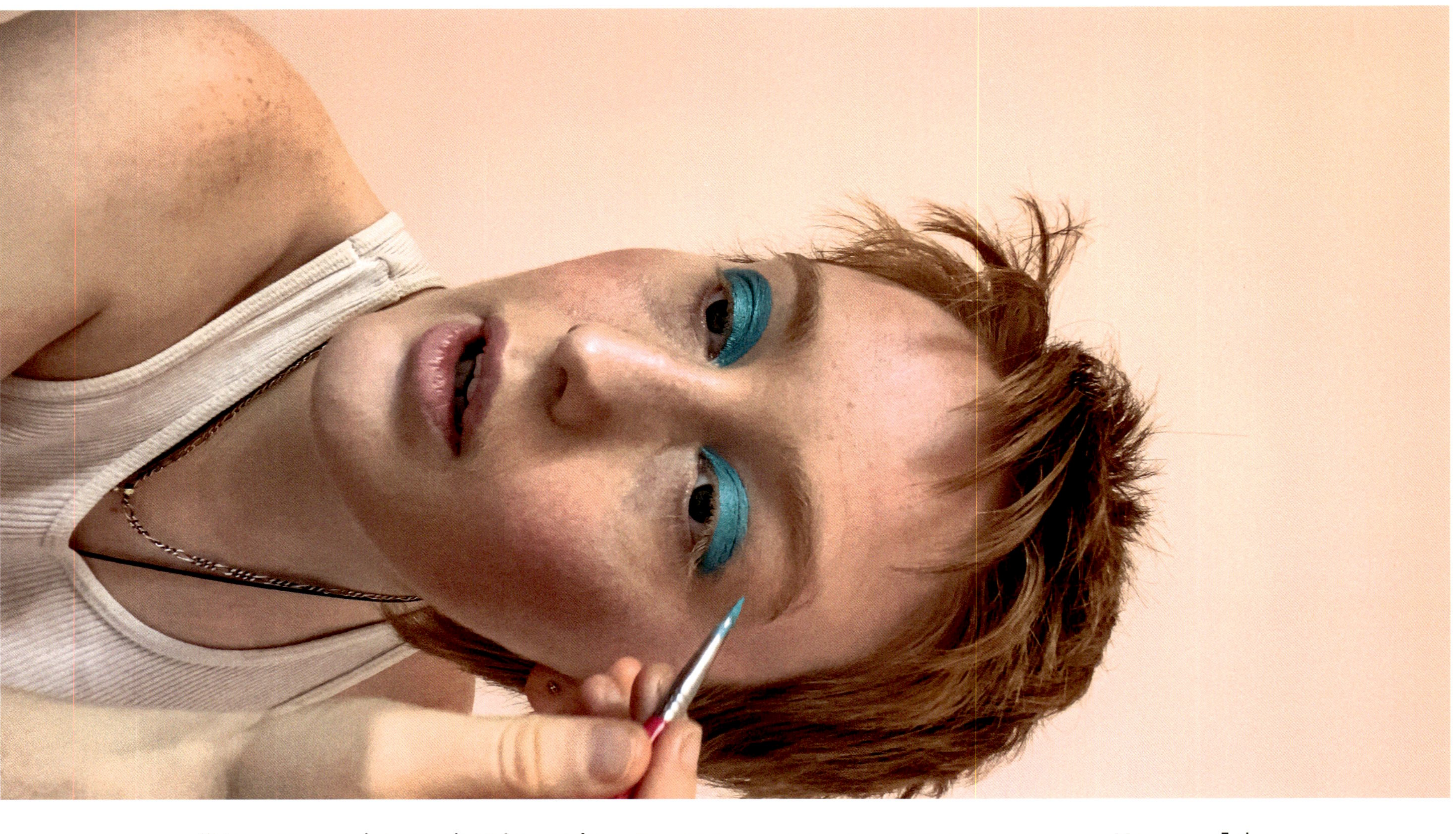

"You never know what's going to pop up on your screen.   You could be there eating and chilling and ... boom!   You'd be screaming 'guys, is this a photo of a child being raped?'. We'd all be shocked. And then we'd move on."

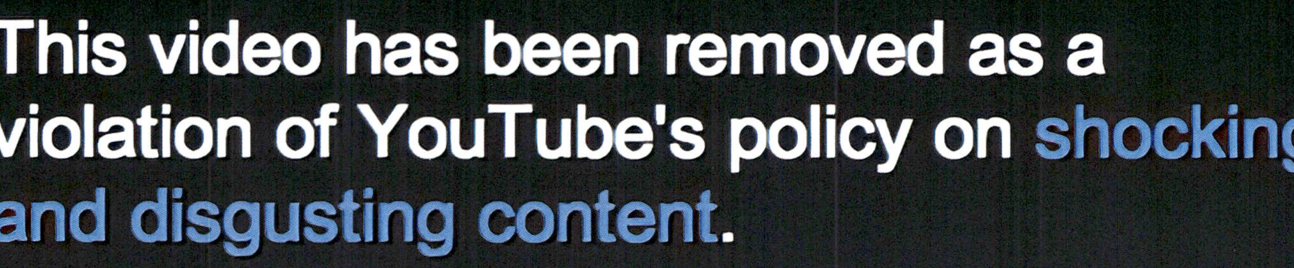

This video has been removed as a violation of YouTube's policy on shocking and disgusting content.
Sorry about that.

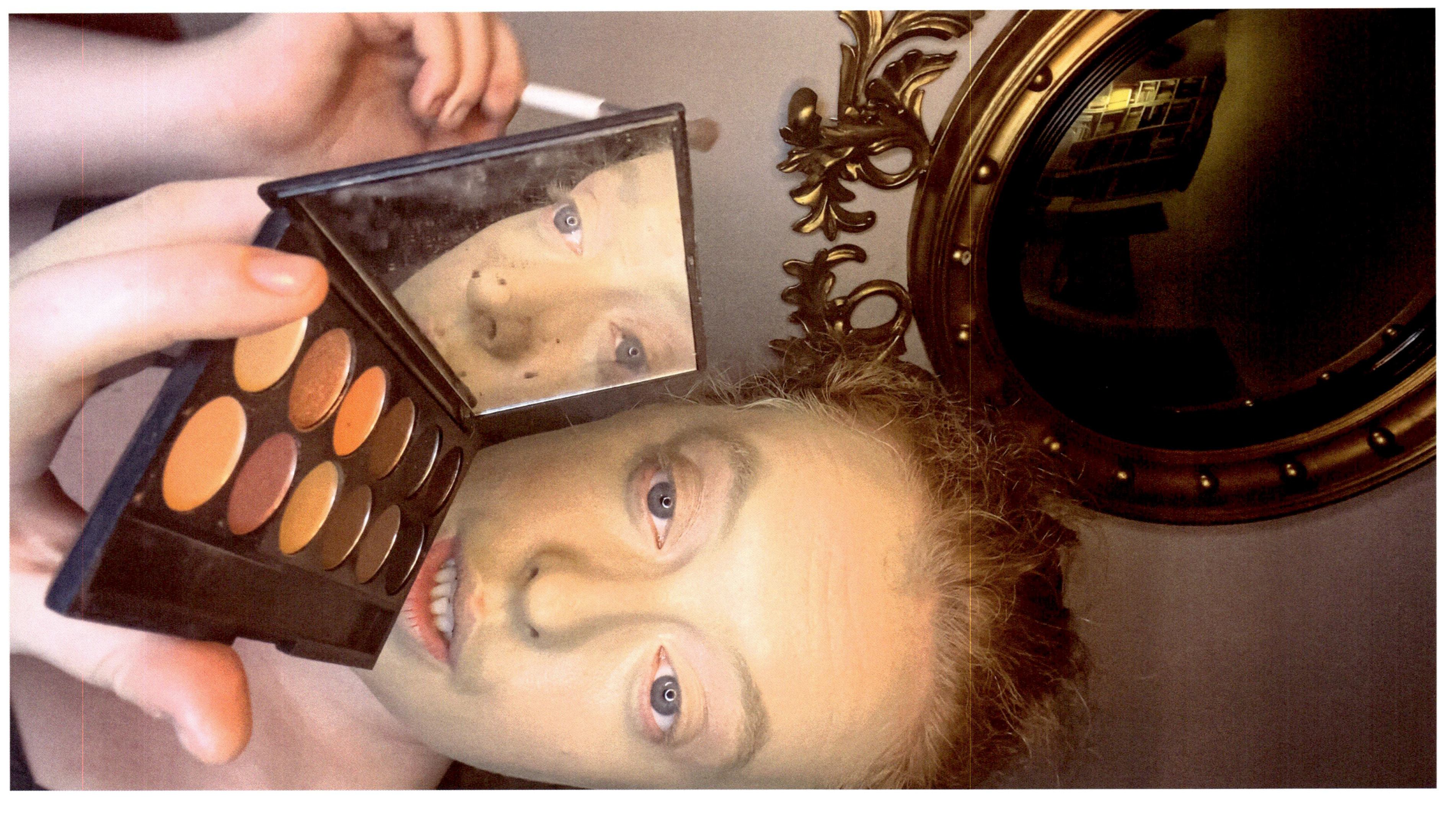

"In the past, before I had the job,   I knew that content moderation existed,   but I thought it was done by a computer, not by real people."

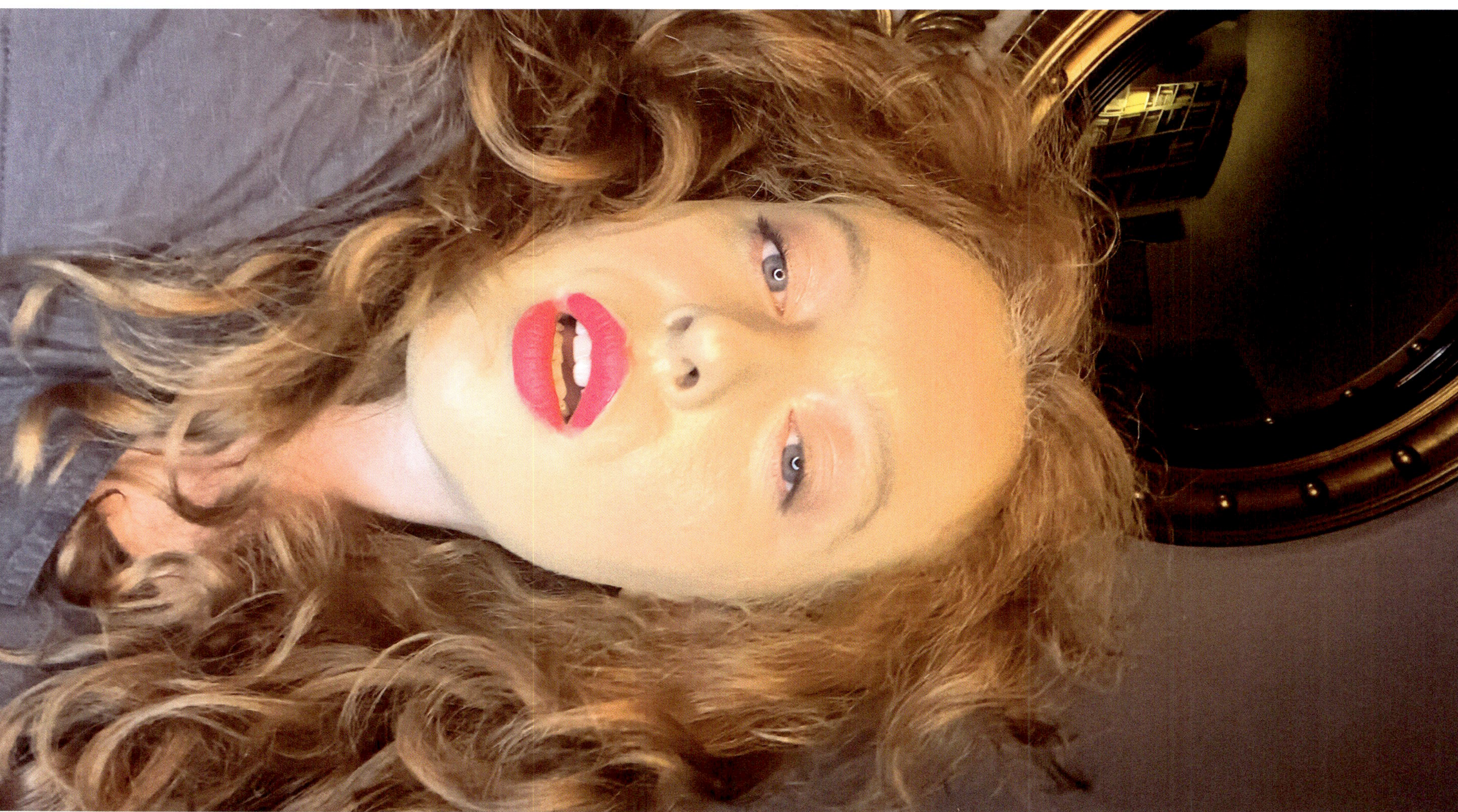

"In fact,   when working,
    we see that people think we're robots."

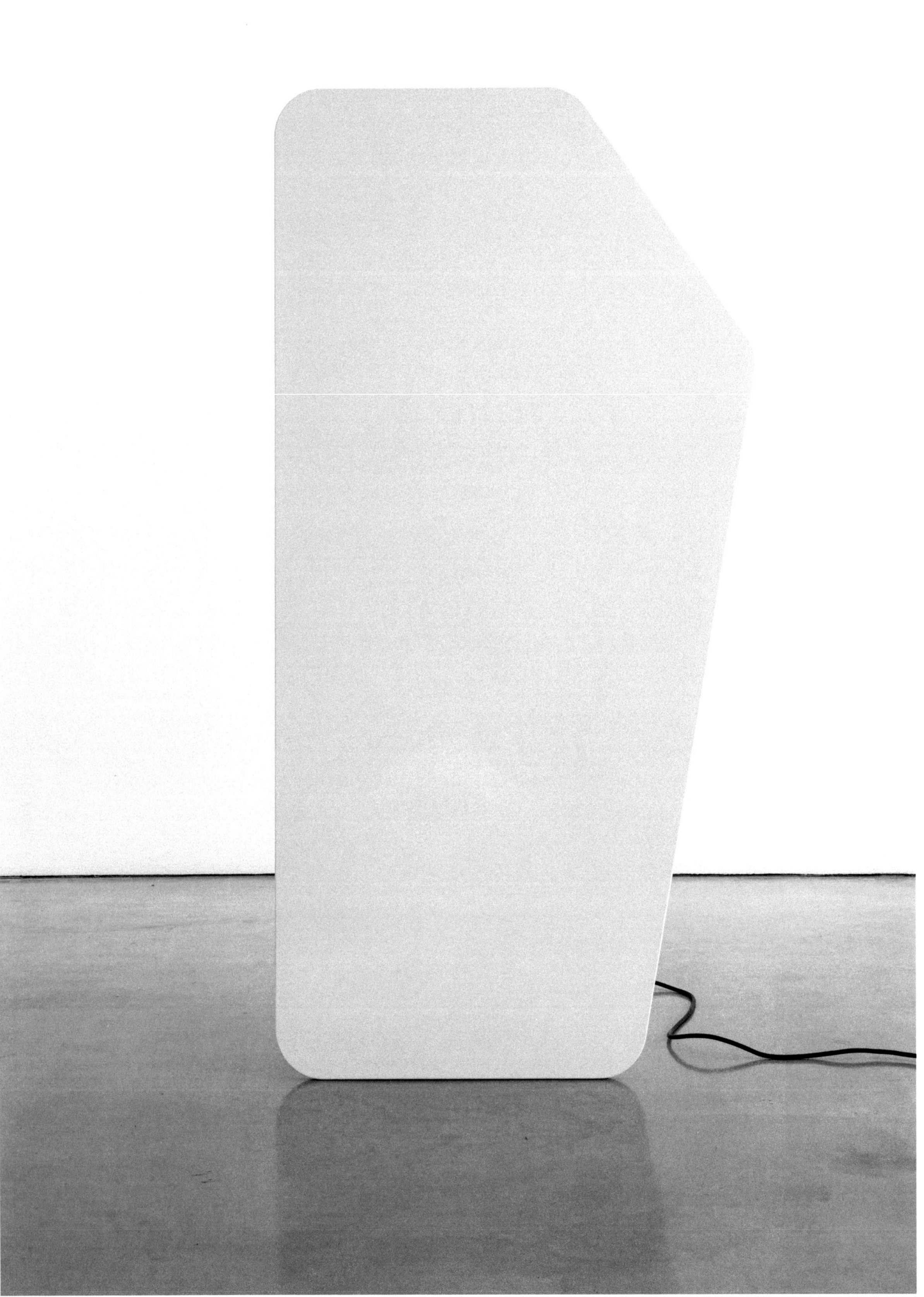

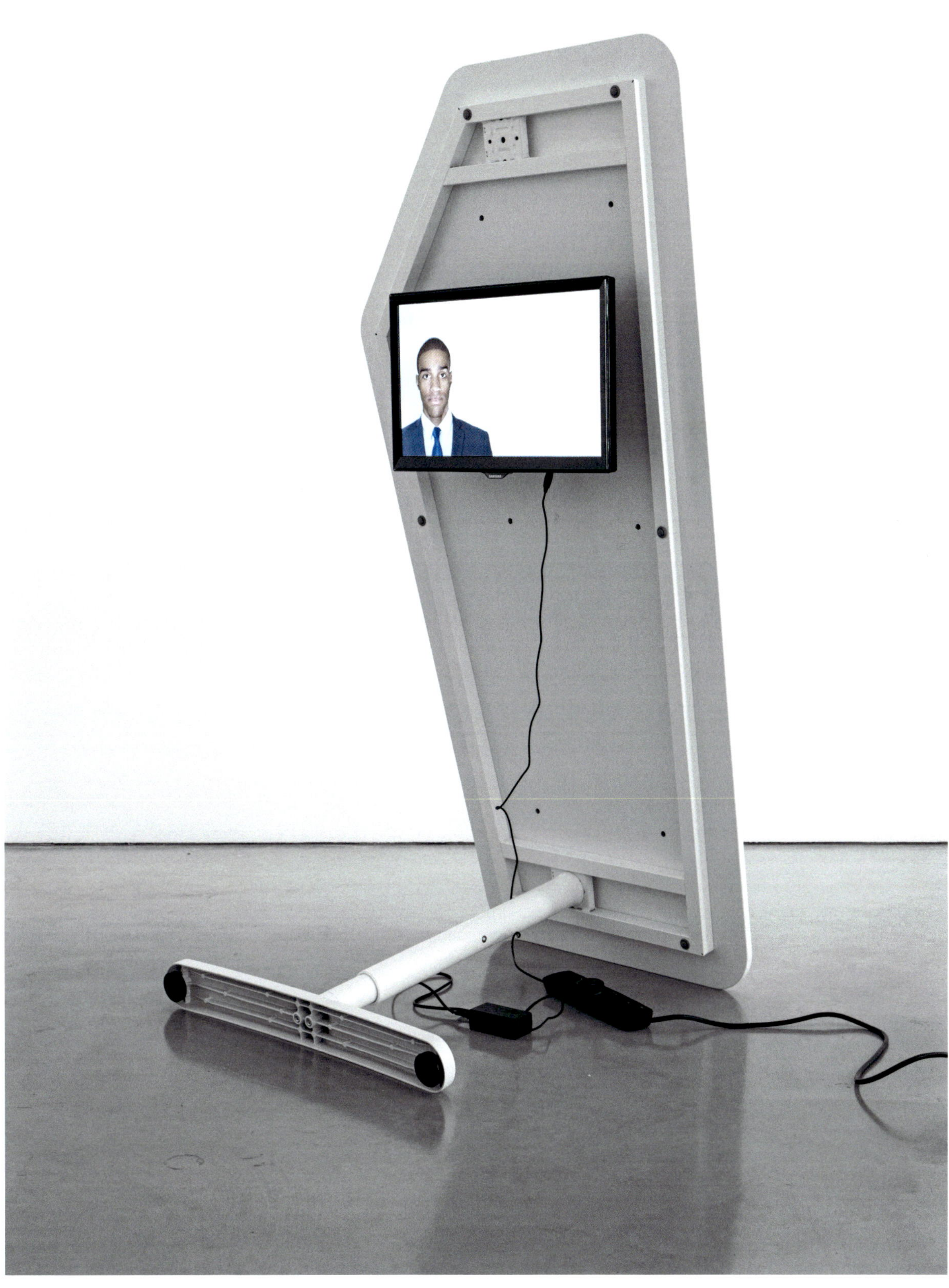

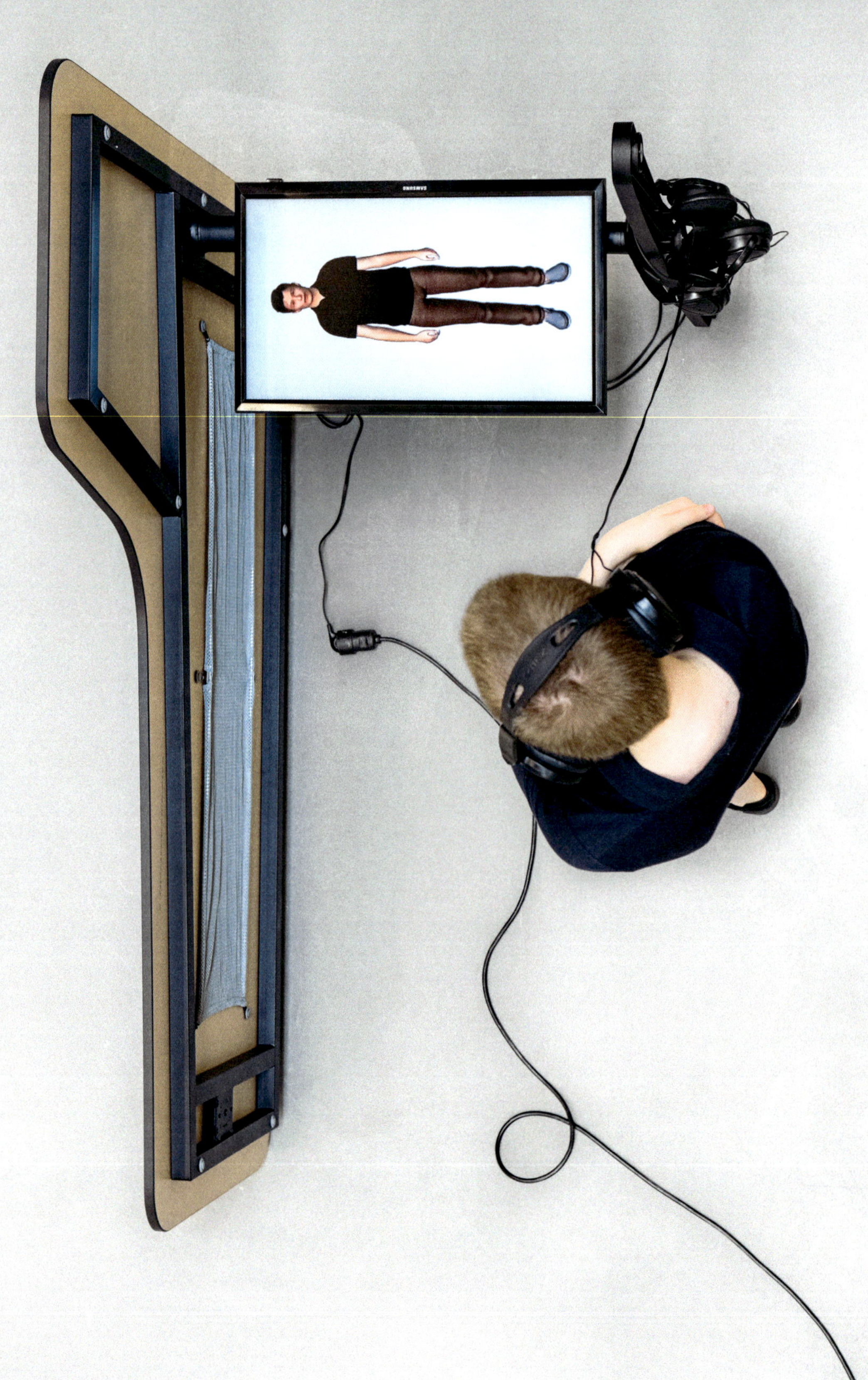

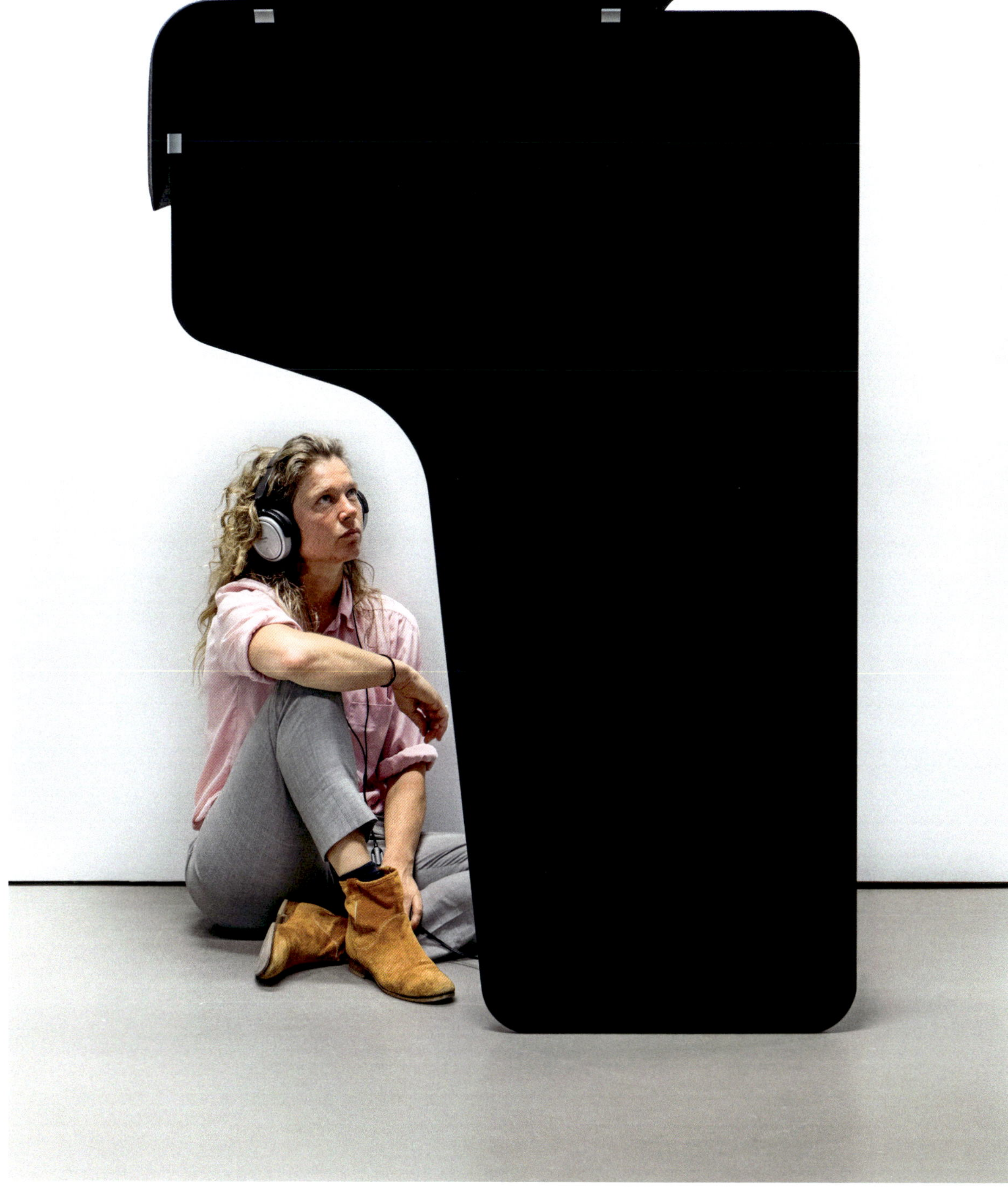

Abuse Standards Violations, 2016–

The job of internet **content moderation**[>p. 133] is often outsourced to workers from emerging economies and developing countries. Hired at low wages through intermediary firms, content moderators have to sign non-disclosure agreements and usually don't know which internet company they are working for.

During their research for *Dark Content* (2015), corporate guidelines were leaked to Eva & Franco Mattes that stipulate how content needs to be classified in order to be removed from the internet.

The wall-mounted insulation panels of *Abuse Standards Violations* show lists of breaches of the norms and standards that need to be filtered out and deleted. Apart from obviously severe cases, such as child abuse or torture, the guidelines are modified on a weekly basis in response to current social and political events and vary locally and culturally.

The standards violations map out morality through the lens of **social media**[>p. 138]. Yet the subtlety with which content is classified as "clean", "safe" or "inappropriate" also conveys the ambivalence of this undertaking: internet giants set out to protect people from the consequences of hate and violence by interfering covertly and largely unchallenged with cultural, societal and governmental processes of normatisation. At the same time, the price of protecting the general public is paid by the content moderators who are exploited by cheap labour and put under psychological stress.

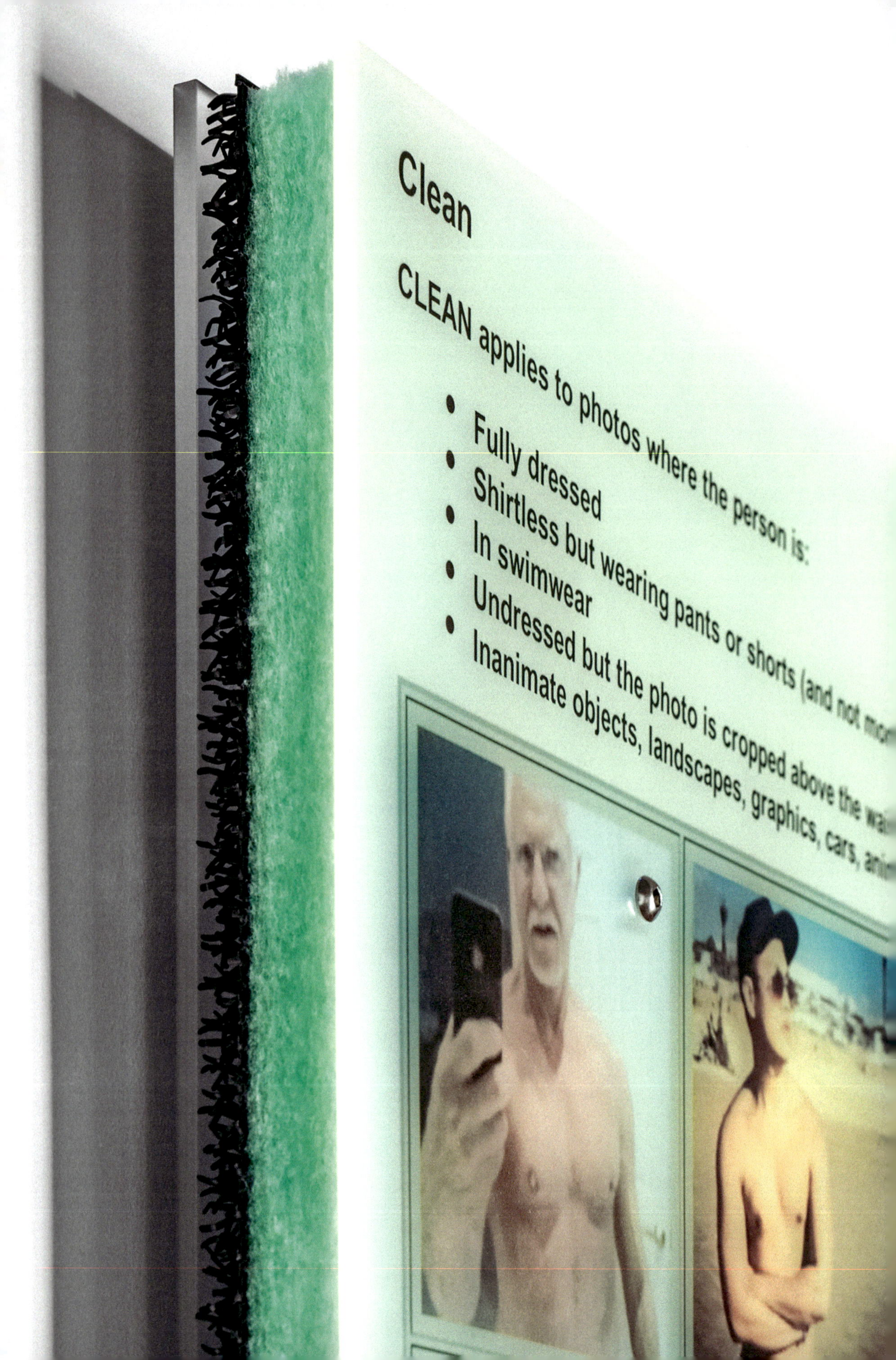

Clean

CLEAN applies to photos where the person is:

- Fully dressed
- Shirtless but wearing pants or shorts (and not mor
- In swimwear
- Undressed but the photo is cropped above the wai
- Inanimate objects, landscapes, graphics, cars, ani

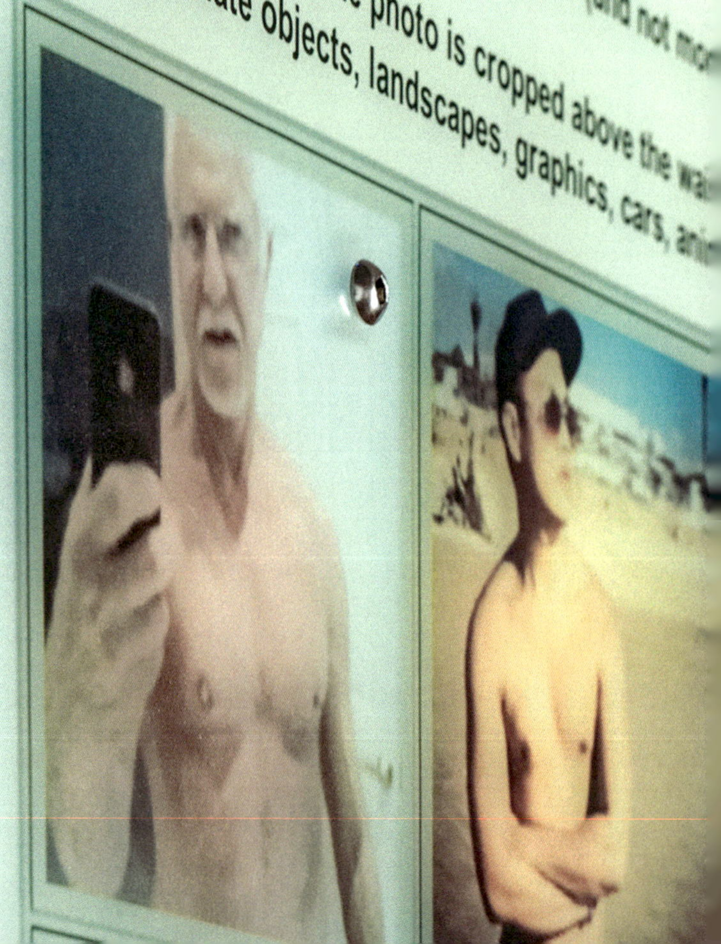

Instructions

Categorizing Images

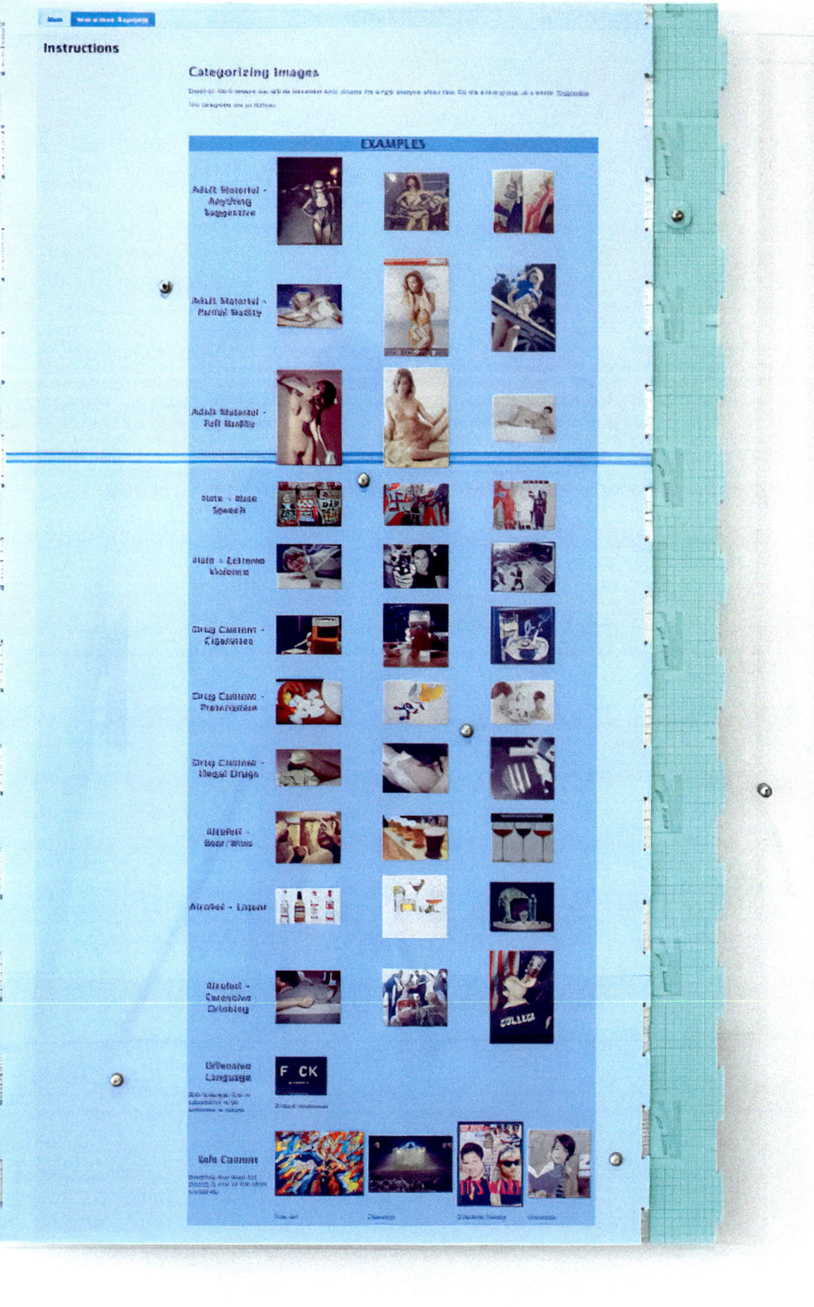

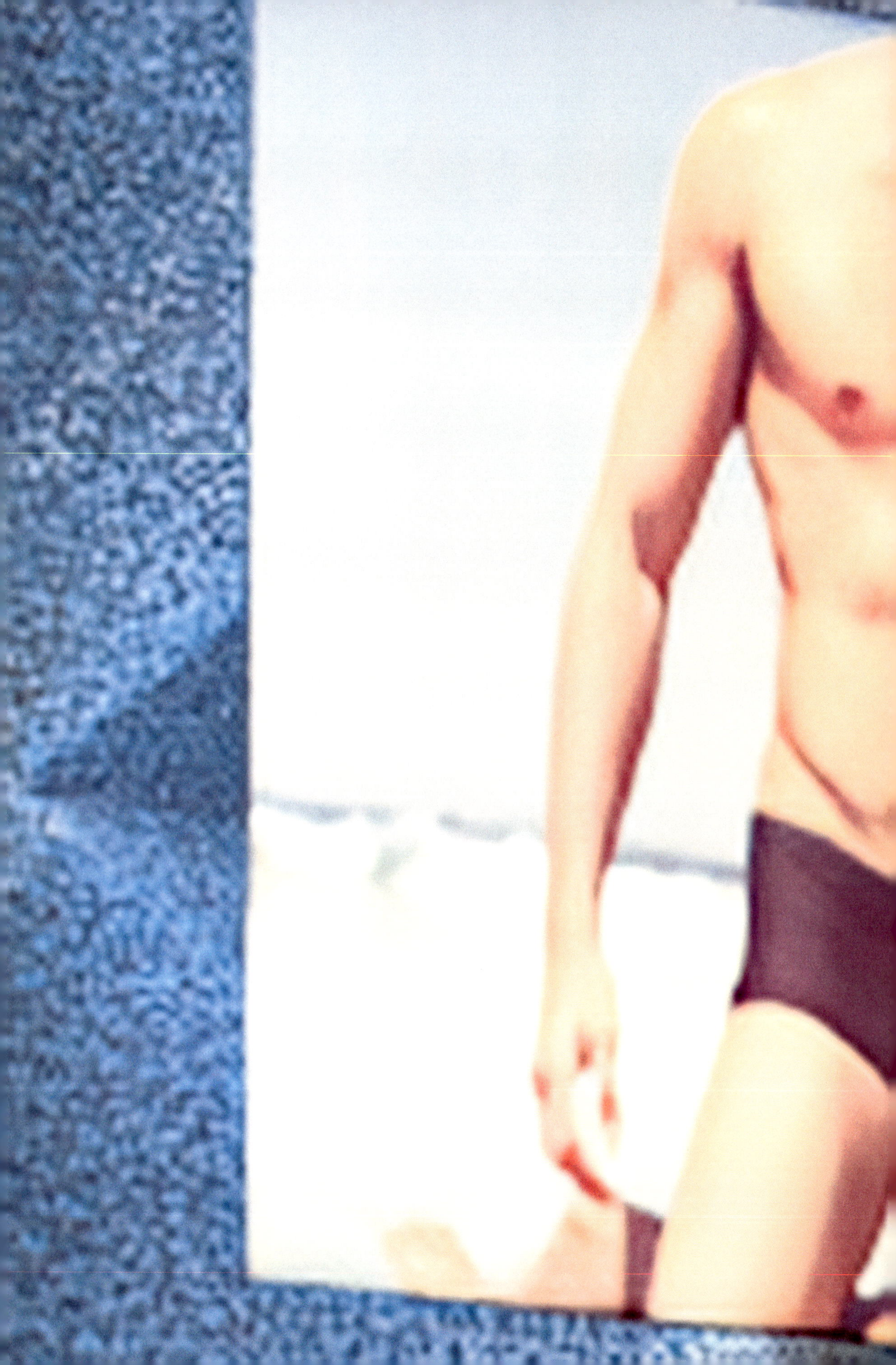

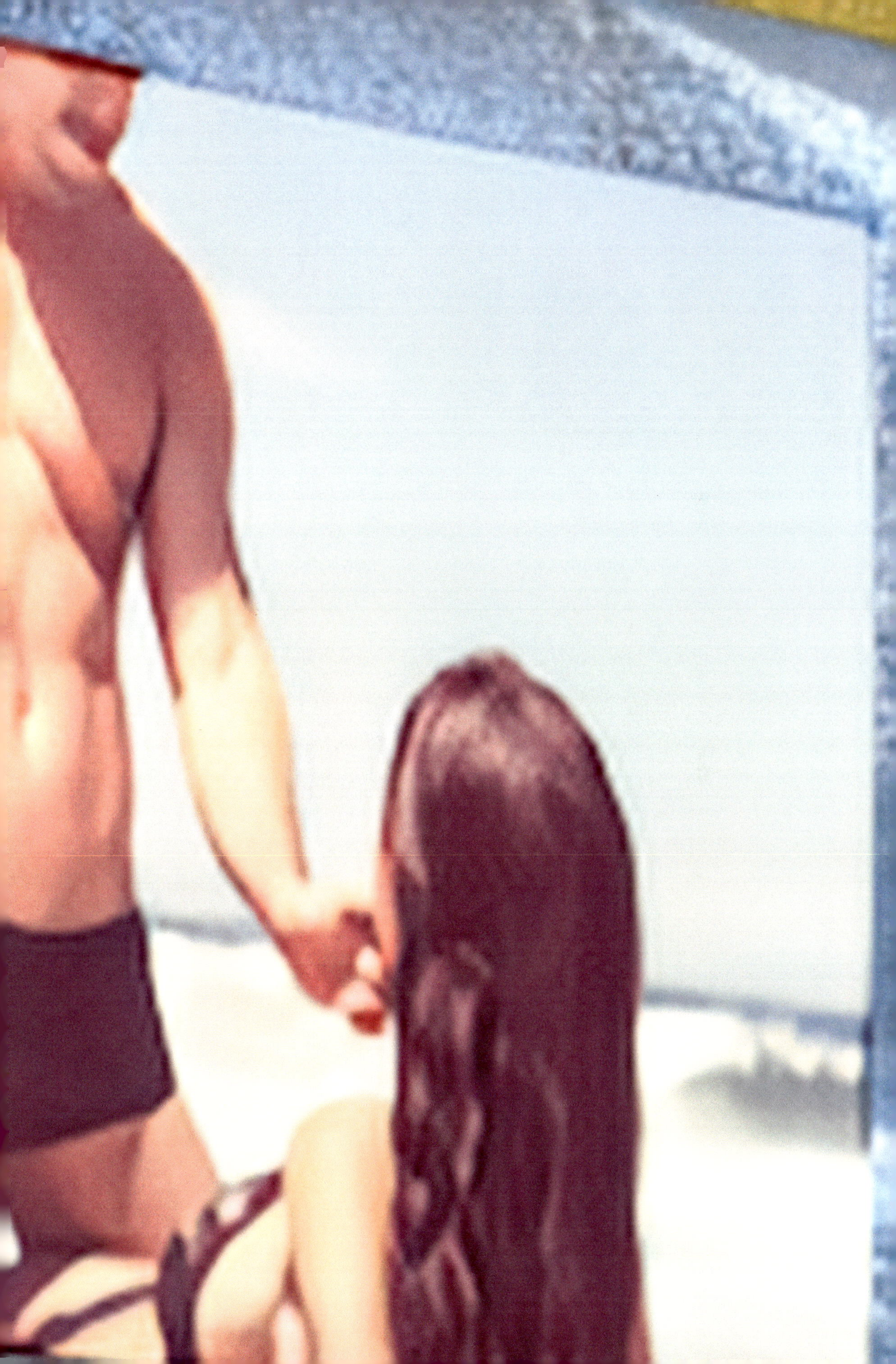

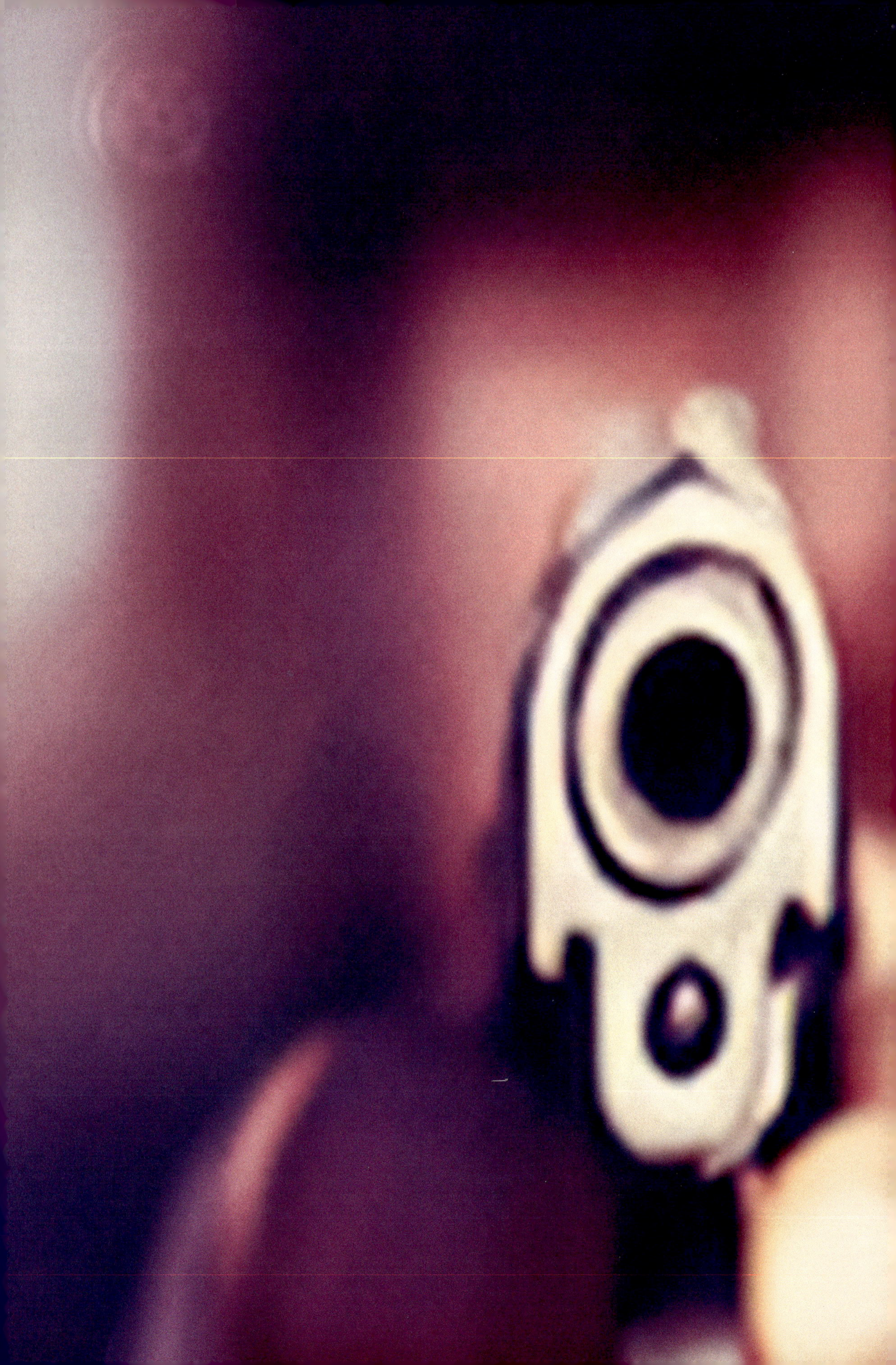

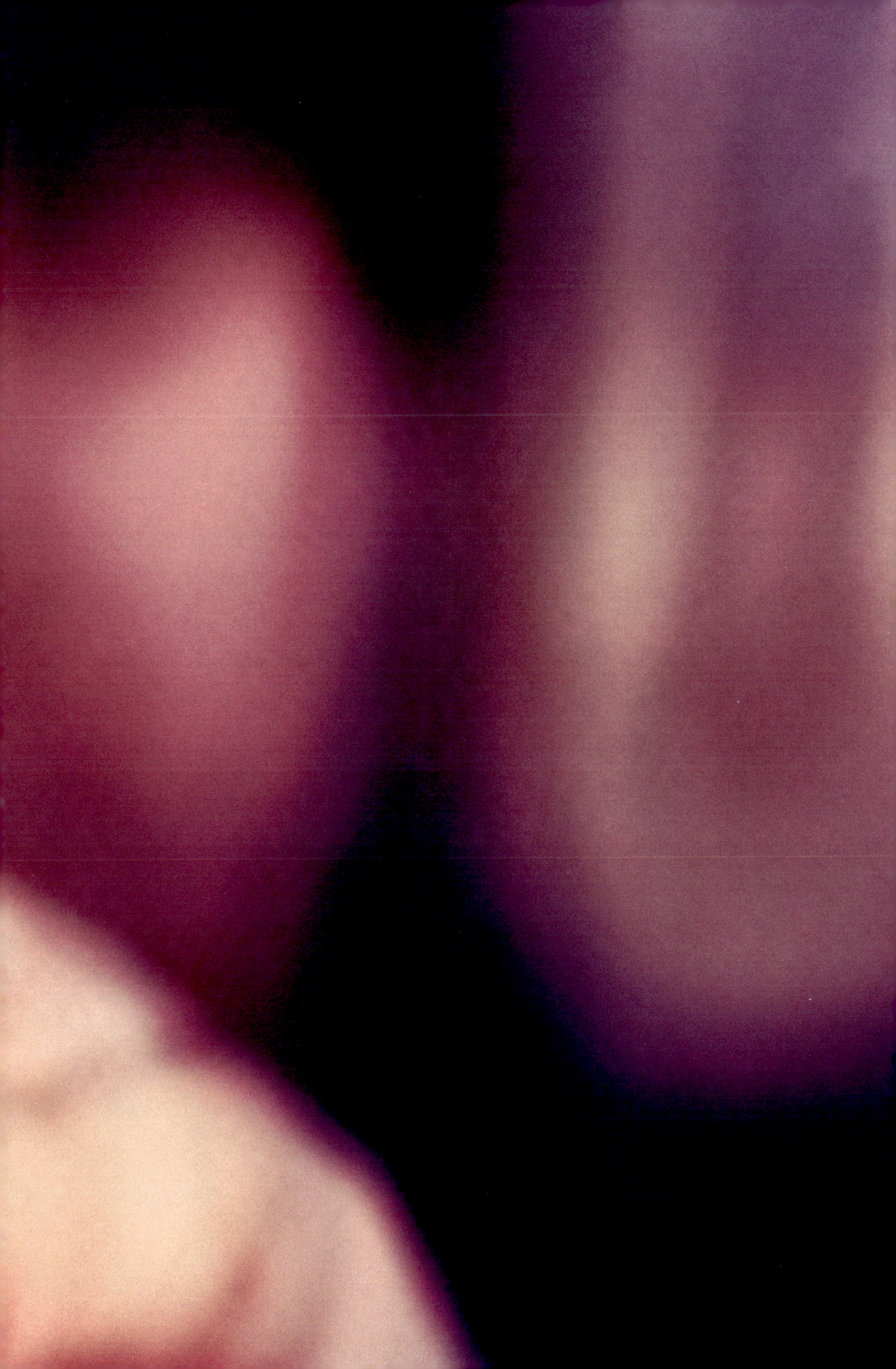

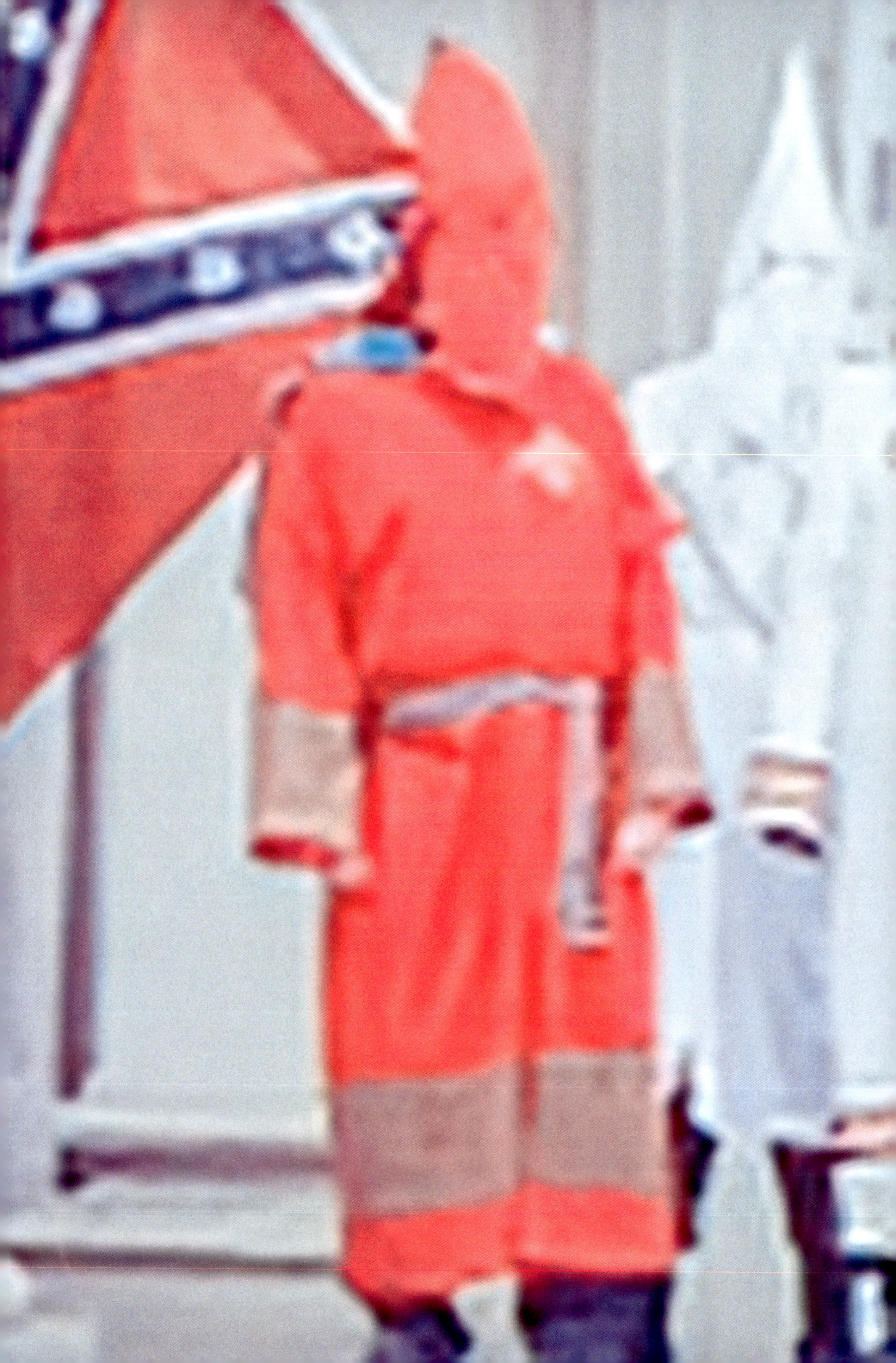

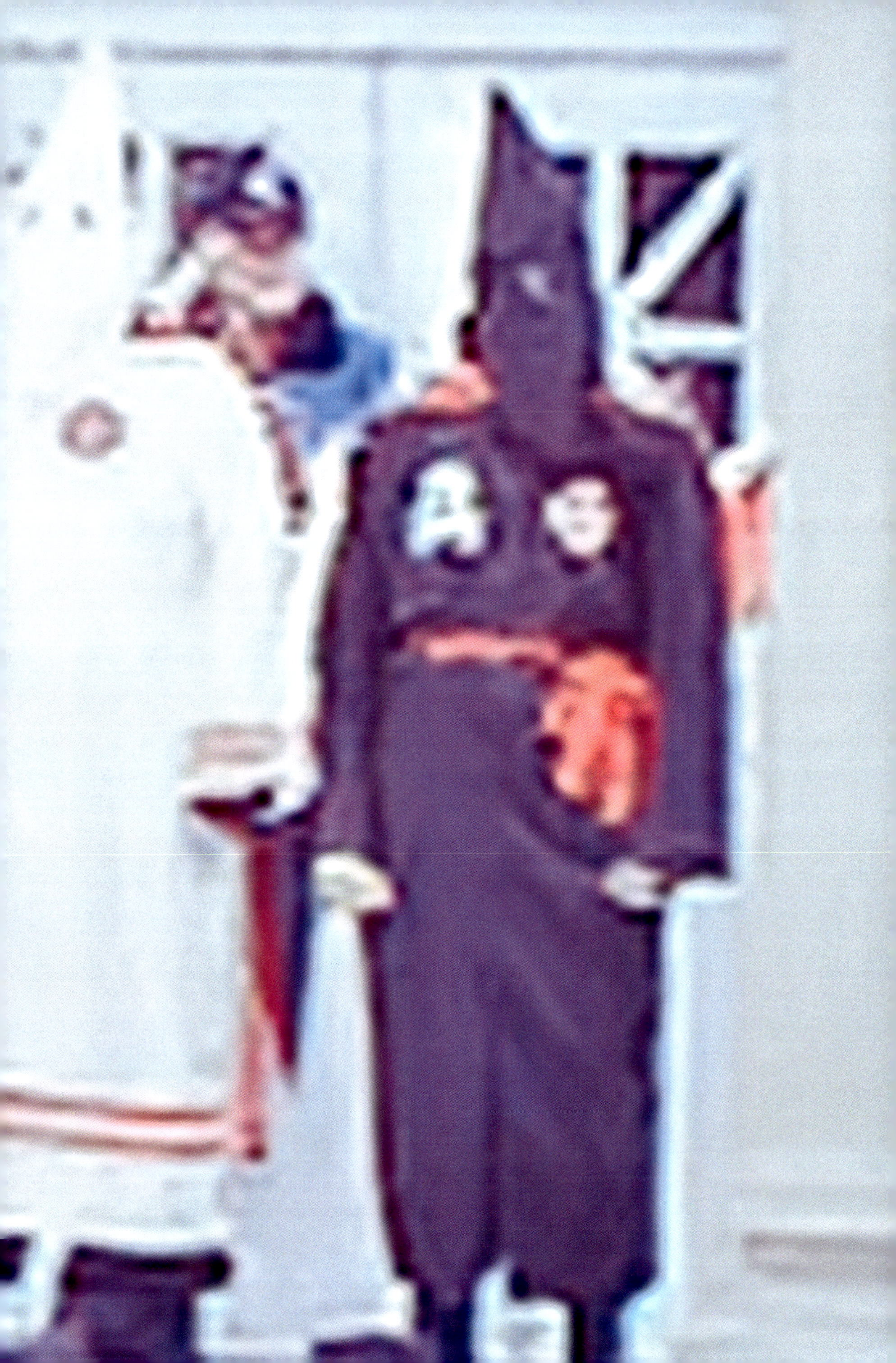

You are assigned with classifying an image, use the following examples as a guide:

Scroll down to continue. You will only been shown this on the first HIT you do with us and periodically after.

Pharmaceutical Elements:

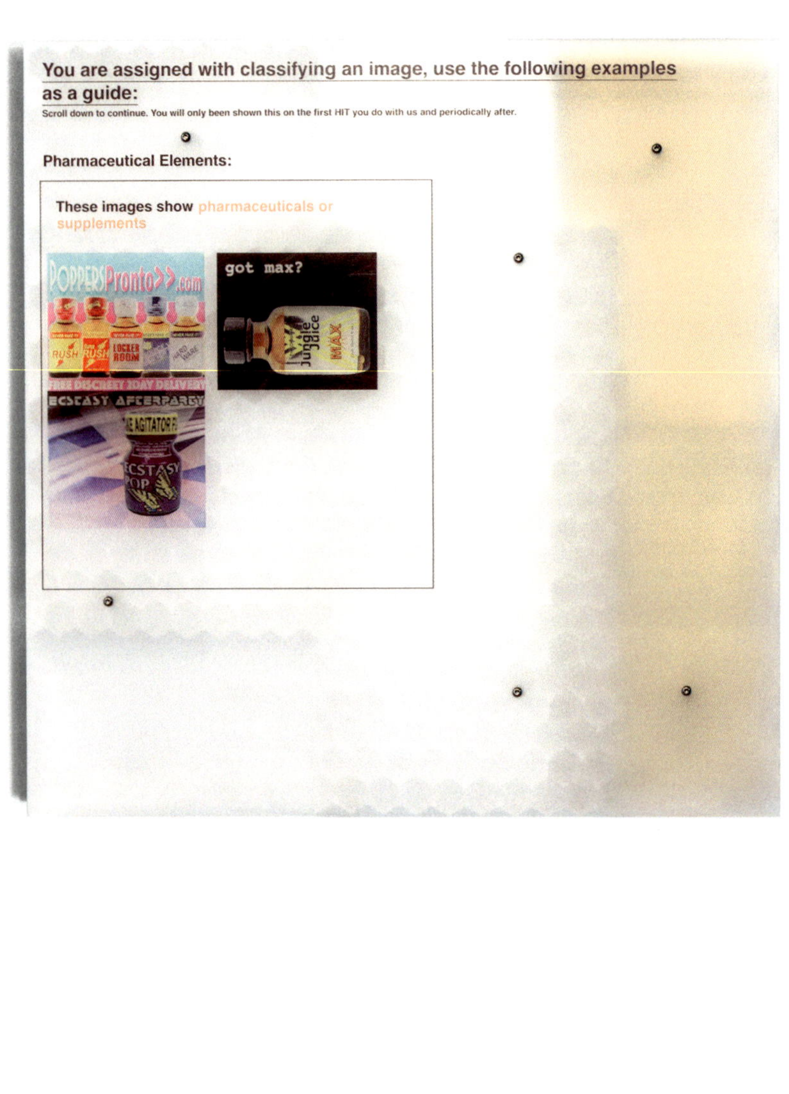

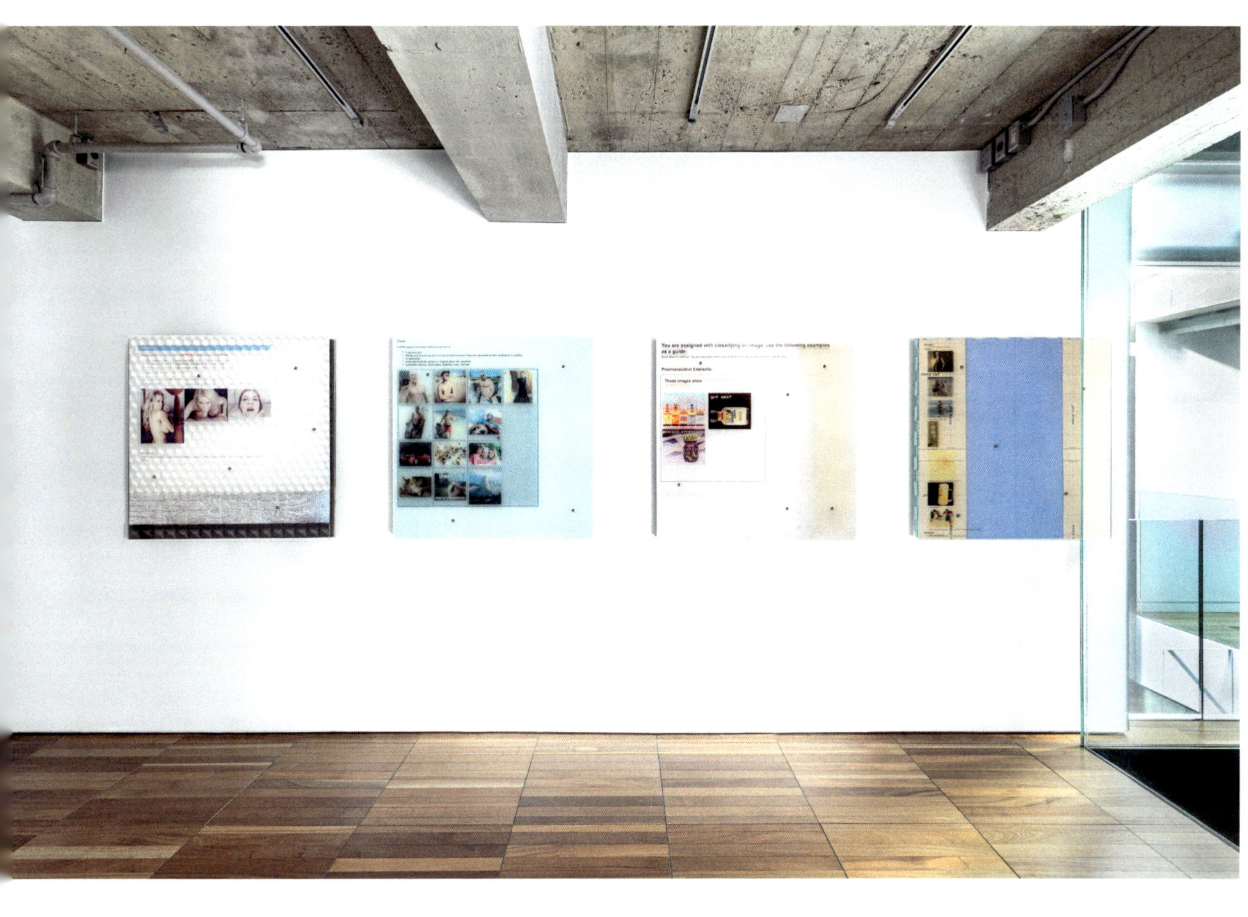

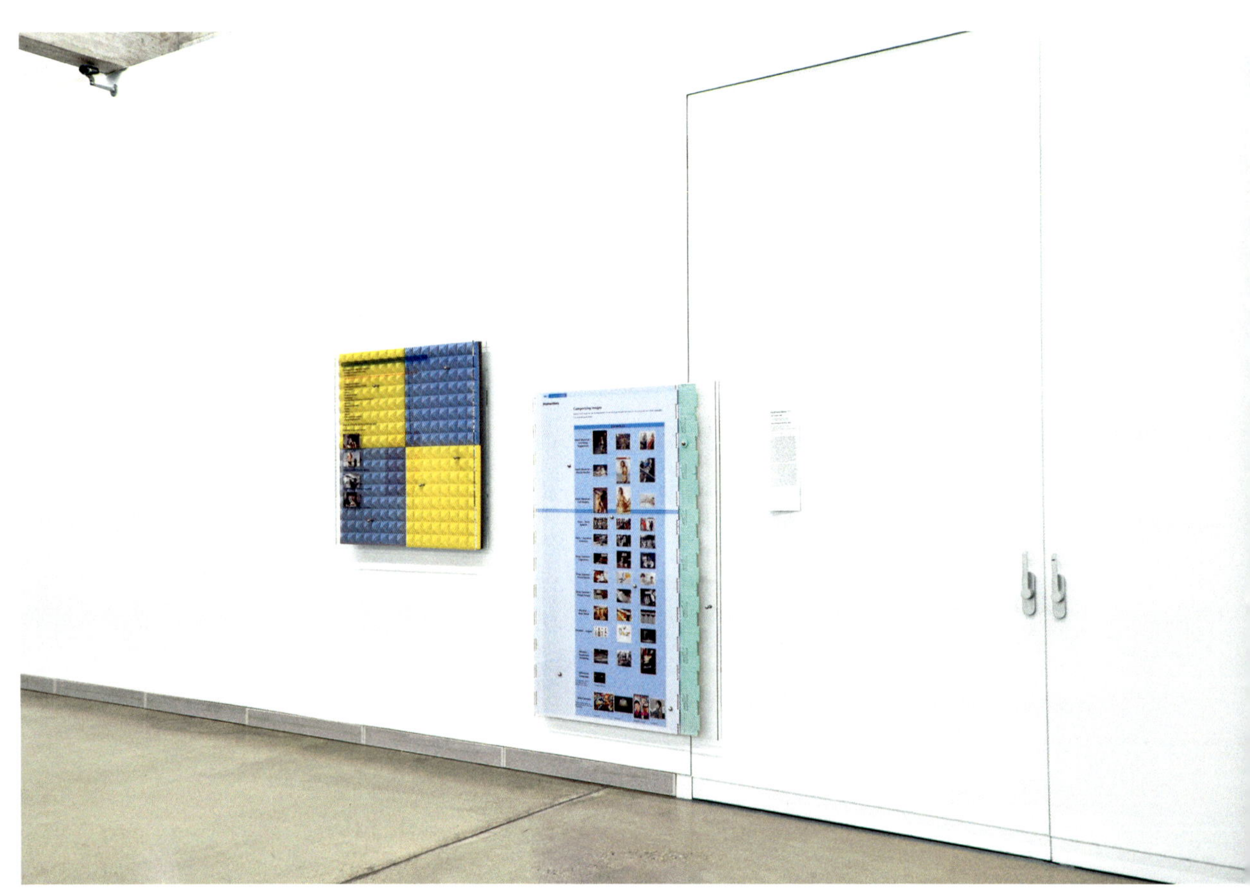

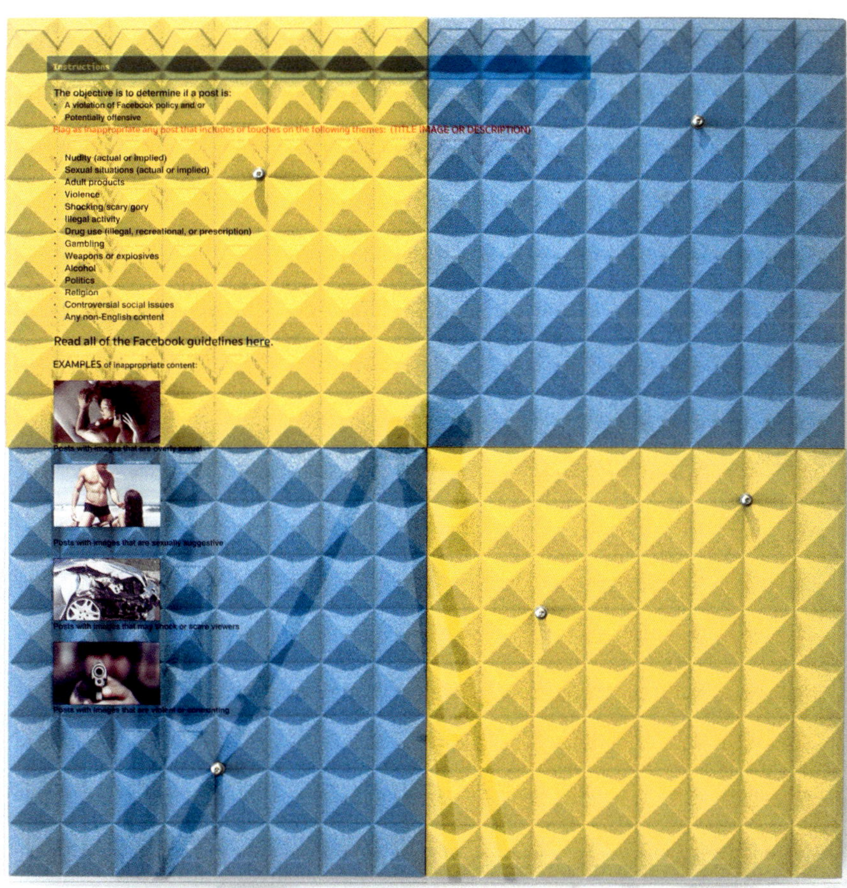

Instructions

The objective is to determine if a post is:
· A violation of Facebook policy and/or
· Potentially offensive
Flag as inappropriate any post that includes or touches on the following themes: (TITLE IMAGE OR DESCRIPTION)

· Nudity (actual or implied)
· Sexual situations (actual or implied)
· Adult products
· Violence
· Shocking/scary/gory
· Illegal activity
· Drug use (illegal, recreational, or prescription)
· Gambling
· Weapons or explosives
· Alcohol
· Politics
· Religion
· Controversial social issues
· Any non-English content

Read all of the Facebook guidelines here.

EXAMPLES of inappropriate content:

Posts with images that are overtly sexual

Posts with images that are sexually suggestive

Posts with images that may shock or scare viewers

Posts with images that are violent or confronting

BEFNOED,
2014–

BEFNOED – an acronym for By Everyone, For No One, Every Day – is a take on the **gig economy**[>p. 135] that both embraces and discloses its mechanisms.

For this screen-based installation, Eva & Franco Mattes **crowdsourced**[>p. 135] various jobs (gigs) to anonymous paid workers, providing them with detailed instructions to perform absurd actions and document them with webcams.

Different workers interpreted the same performance with slight variations.

In accordance with the crowdsourcing platform's rules, neither the identity of the commissioner nor the purpose or usage of the videos is disclosed to the contractors.

The artists uploaded the videos to largely peripheral or outdated **social media**[>p. 138] platforms in China, Cambodia, Pakistan or Brazil, where they circulate without any captions or further context, some with few views and some with no views at all.

BEFNOED not only reflects the morally questionable actions and capitalist sadism of the gig economy but also exposes the complicity of the consumers, in this case the viewers.

This aspect is further enhanced by the arrangement of the screens: like the commissioned workers, visitors have to strain, stretch and bend to consume the videos – and are confronted in the process with their own participation in an exploitative global economy.

初月に40万稼げるスマホを使ったバイト

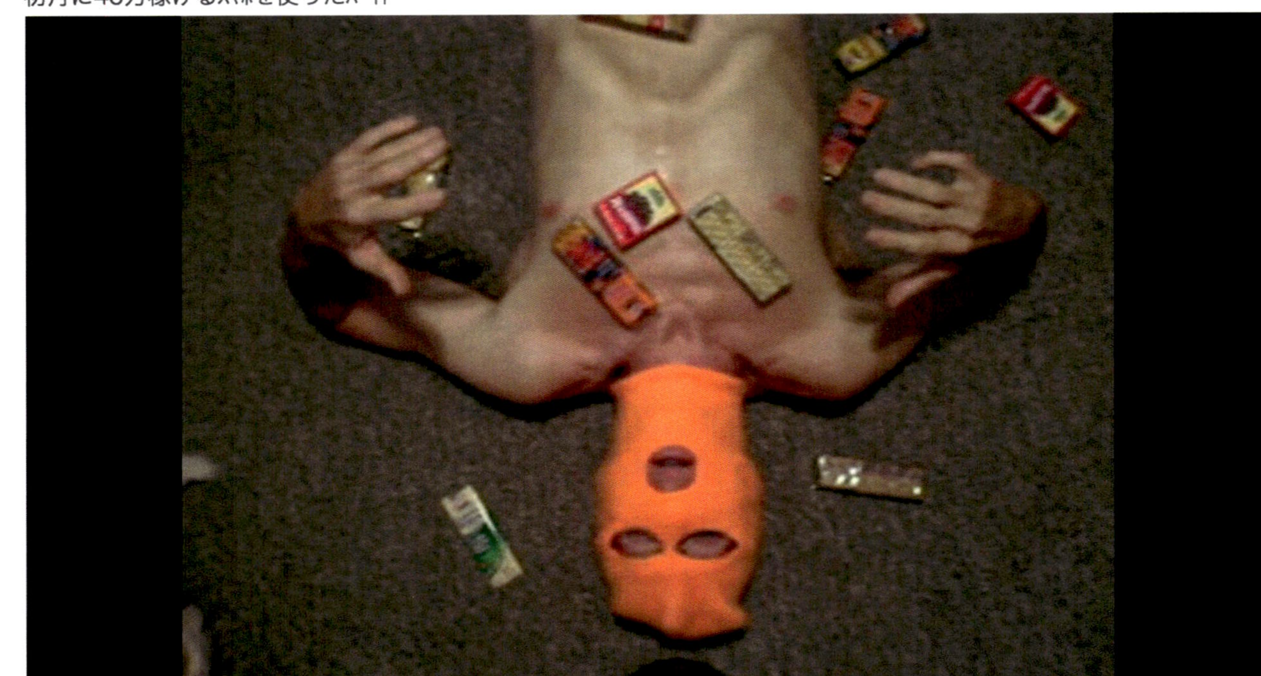

Balaclava Snacks

2016-05-29 アップロード · 2 視聴

Balaclava Snacks

tag Balaclava Snacks

[HD] おすすめ動画

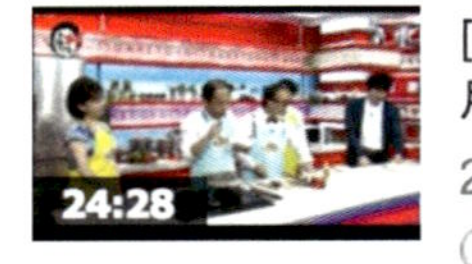

[HD]有吉弘行の
月31日)
2016-05-31 ·
⊙楽Room

国際報道２０１
2016-05-31 ·

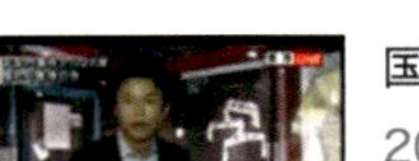

初月に40万稼げるスマホを使ったバイト

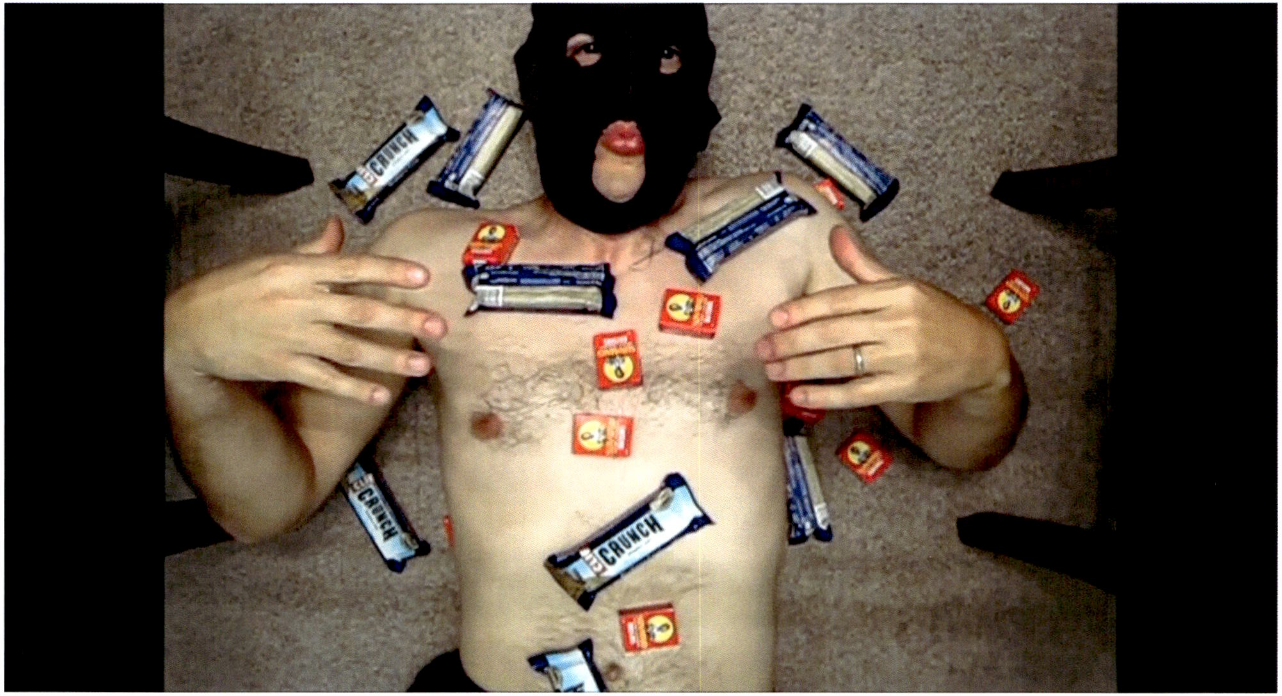

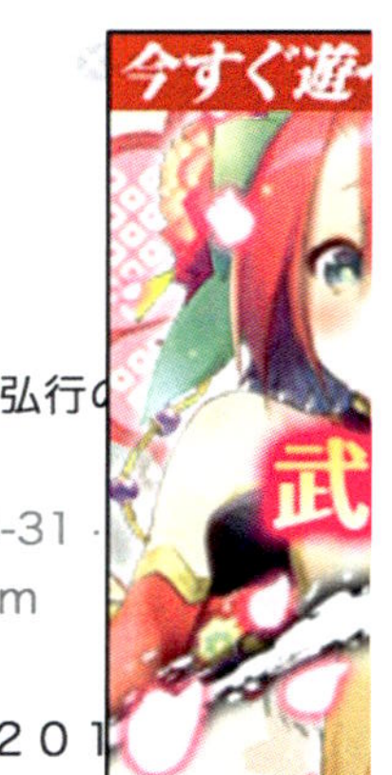

Balaclava Snacks

2016-05-29 アップロード・２ 視聴

Balaclava Snacks

tag: Balaclava Snacks

[HD] おすすめ動画

[HD]有吉弘行の
月31日)
2016-05-31・
⊙楽Room

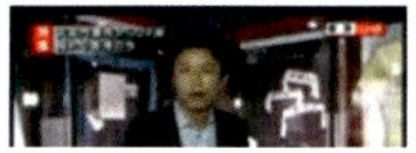

国際報道２０１
2016-05-31・

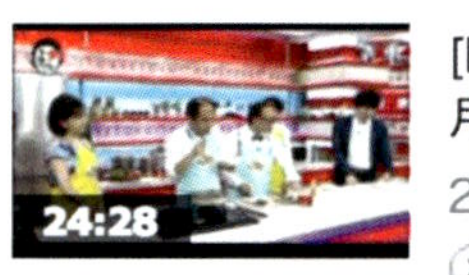

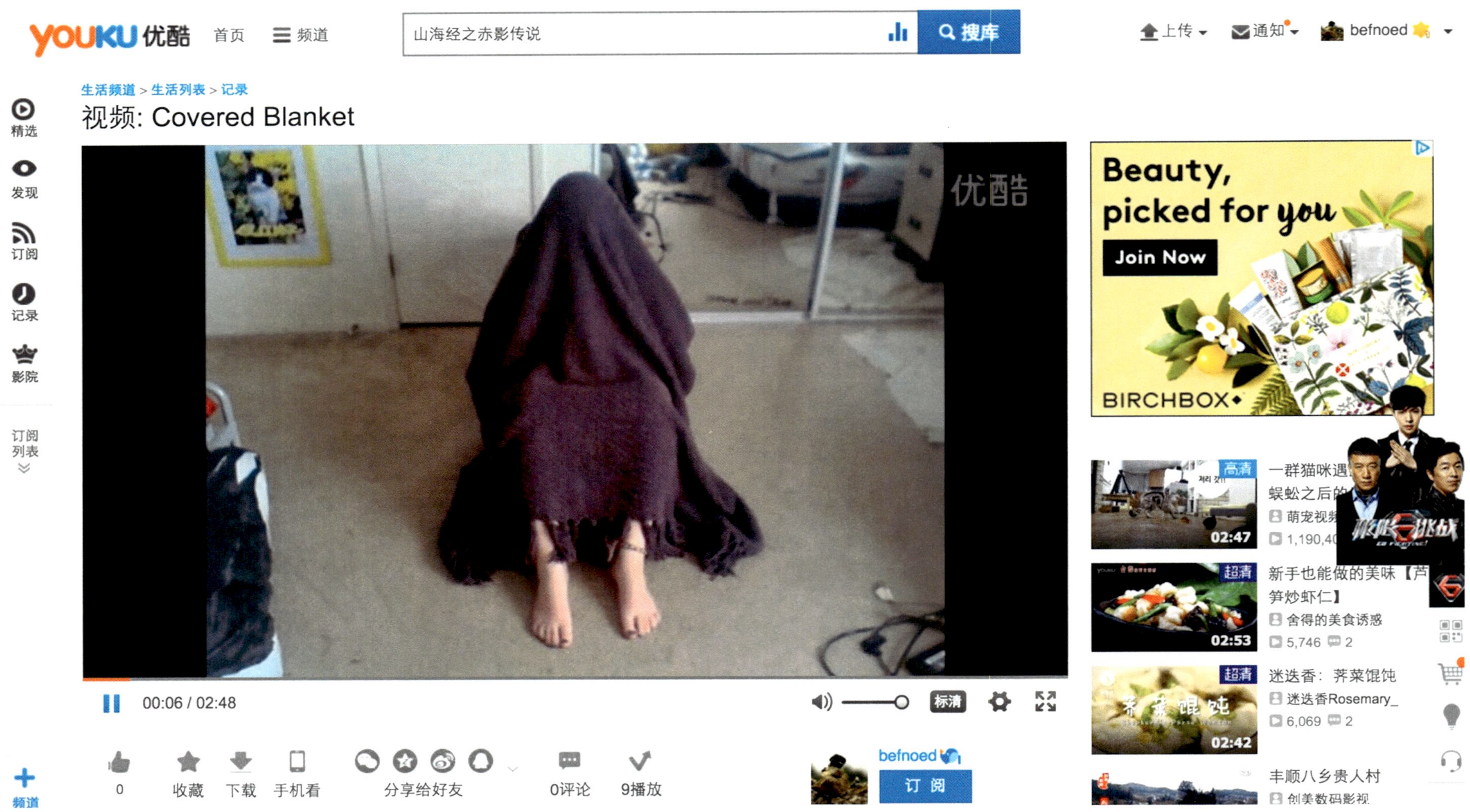

YOUKU 优酷   首页   频道   山海经之赤影传说   搜库   上传   通知   befnoed
生活频道 > 生活列表 > 记录
视频: Covered Blanket
精选
发现
订阅
记录
影院
订阅列表
优酷
00:06 / 02:48   标清
收藏   下载   手机看   分享给好友   0评论   9播放
0
befnoed   订阅
频道
Beauty, picked for you
Join Now
BIRCHBOX
一群猫咪遇
蜈蚣之后的
萌宠视频
02:47   1,190,40
新手也能做的美味【芦笋炒虾仁】
舍得的美食诱惑
02:53   5,746   2
迷迭香：荠菜馄饨
迷迭香Rosemary_
02:42   6,069   2
丰顺八乡贵人村
创美数码影视
高清
超清
超清
荠菜馄饨

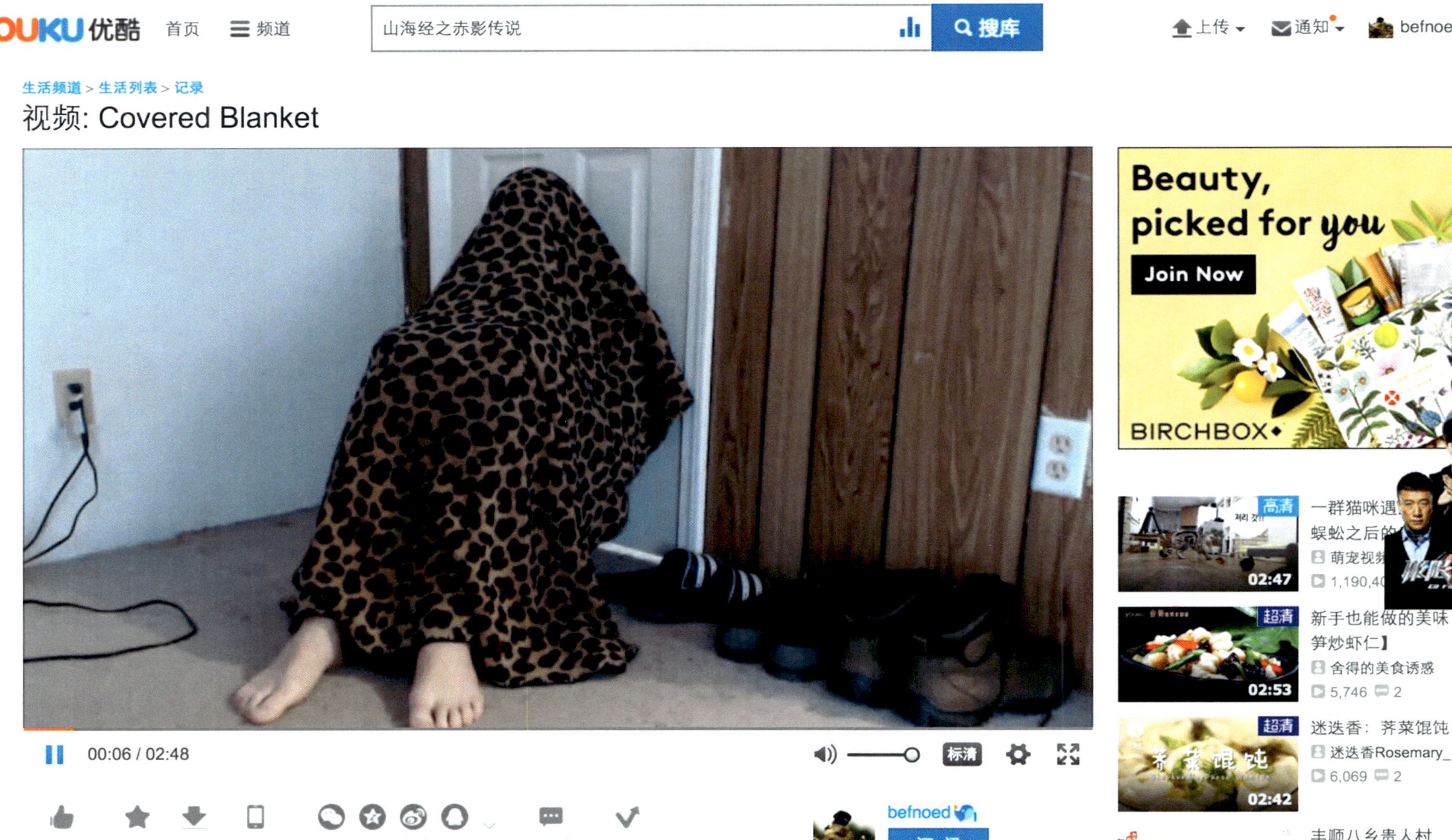
YOUKU 优酷
首页
频道
山海经之赤影传说
搜库
上传
通知
befnoed
生活频道 > 生活列表 > 记录
视频: Covered Blanket
精选
发现
订阅
记录
影院
订阅列表
Beauty, picked for you
Join Now
BIRCHBOX
00:06 / 02:48
标清
一群猫咪遇蜈蚣之后的
萌宠视频
1,190,40
02:47
新手也能做的美味【芦笋炒虾仁】
舍得的美食诱惑
5,746
2
02:53
迷迭香：荠菜馄饨
迷迭香Rosemary_
6,069
2
02:42
丰顺八乡贵人村
创美数码影视
0
收藏
下载
手机看
分享给好友
0评论
9播放
befnoed
订阅
频道

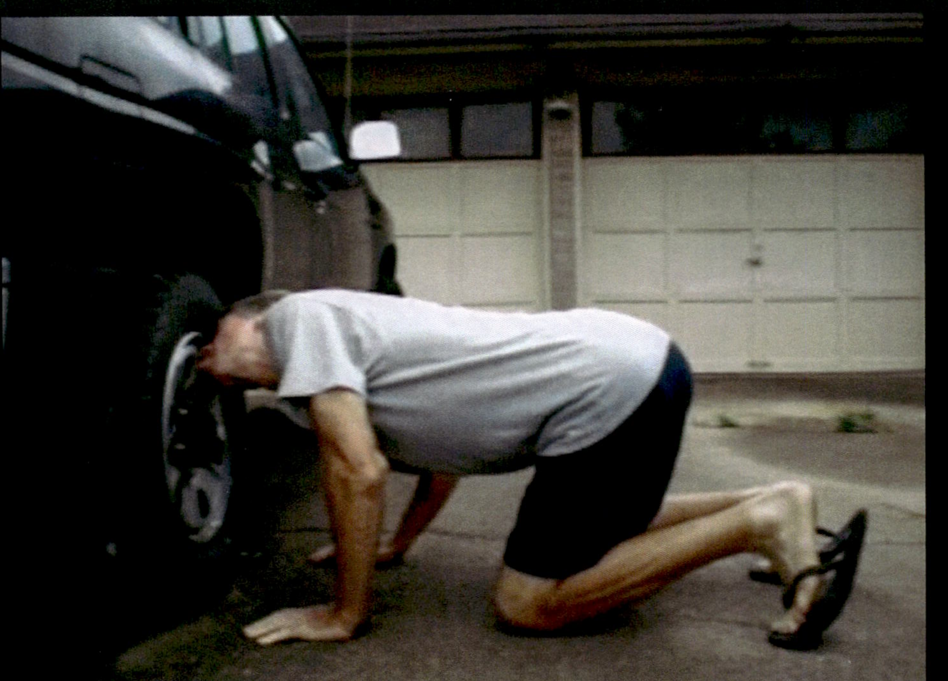

Licking Rim

Bef Noed
May 26, 2016 at 3:15 pm · 8 views

Commenting for this video disabled by the owner.

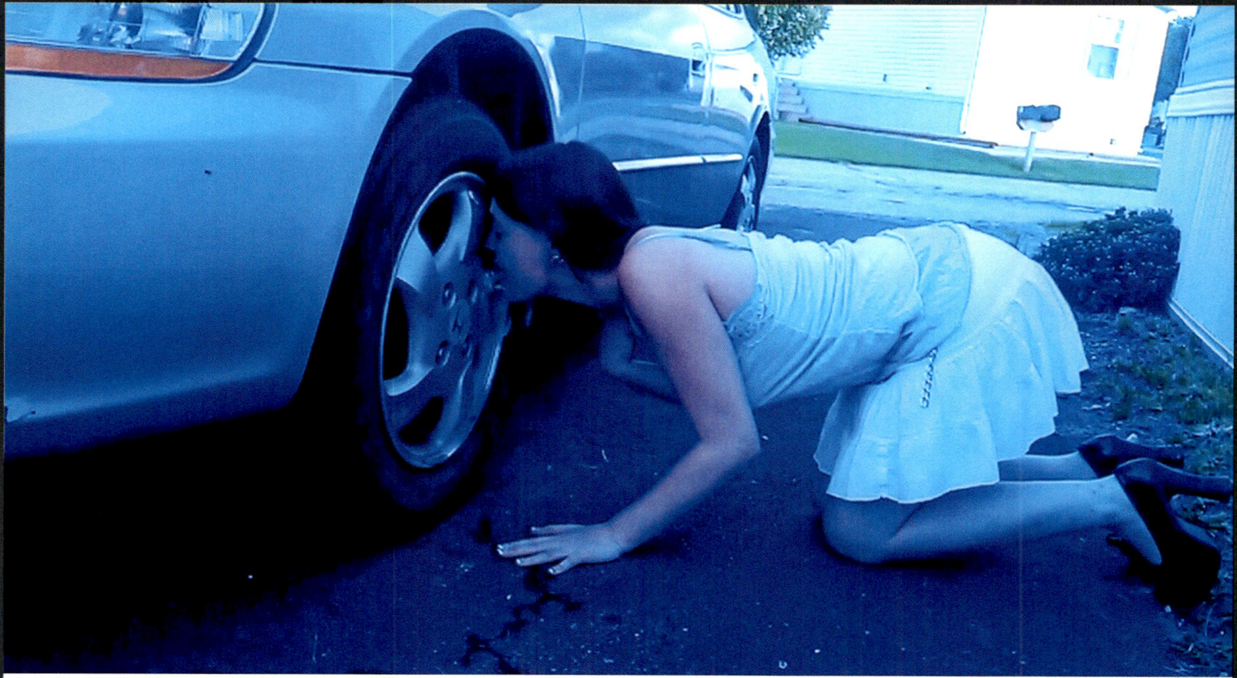

Licking Rim

Bef Noed
May 26, 2016 at 3:15 pm · 8 views

Commenting for this video disabled by the owner.

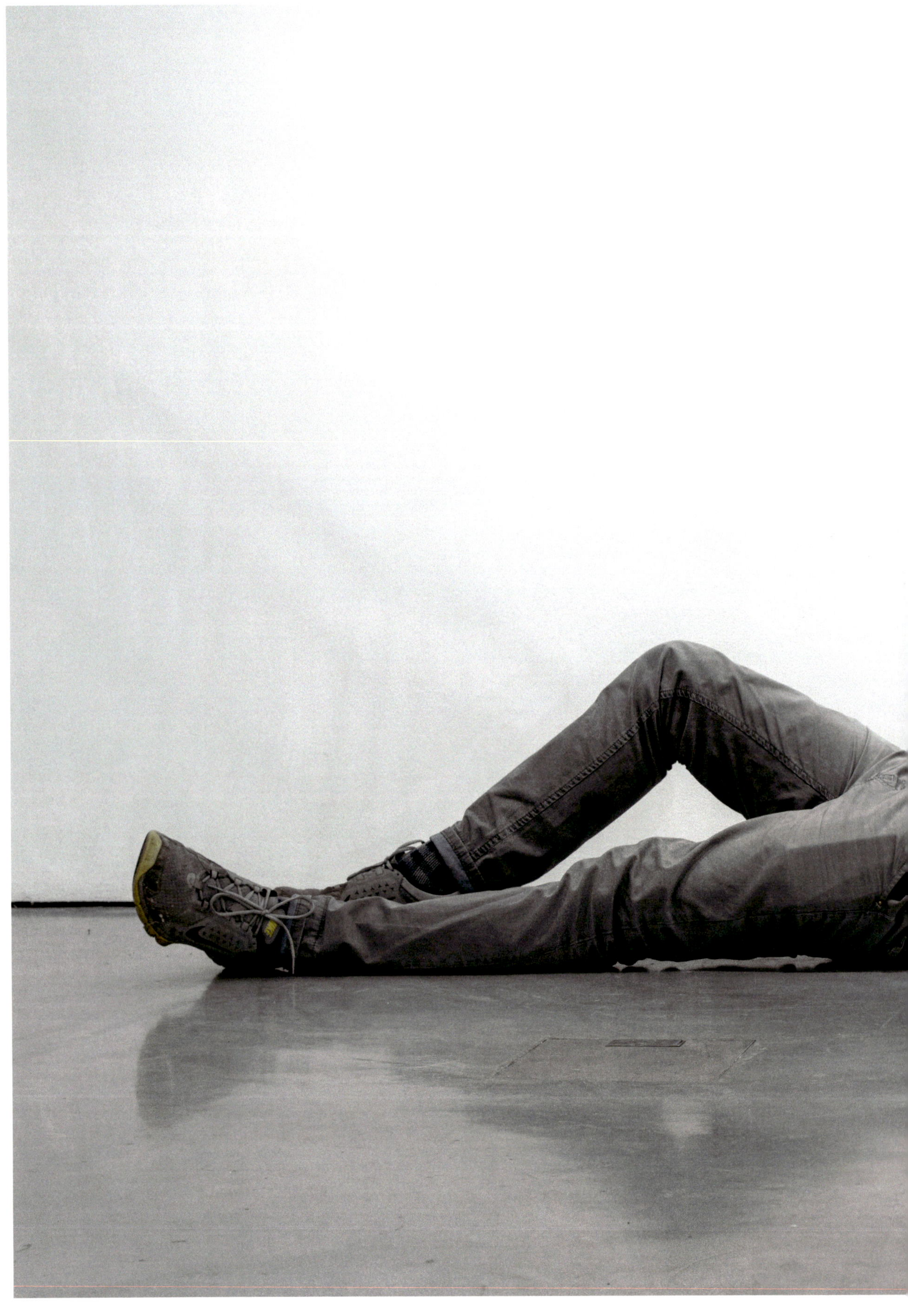

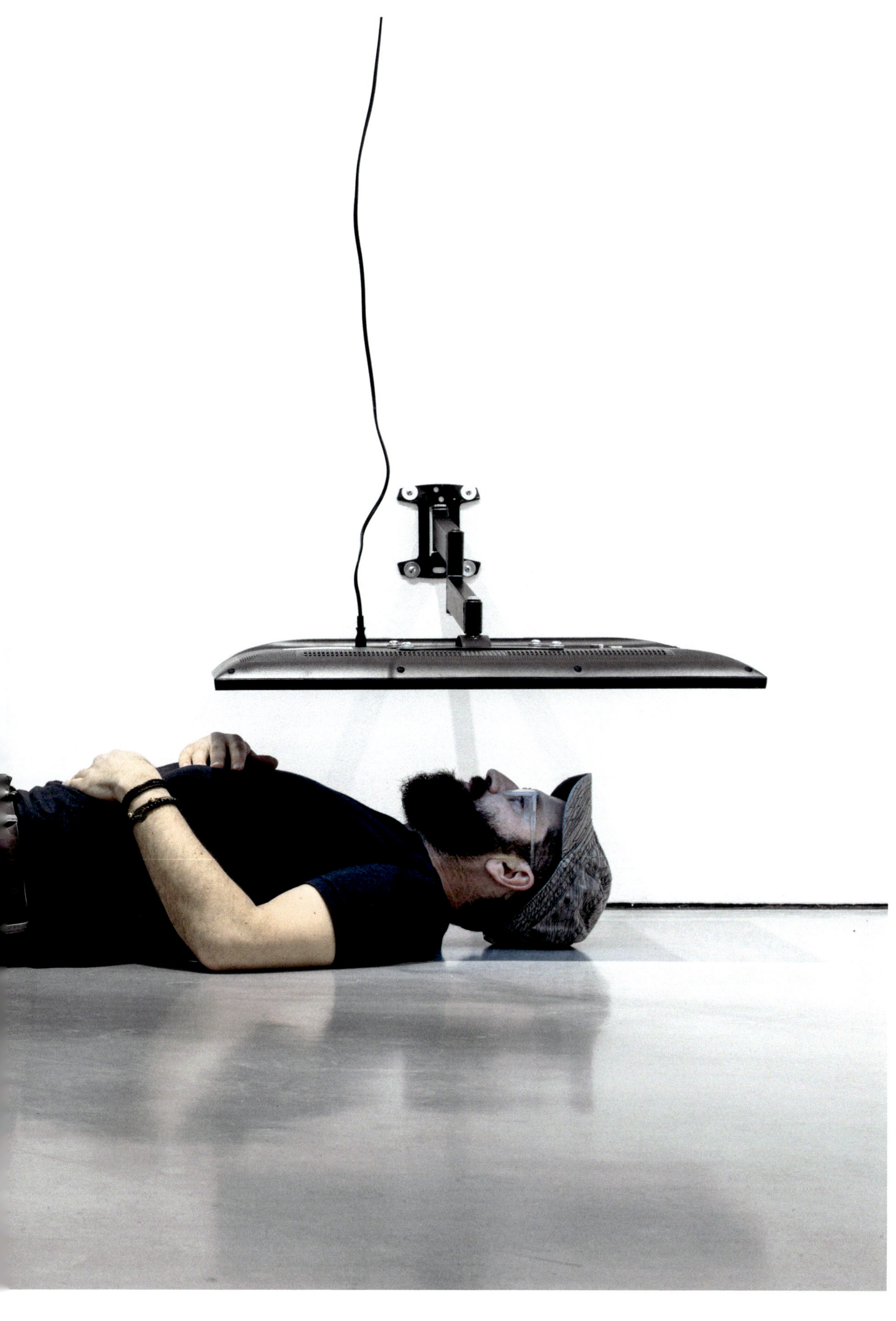

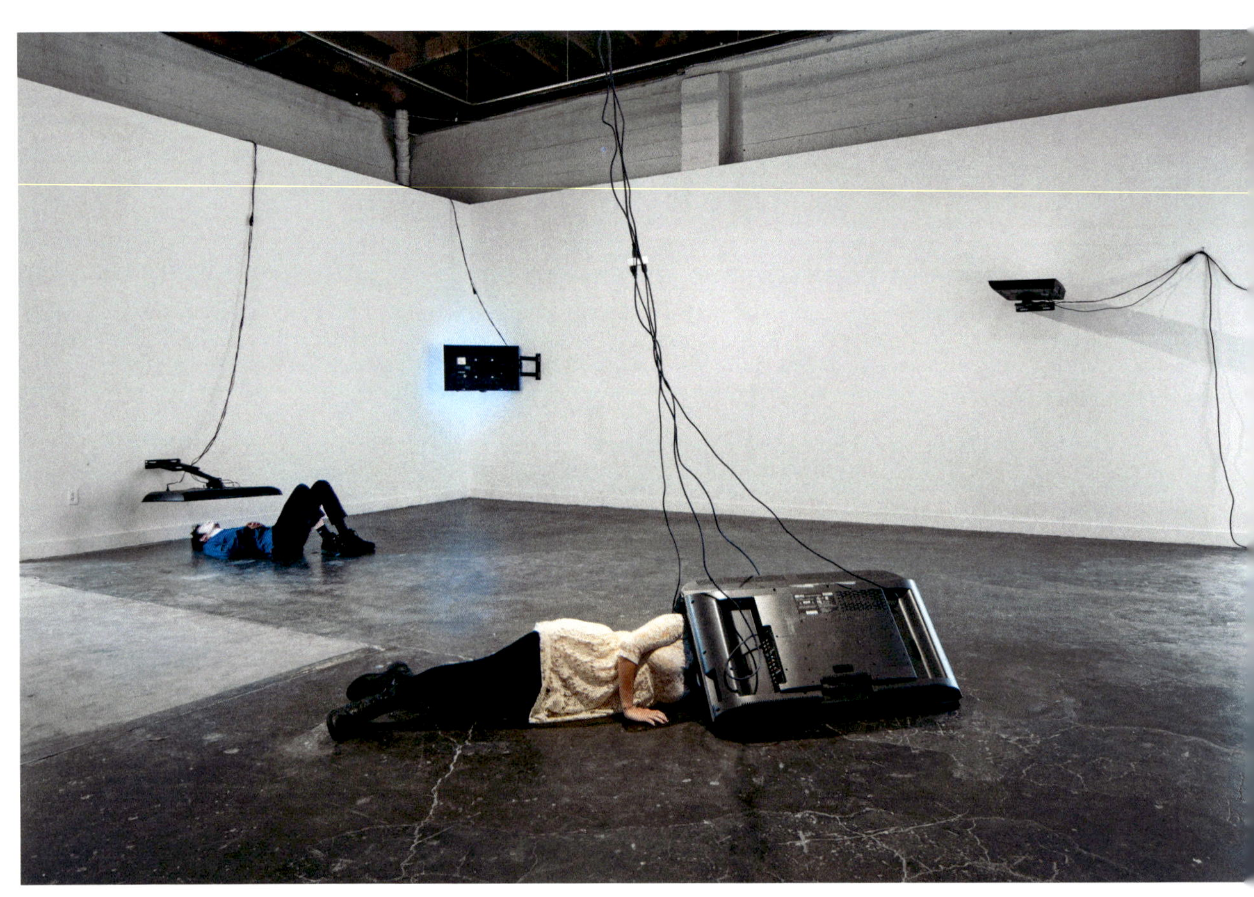

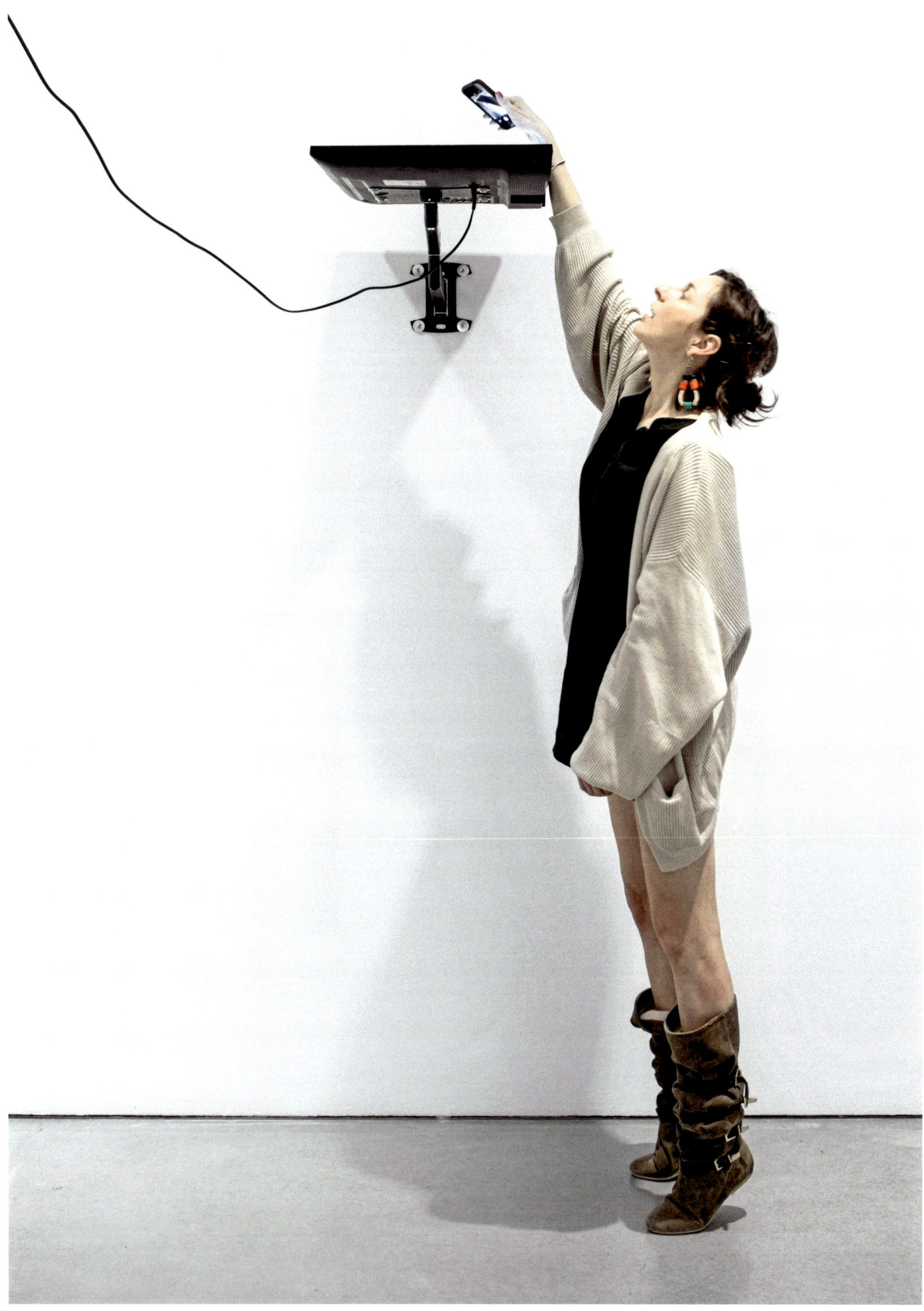

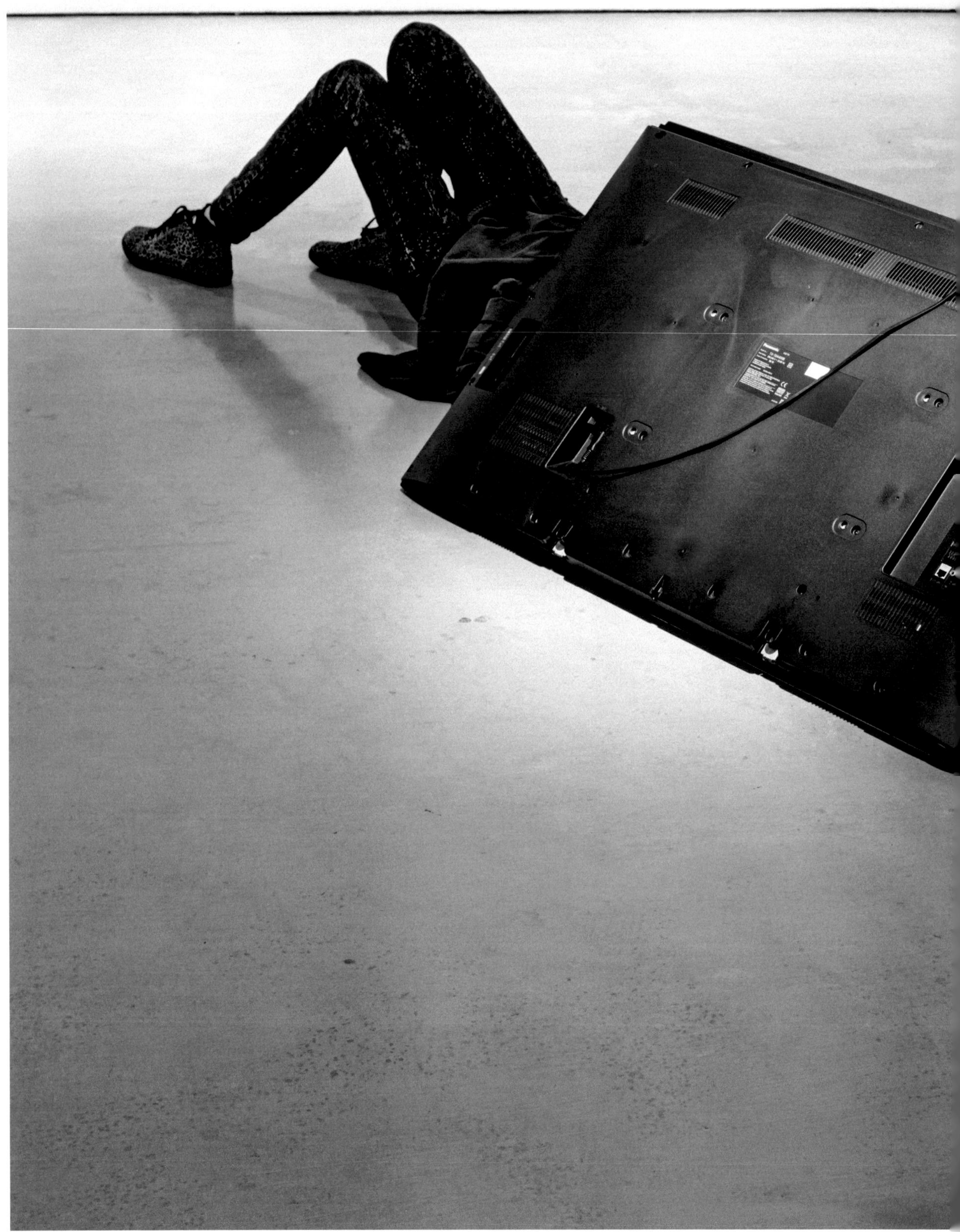

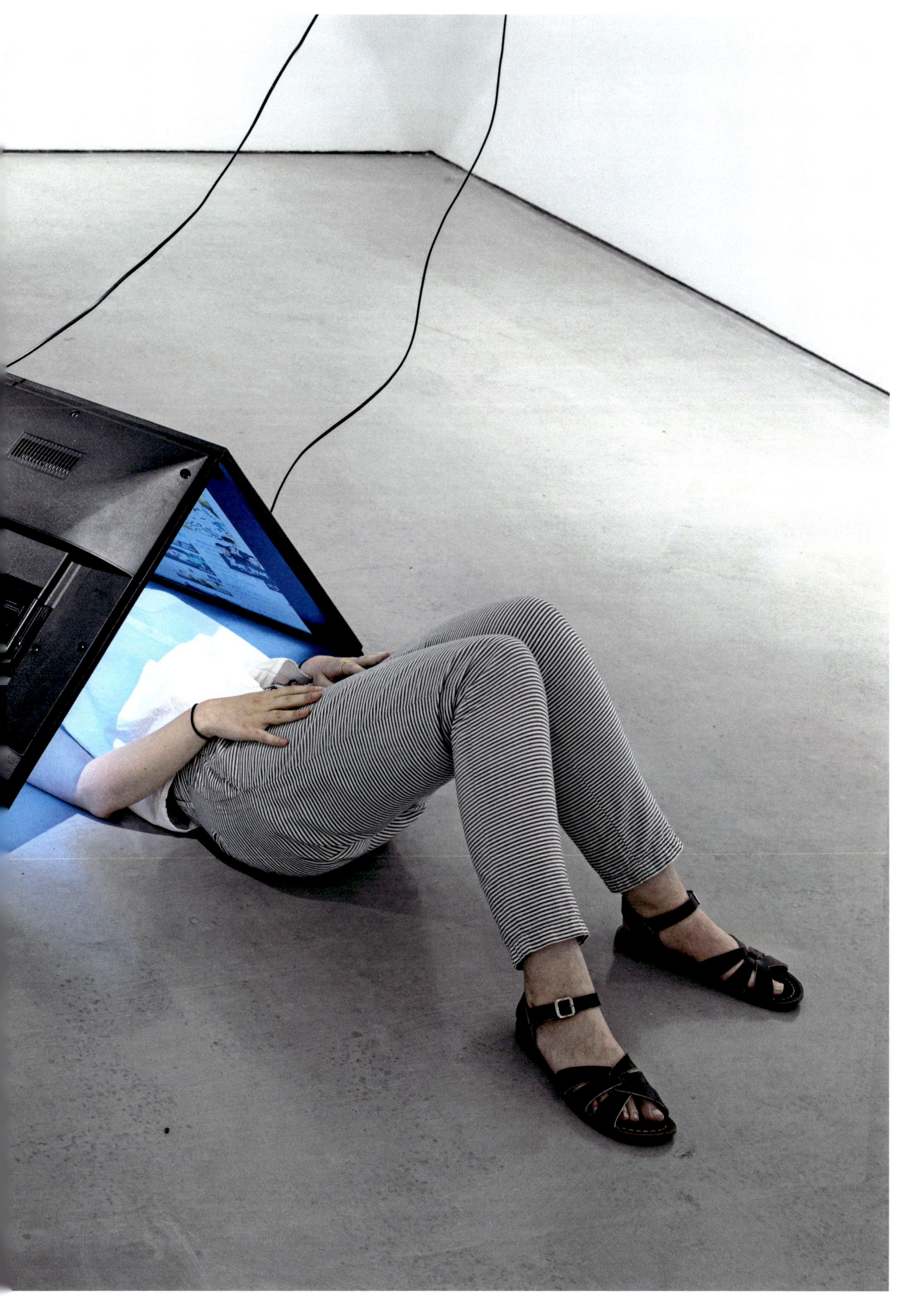

Emily's Video, 2012

Emily's Video is based on an online open call put out by Eva & Franco Mattes that invited anyone willing to watch "the worst video ever" to take part in an art project.
The participants had to consent to having a stranger named Emily visit their home and film them with a webcam while they were watching the video.

Sourced from the **darknet**[>p. 133], a digital underground in which disturbing content can circulate uncensored, the mysterious video triggers reactions that indeed tally with the artists' description: they range from startled frowns, sheepish laughter and abrupt aversion of the eyes all the way to gag reflexes triggered by disgust and people leaving the room.

As we never get to see the actual footage, we are left to speculate on the nature of what is causing such reactions.
Instead, the responses reflect our own conflicted and morbid curiosity back at us, mirroring the voyeuristic and sensationalist impulses our gaze is driven by.
Moreover, these **reaction videos**[>p. 136], an online genre that began to proliferate in the mid-2000s, expose our own entanglement in the networked **attention economy**[>p. 136], in which the simple fact of looking at something – no matter how passive it may seem – can become a catalyst that helps amplify the popularity of the content and thus contributes to its increased circulation and visibility.

Emily's Video is displayed on a large vertical monitor leaning against a column, positioned where visitors can only see the back of it upon entering the room.
The video occupies just a third of the screen, turning the rest into a black mirror in which the viewers see their own reflection.

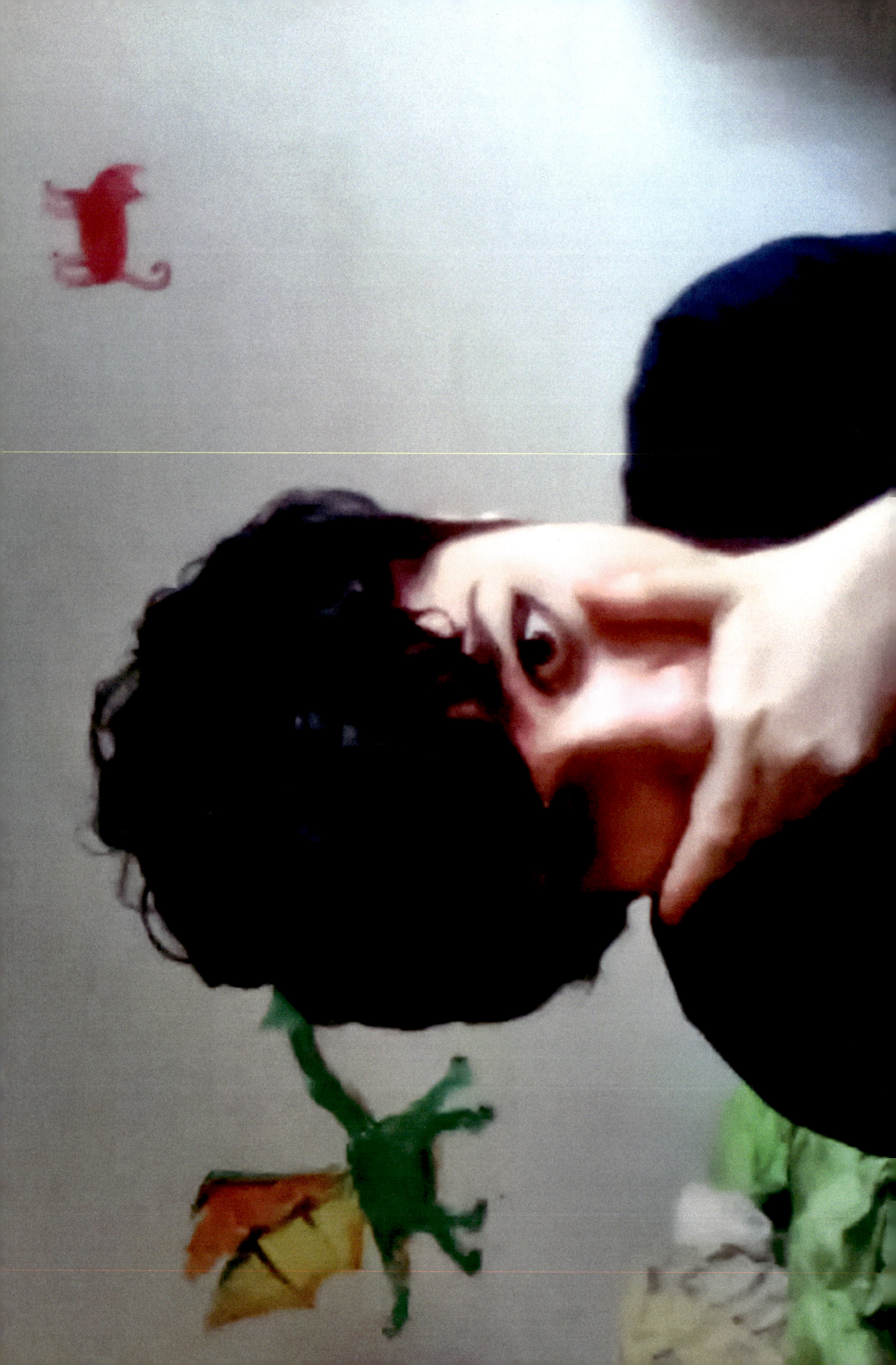

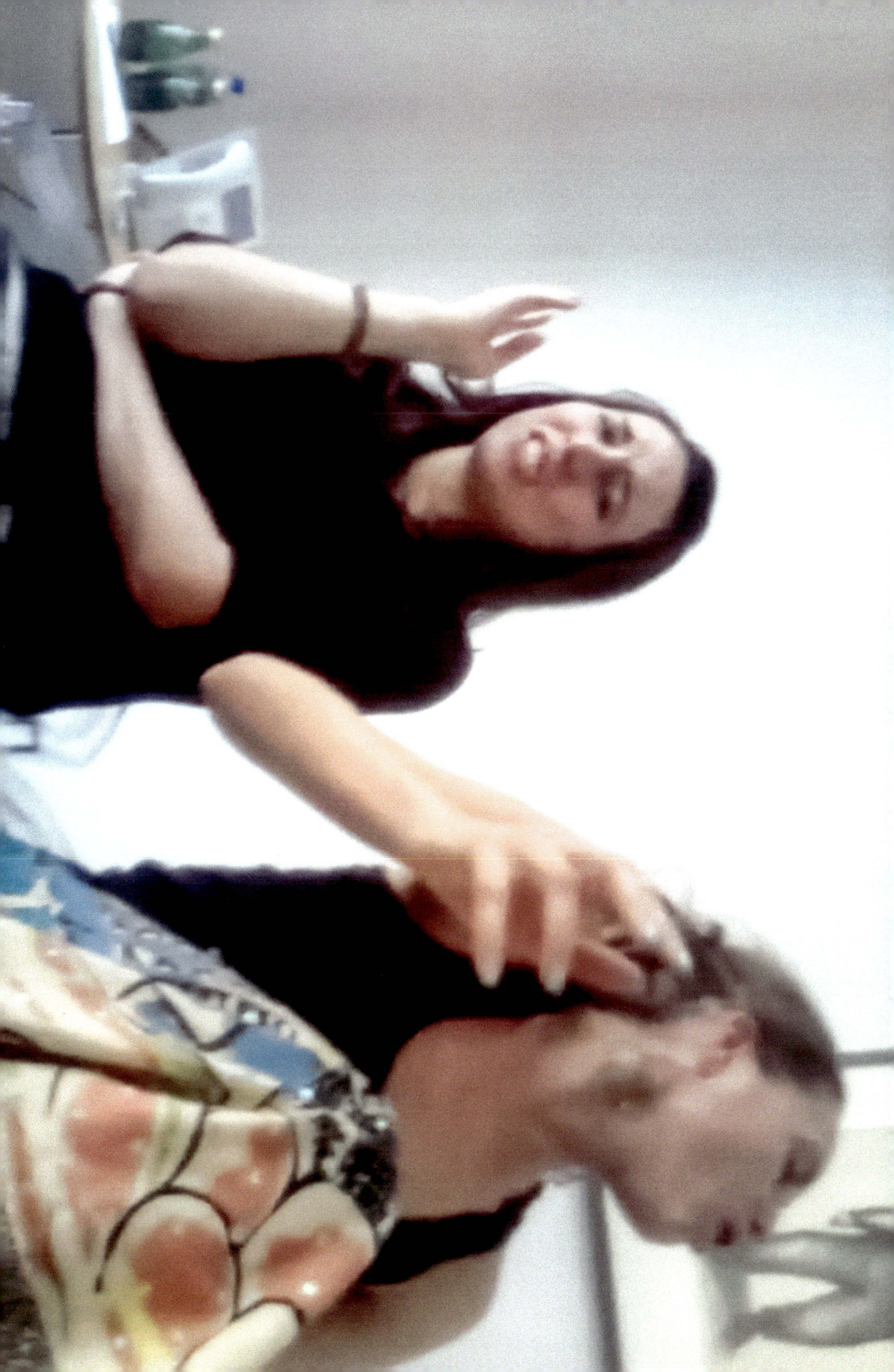

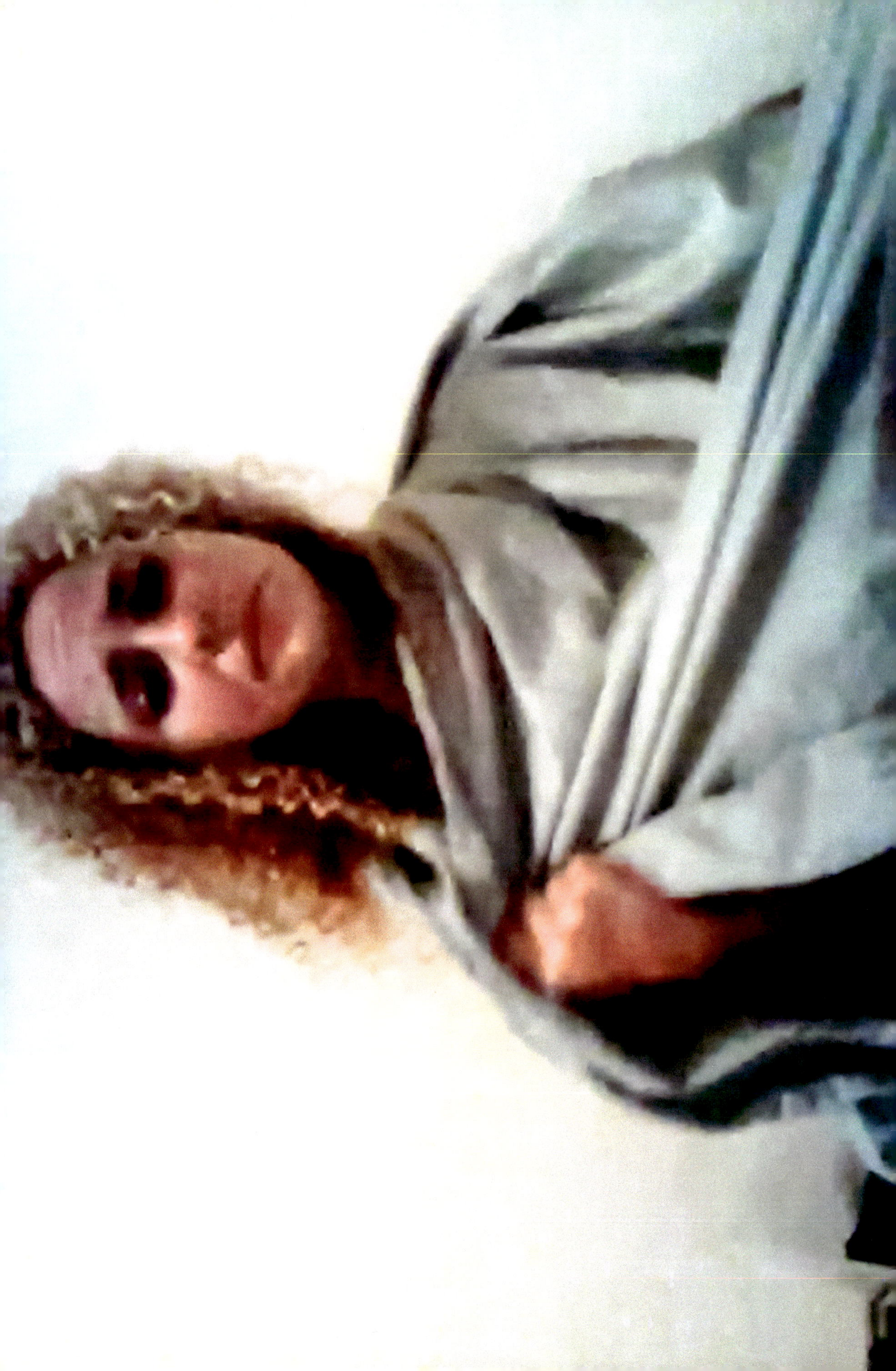

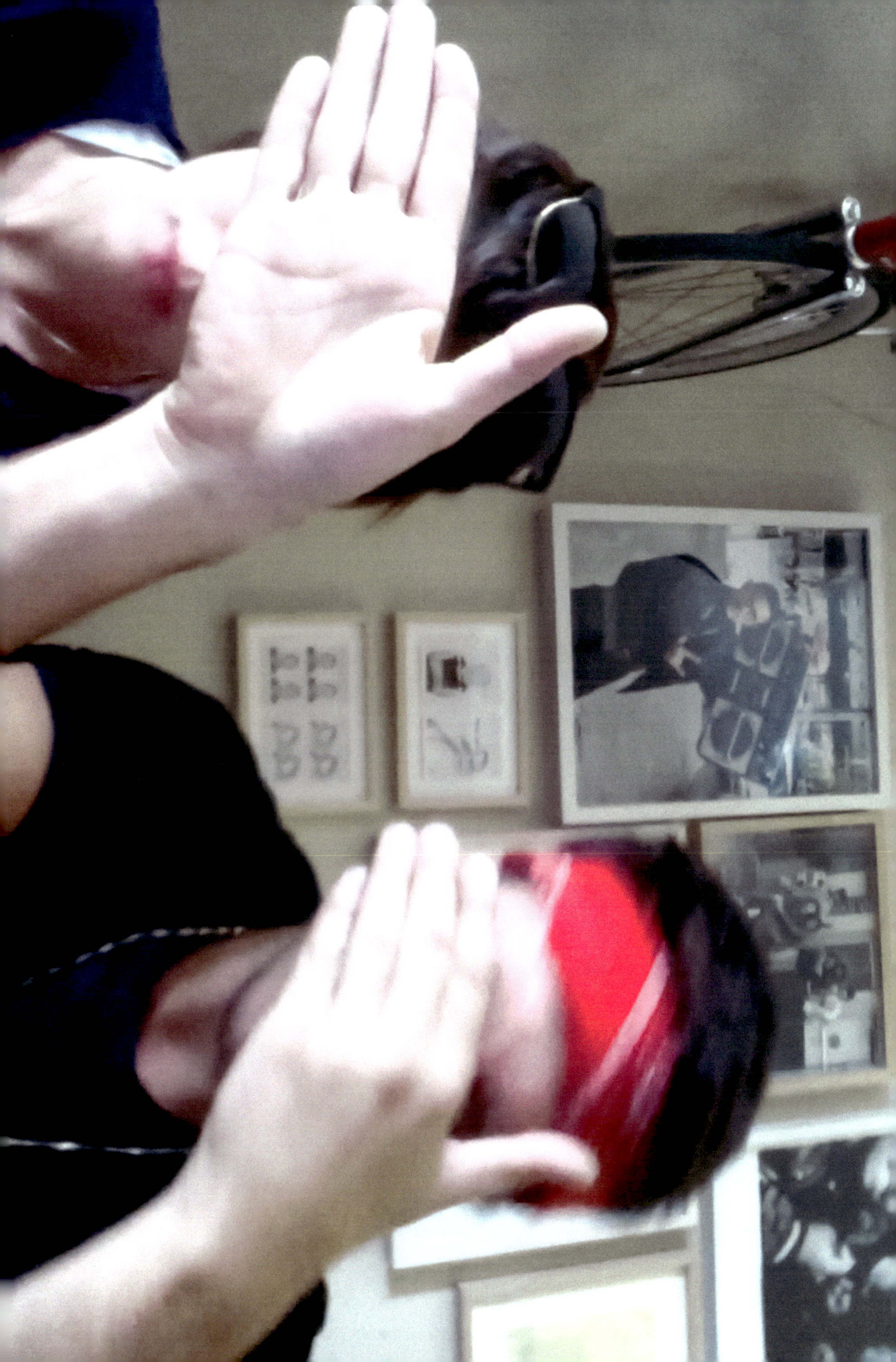

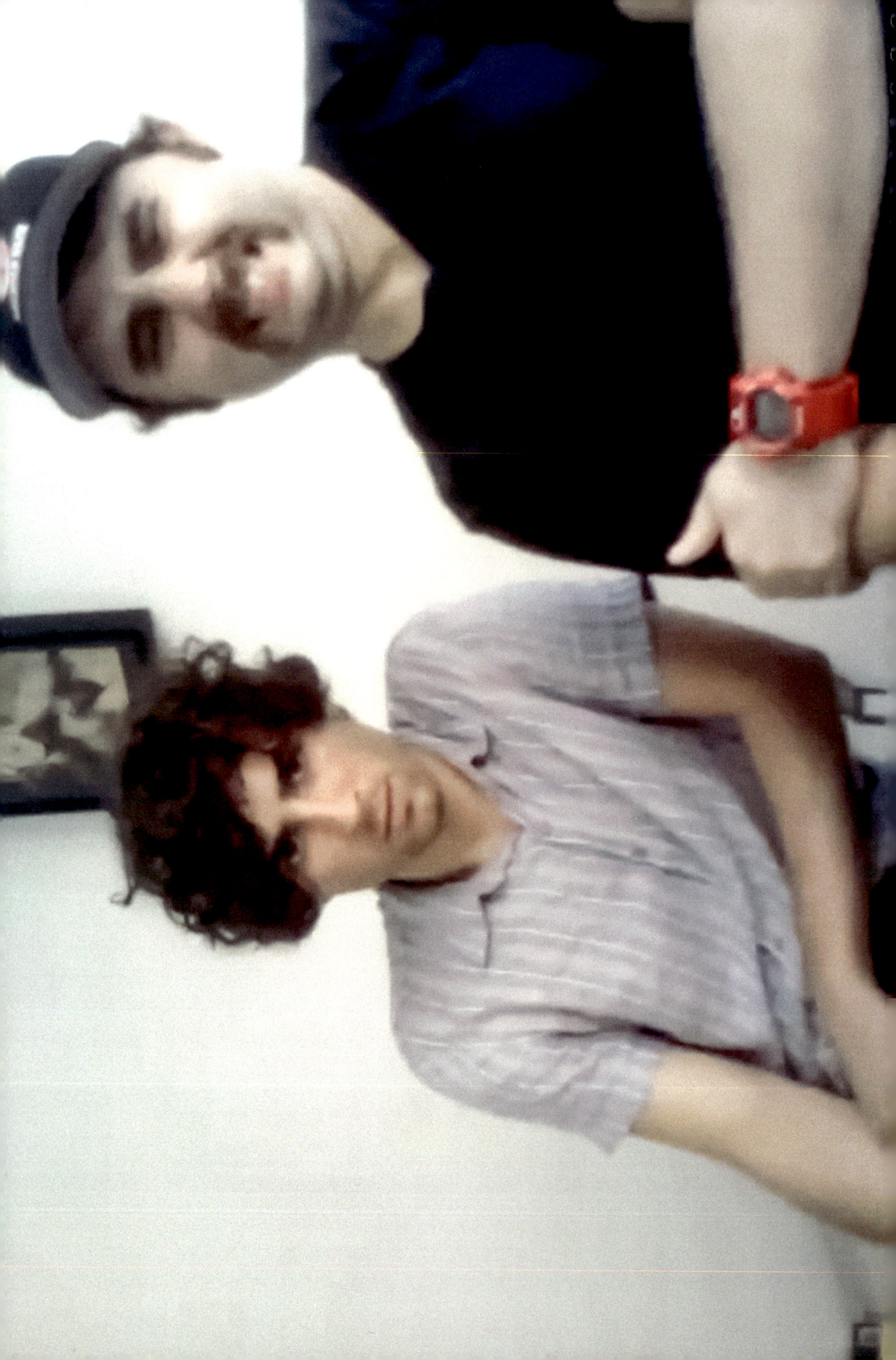

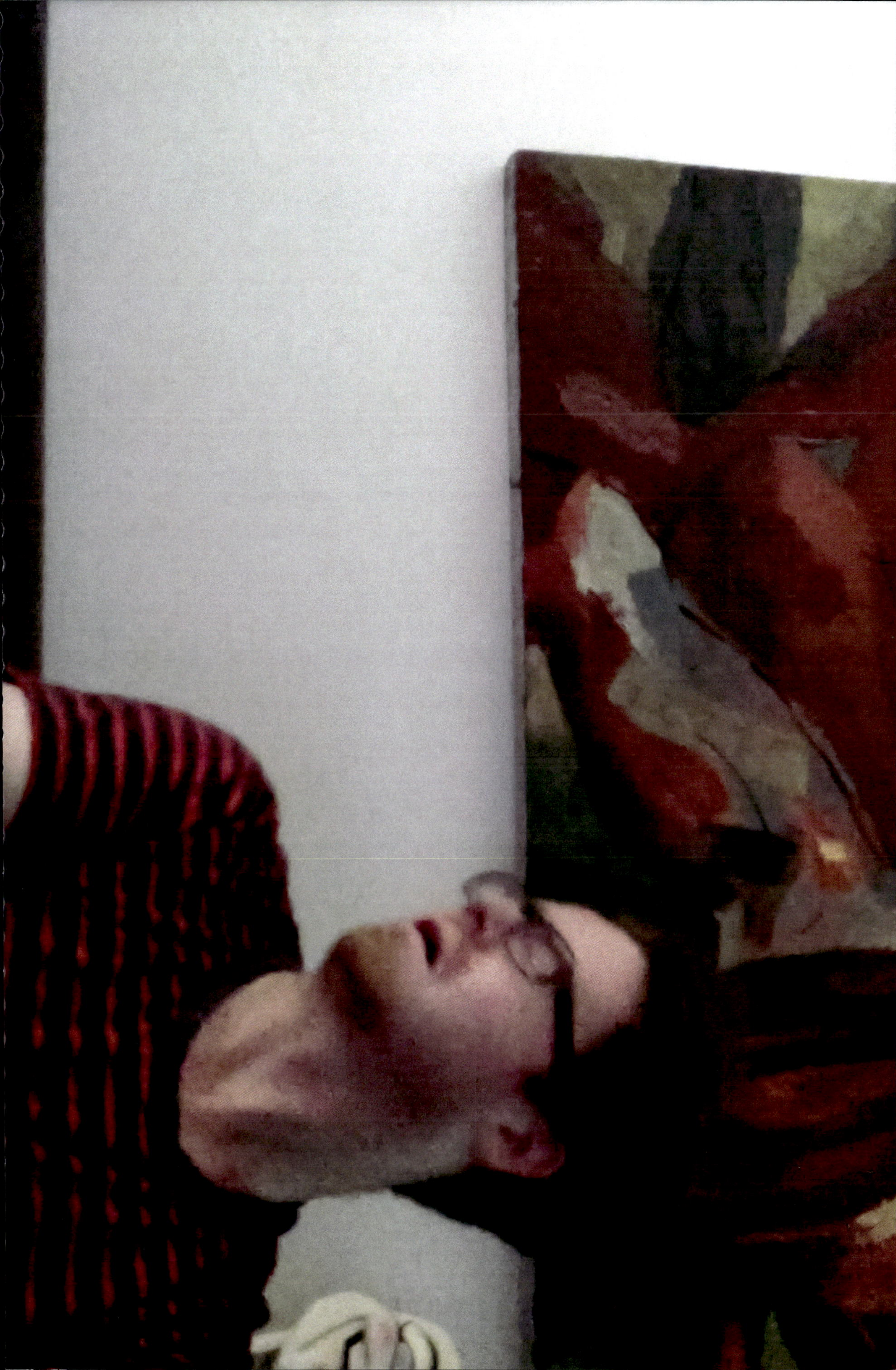

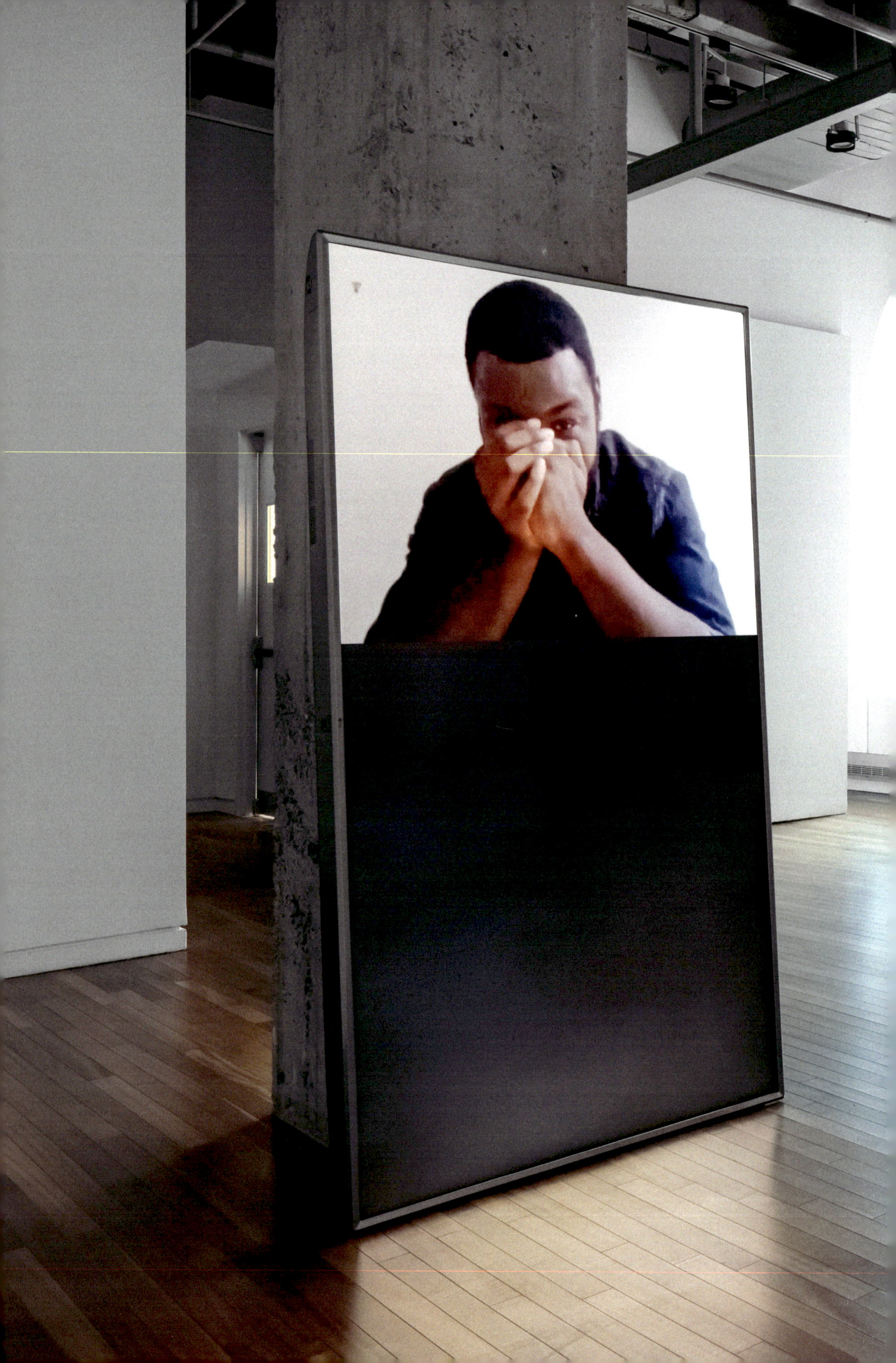

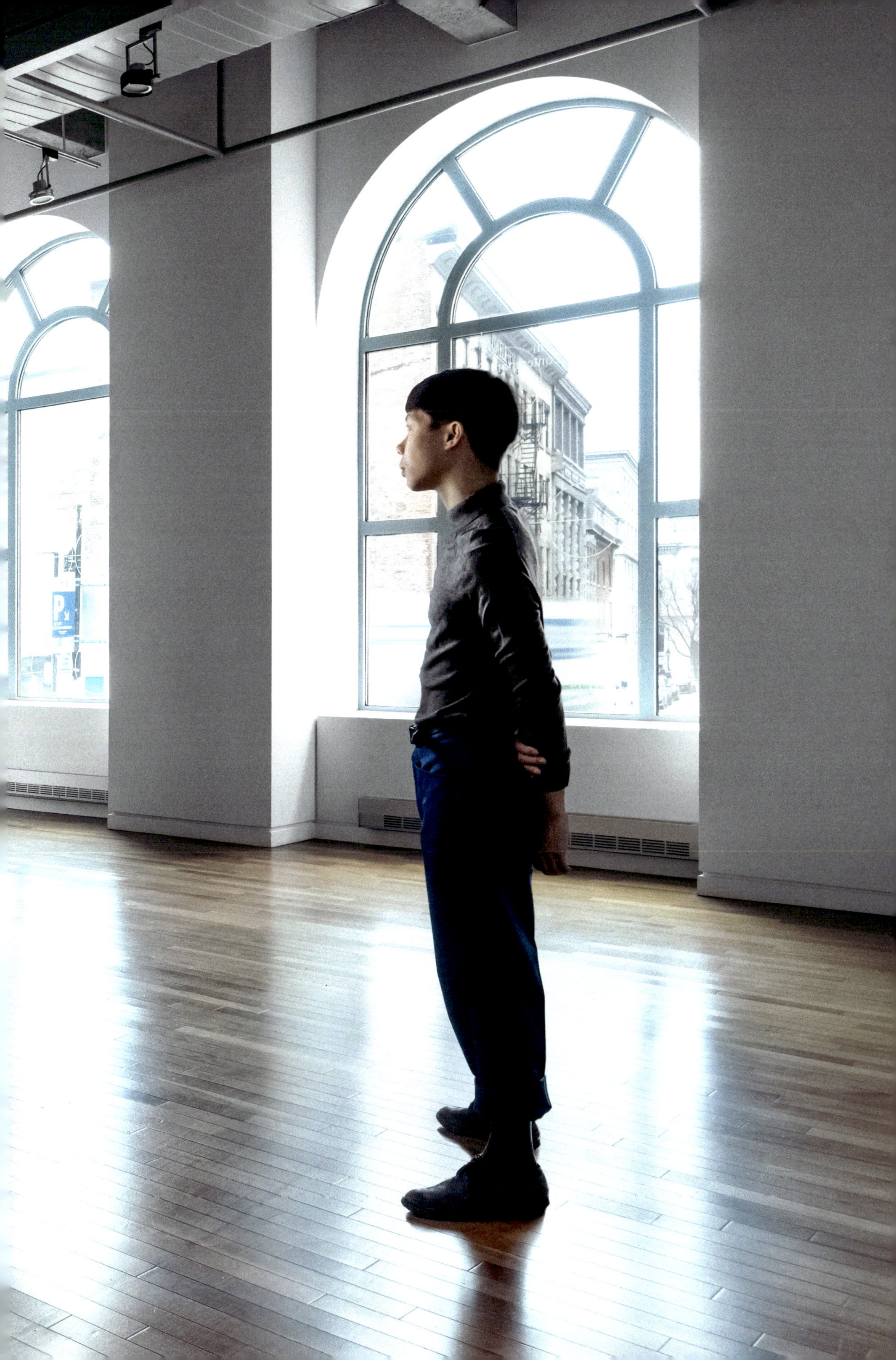

Personal Photographs, 2019–

The increasing precariousness of privacy through the impact of digital networks – tied to the social practice of oversharing as well as to mechanisms of surveillance – was already a main focus of Eva & Franco Mattes's artistic explorations back in the early 2000s.
At that time, their three-year-long performance *Life Sharing* (2000–2003) provided direct access to the artists' personal computer and all the private data it contained.

In their site-specific installation *Personal Photographs*, they expand this practice by **sharing**[>p. 137] private images that they had shot in a given month – September 2009, January 2012 or October 2016.
Yet rather than giving us a sneak peek into Eva & Franco Mattes's private lives, the installation re-directs our gaze to the underlying infrastructure of image circulation.

Materialised through a network of modular cable trays that wind through the exhibition space and ultimately control the movement of the visitors, what we usually only perceive as abstract flows of information is made conspicuously present and physically palpable.
The photographs circulate as data through cables that connect two microcomputers placed at either end of the installation.

The **software**[>p. 138], coded in collaboration with David Huerta, digital security trainer at the Freedom of the Press Foundation, transfers the images back and forth endlessly.
As much as anything, *Personal Photographs* reveals the **networked**[>p. 136] and distributed character of today's **data images**[>p. 133].

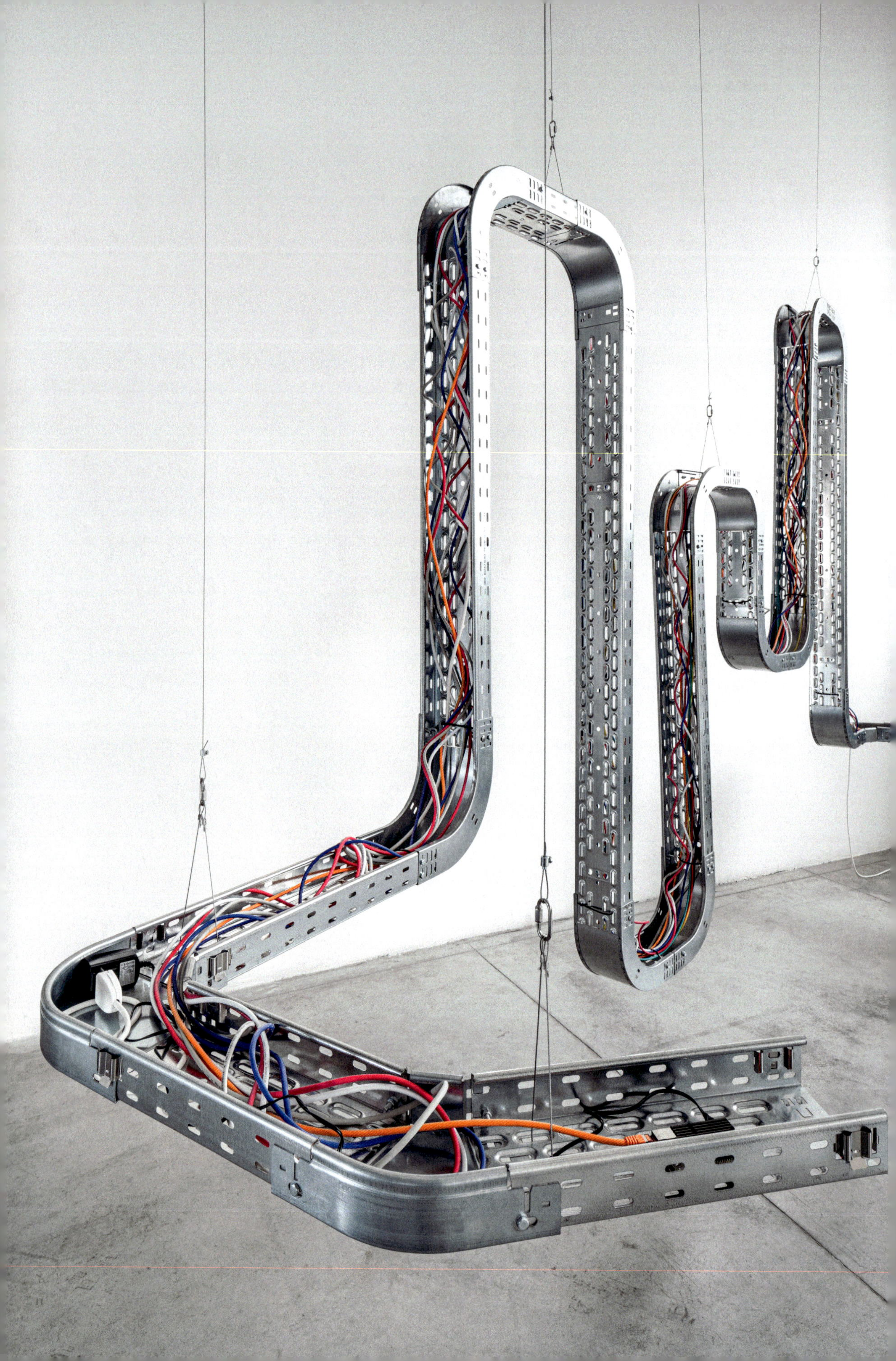

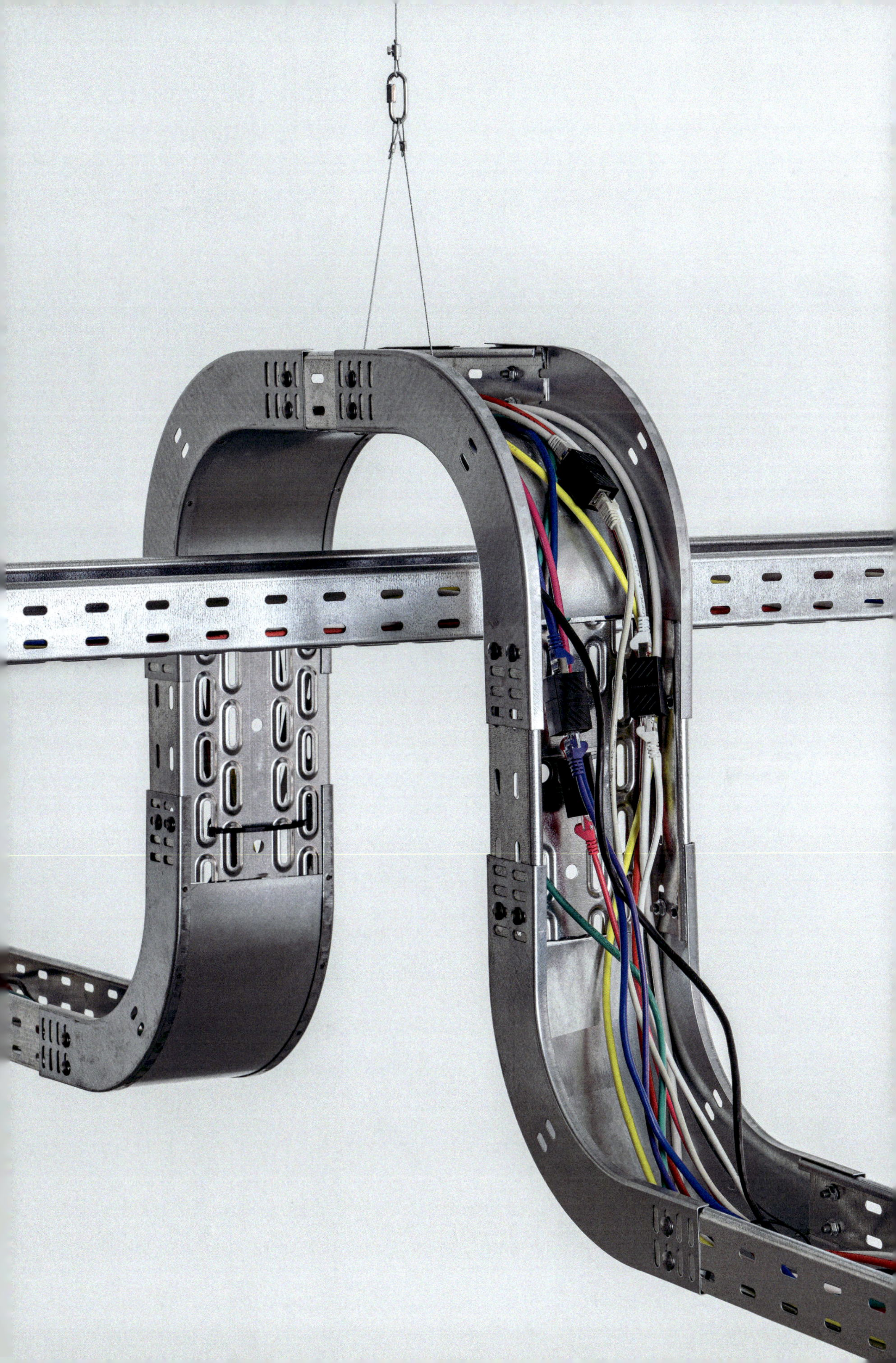

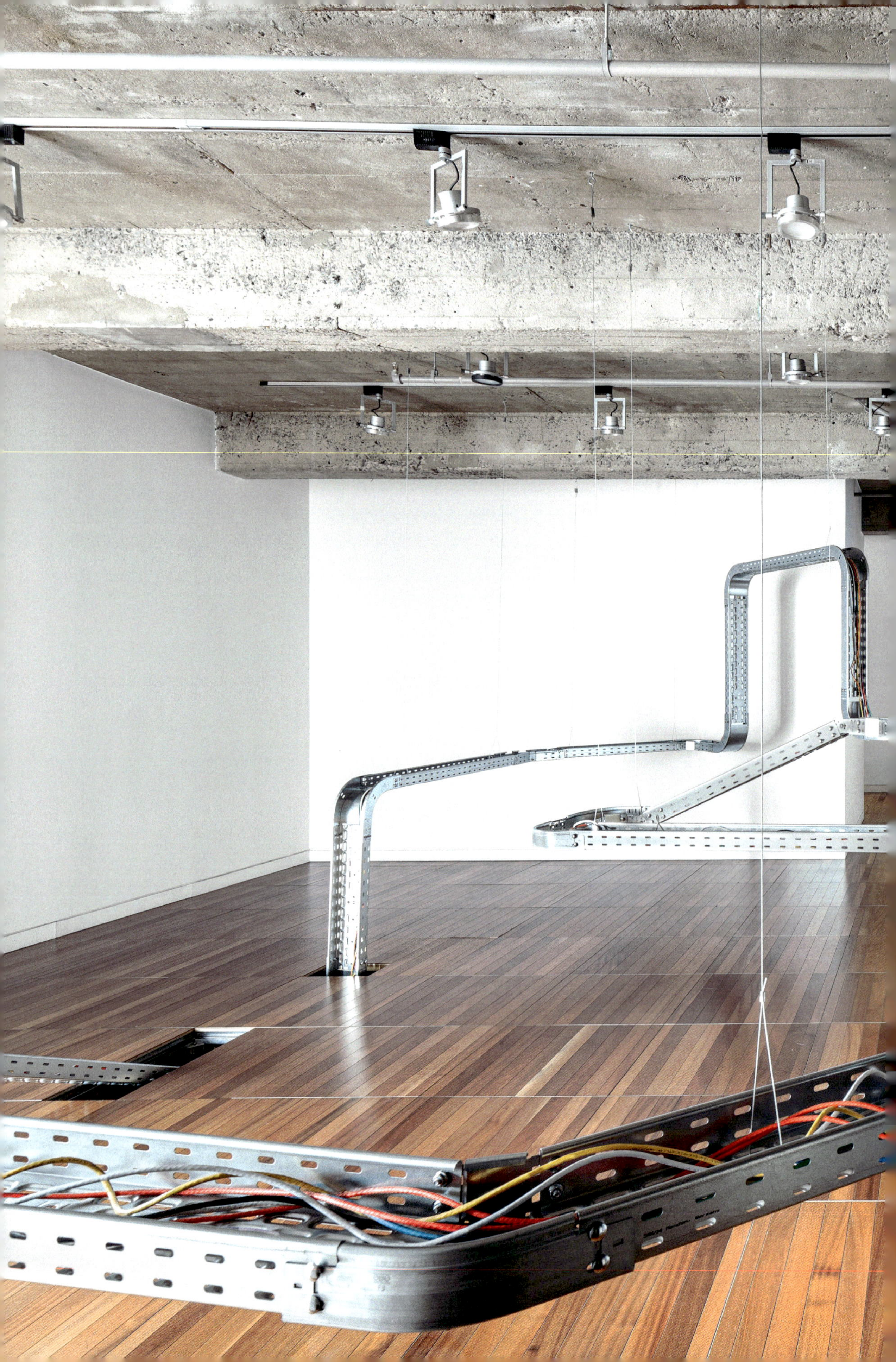

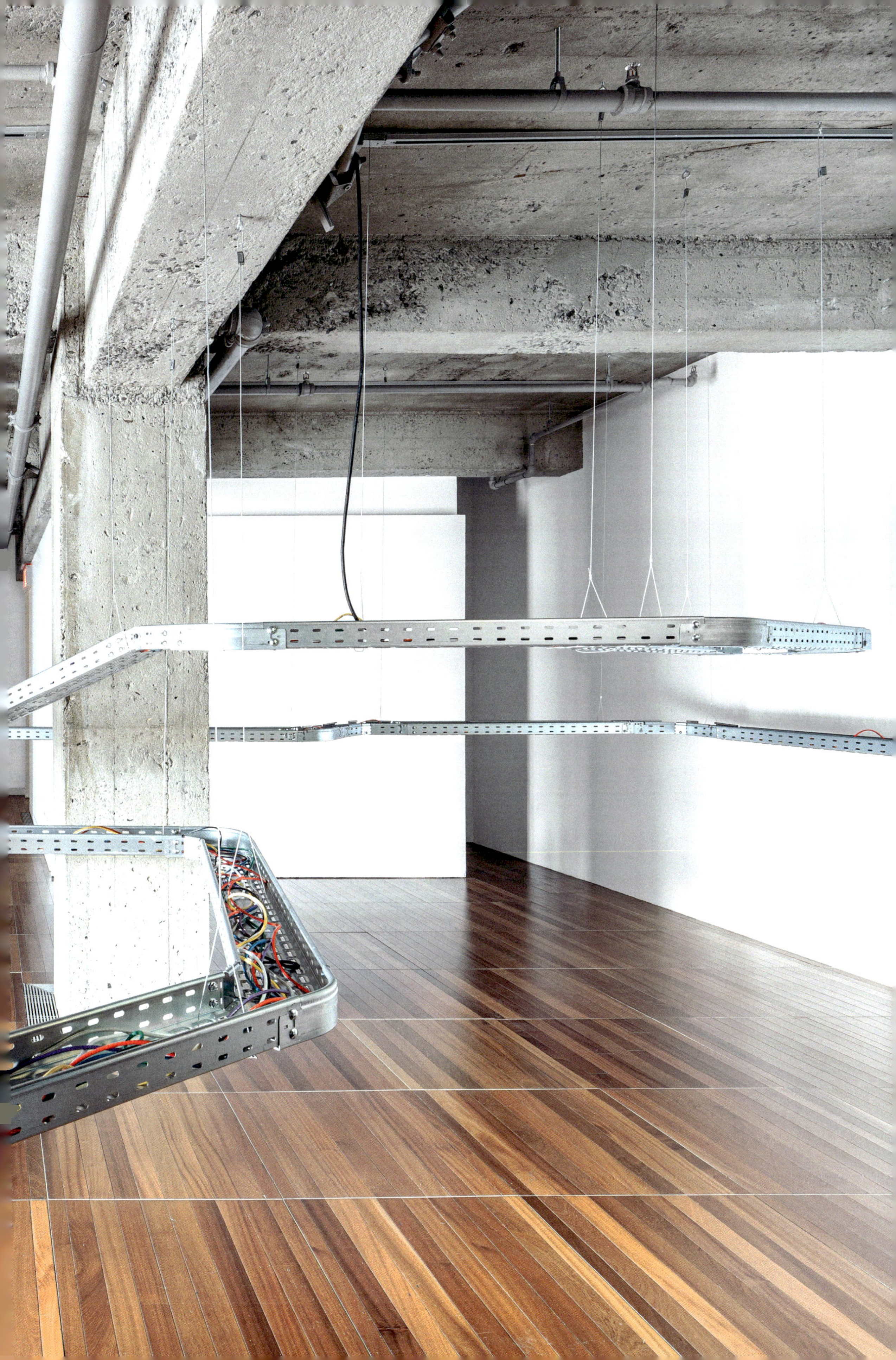

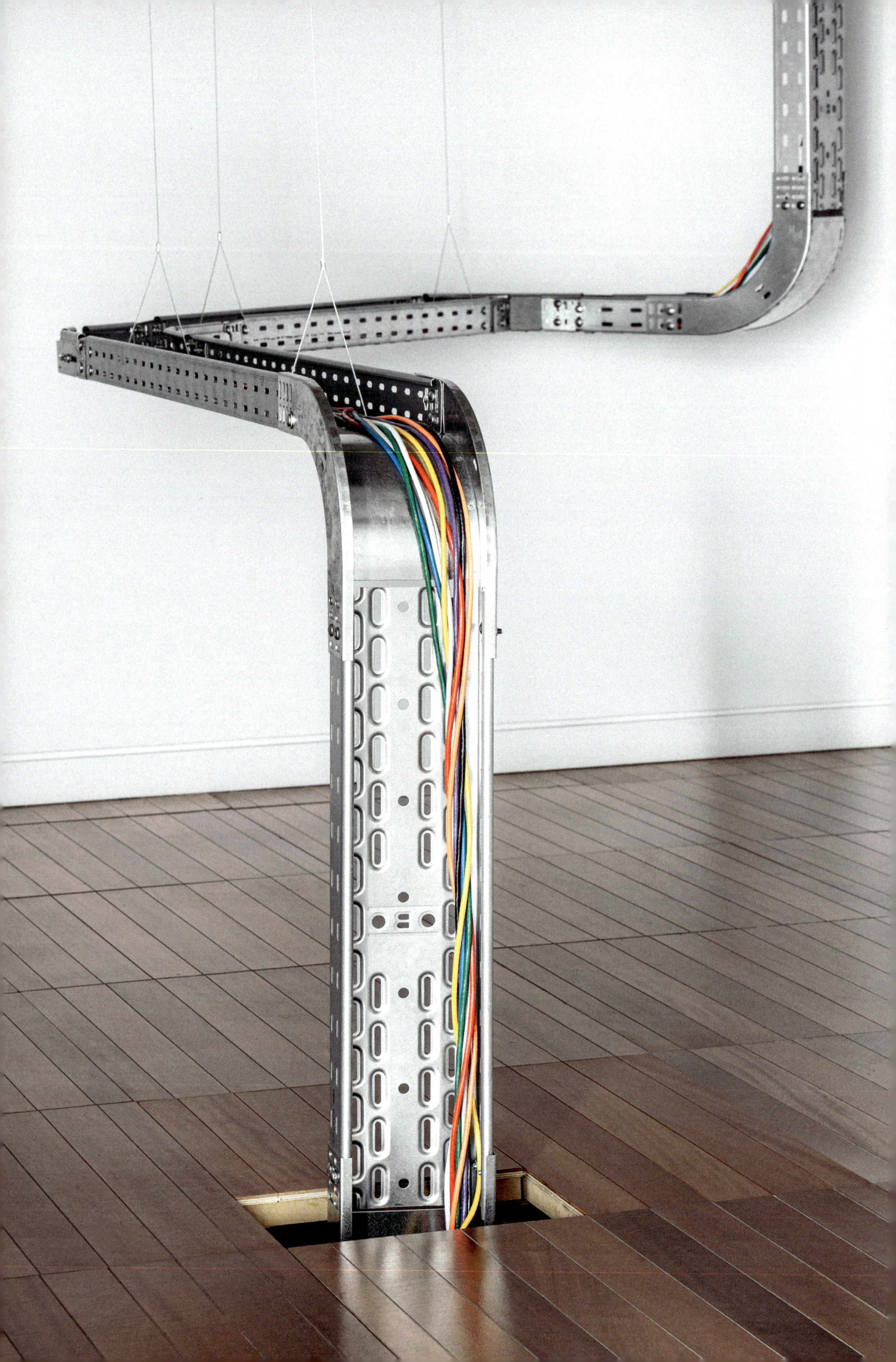

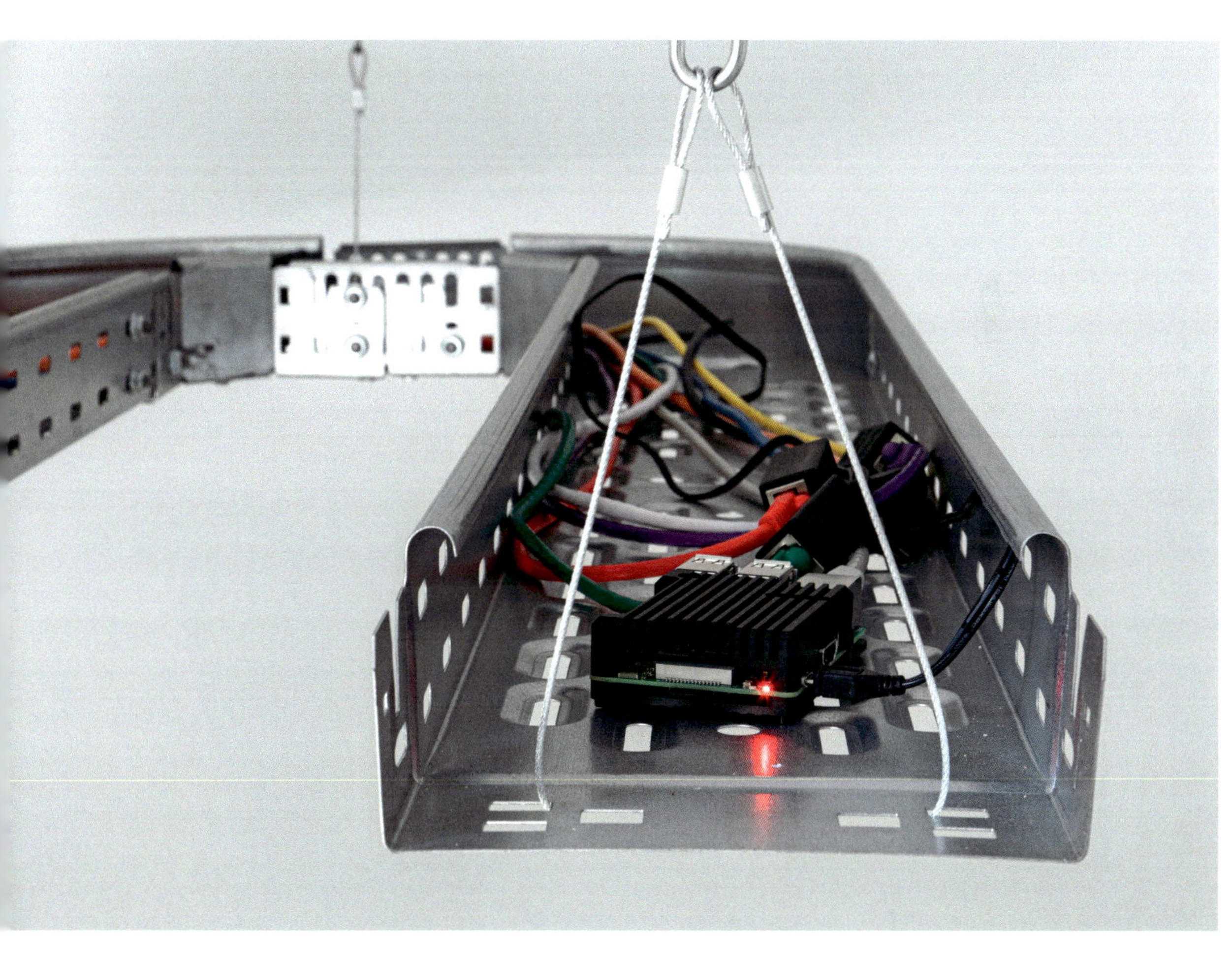

Name	Date	Size
▼ 🖥 2009-09	May 11, 2019 at 9:26 AM	294.3 MB
▶ 📁 receiving	May 10, 2019 at 5:21 PM	--
▼ 📁 sending	May 11, 2019 at 9:18 AM	--
_BVD7671.JPG	Sep 15, 2009 at 9:09 AM	3.2 MB
_BVD7682.JPG	Sep 15, 2009 at 9:09 AM	2.3 MB
_BVD7698.JPG	Sep 15, 2009 at 9:09 AM	2.8 MB
_BVD7710.JPG	Sep 15, 2009 at 9:09 AM	2.8 MB
_BVD7722.JPG	Sep 15, 2009 at 9:09 AM	3.4 MB
10092009_001.jpg	Oct 6, 2009 at 1:35 PM	498 KB
10092009.jpg	Oct 6, 2009 at 1:35 PM	496 KB
12092009_001.jpg	Oct 6, 2009 at 1:35 PM	322 KB
12092009.jpg	Oct 6, 2009 at 1:35 PM	351 KB
21102009_001.jpg	Mar 5, 2010 at 9:45 AM	116 KB
21102009.jpg	Mar 5, 2010 at 9:45 AM	95 KB
30112009_001.jpg	Mar 5, 2010 at 9:45 AM	150 KB
30112009.jpg	Mar 5, 2010 at 9:45 AM	157 KB
20099129754720.JPG.jpeg	Oct 1, 2009 at 4:13 PM	46 KB
20099129754721.JPG.jpeg	Oct 1, 2009 at 4:13 PM	46 KB
20099129754722.JPG.jpeg	Oct 1, 2009 at 4:13 PM	50 KB
20099129754723.JPG.jpeg	Oct 1, 2009 at 4:13 PM	50 KB
20099129754724.JPG.jpeg	Oct 1, 2009 at 4:13 PM	56 KB
DSCF7204.jpg	Sep 10, 2009 at 10:53 AM	1.5 MB
DSCF8923.JPG	Sep 2, 2009 at 4:15 PM	1.9 MB
DSCF8935.JPG	Sep 2, 2009 at 5:47 PM	1.8 MB
DSCF8971.JPG	Sep 6, 2009 at 11:25 AM	1.9 MB
DSCF8972.JPG	Sep 6, 2009 at 11:26 AM	1.9 MB
DSCF8975.JPG	Sep 6, 2009 at 11:27 AM	1.9 MB
DSCF8980.JPG	Sep 6, 2009 at 11:28 AM	1.8 MB
DSCF8981.JPG	Sep 6, 2009 at 12:15 PM	1.8 MB
DSCF8984.JPG	Sep 6, 2009 at 12:29 PM	1.9 MB
DSCF8987.JPG	Sep 6, 2009 at 6:06 PM	1.8 MB
DSCF8988.JPG	Sep 6, 2009 at 6:08 PM	1.9 MB
DSCF8990.JPG	Sep 6, 2009 at 7:00 PM	1.8 MB
DSCF8992.JPG	Sep 7, 2009 at 4:44 PM	2 MB
DSCF8995.JPG	Sep 7, 2009 at 4:53 PM	1.9 MB
DSCF8997.JPG	Sep 7, 2009 at 6:12 PM	2 MB
DSCF8998.JPG	Sep 7, 2009 at 6:13 PM	2 MB
DSCF8999.JPG	Sep 7, 2009 at 11:26 PM	1.9 MB
DSCF9001.JPG	Sep 9, 2009 at 8:50 PM	1.9 MB
DSCF9003.JPG	Sep 9, 2009 at 8:51 PM	1.9 MB
DSCF9004.JPG	Sep 9, 2009 at 10:36 PM	1.9 MB
DSCF9005.JPG	Sep 10, 2009 at 4:11 PM	2 MB
DSCF9021.JPG	Sep 15, 2009 at 3:02 PM	1.9 MB
DSCF9022.JPG	Sep 15, 2009 at 7:21 PM	1.9 MB
DSCF9024.JPG	Sep 15, 2009 at 7:21 PM	1.9 MB
DSCF9025.JPG	Sep 15, 2009 at 7:22 PM	1.9 MB
DSCF9026.JPG	Sep 15, 2009 at 7:22 PM	1.8 MB
DSCF9027.JPG	Sep 15, 2009 at 7:27 PM	1.9 MB
DSCF9028.JPG	Sep 15, 2009 at 7:28 PM	1.8 MB
DSCF9032.JPG	Sep 15, 2009 at 7:30 PM	1.9 MB
DSCF9036.JPG	Sep 15, 2009 at 7:33 PM	1.9 MB
DSCF9037.JPG	Sep 15, 2009 at 7:34 PM	2 MB
DSCF9038.JPG	Sep 15, 2009 at 7:35 PM	1.9 MB
DSCF9040.JPG	Sep 15, 2009 at 7:38 PM	2 MB
DSCF9042.JPG	Sep 15, 2009 at 7:38 PM	1.9 MB
DSCF9044.JPG	Sep 15, 2009 at 7:39 PM	1.9 MB
DSCF9050.JPG	Sep 15, 2009 at 8:11 PM	1.9 MB
DSCF9054.JPG	Sep 16, 2009 at 11:26 PM	1.9 MB
DSCF9062.JPG	Sep 16, 2009 at 11:28 PM	1.9 MB
DSCF9066.JPG	Sep 16, 2009 at 11:29 PM	1.9 MB
DSCF9067.JPG	Sep 16, 2009 at 11:31 PM	1.9 MB
DSCF9068.JPG	Sep 17, 2009 at 3:43 PM	1.9 MB
DSCF9069.JPG	Sep 17, 2009 at 3:43 PM	1.9 MB
DSCF9070.JPG	Sep 18, 2009 at 6:52 PM	1.9 MB
DSCF9075.JPG	Sep 20, 2009 at 5:21 PM	2 MB
DSCF9076.JPG	Sep 20, 2009 at 5:22 PM	1.9 MB
DSCF9078.JPG	Sep 20, 2009 at 5:28 PM	2 MB
DSCF9081.JPG	Sep 20, 2009 at 5:32 PM	2 MB
DSCF9083.JPG	Sep 20, 2009 at 5:36 PM	2 MB
DSCF9084.JPG	Sep 20, 2009 at 5:36 PM	1.9 MB
DSCF9085.JPG	Sep 20, 2009 at 5:38 PM	1.9 MB
DSCF9089.JPG	Sep 20, 2009 at 8:52 PM	1.9 MB
flushing farm_001.jpg	Oct 6, 2009 at 1:35 PM	537 KB
flushing farm_001.jpg	Oct 6, 2009 at 1:35 PM	537 KB
flushing farm_02.jpg	Oct 6, 2009 at 1:35 PM	502 KB
foto di blu - 6894.JPG	Sep 21, 2009 at 5:43 AM	4.6 MB
foto di blu - 6895.JPG	Sep 21, 2009 at 5:43 AM	4.6 MB
foto di blu - 6897.JPG	Sep 21, 2009 at 5:56 AM	4.5 MB
foto di blu - 6898.JPG	Sep 21, 2009 at 6:04 AM	4.4 MB
GraphicArt1.jpg	Sep 10, 2009 at 10:44 AM	56 KB
GraphicArt2.jpg	Sep 10, 2009 at 10:44 AM	53 KB
GraphicArt3.jpg	Sep 10, 2009 at 10:44 AM	50 KB
Image002.jpg	Oct 26, 2009 at 4:47 PM	579 KB
Image003.jpg	Oct 26, 2009 at 4:47 PM	92 KB
Image004.jpg	Dec 2, 2009 at 8:36 AM	110 KB
Image005.jpg	Dec 2, 2009 at 8:36 AM	101 KB
IMG_6497.JPG	Sep 21, 2009 at 7:35 AM	2.7 MB
IMG_6498.JPG	Sep 21, 2009 at 7:36 AM	2.5 MB
IMG_6499.JPG	Sep 21, 2009 at 7:36 AM	2.6 MB
IMG_6501.JPG	Sep 21, 2009 at 7:36 AM	2.9 MB
IMG_6503.JPG	Sep 21, 2009 at 7:36 AM	3.2 MB
IMG_6505.JPG	Sep 21, 2009 at 7:37 AM	2.3 MB
IMG_6506.JPG	Sep 21, 2009 at 7:37 AM	2.7 MB
IMG_6507.JPG	Sep 21, 2009 at 7:37 AM	2.7 MB
IMG_6508.JPG	Sep 21, 2009 at 7:37 AM	3 MB
IMG_6509.JPG	Sep 21, 2009 at 7:37 AM	2.7 MB
IMG_6511.JPG	Sep 21, 2009 at 7:37 AM	3.1 MB
IMG_6512.JPG	Sep 21, 2009 at 7:38 AM	3.3 MB
IMG_6513.JPG	Sep 21, 2009 at 7:38 AM	2.4 MB
IMG_6514.JPG	Sep 21, 2009 at 7:38 AM	2.4 MB
IMG_6515.JPG	Sep 21, 2009 at 7:38 AM	3.4 MB
IMG_6516.JPG	Sep 21, 2009 at 7:38 AM	2.8 MB
IMG_6517.JPG	Sep 21, 2009 at 7:38 AM	2.4 MB
IMG_6521.JPG	Sep 21, 2009 at 7:39 AM	2.7 MB
IMG_6522.JPG	Sep 21, 2009 at 7:39 AM	2.5 MB
IMG_6523.JPG	Sep 21, 2009 at 7:39 AM	2.9 MB
IMG_6525.JPG	Sep 21, 2009 at 7:39 AM	2.5 MB
IMG_6526.JPG	Sep 21, 2009 at 7:40 AM	2.8 MB
IMG_6527.JPG	Sep 21, 2009 at 7:40 AM	2.5 MB
IMG_6528.JPG	Sep 21, 2009 at 7:40 AM	2.9 MB
IMG_6530.JPG	Sep 21, 2009 at 7:40 AM	3.4 MB
IMG_6531.JPG	Sep 21, 2009 at 7:40 AM	2.8 MB
IMG_6532.JPG	Sep 21, 2009 at 7:40 AM	2.8 MB
IMG_6533.JPG	Sep 21, 2009 at 7:41 AM	2.9 MB
IMG_6534.JPG	Sep 21, 2009 at 7:41 AM	2.8 MB
IMG_6535.JPG	Sep 21, 2009 at 7:41 AM	3.6 MB
IMG_6537.JPG	Sep 21, 2009 at 7:41 AM	2.1 MB
IMG_6539.JPG	Sep 21, 2009 at 7:41 AM	2.8 MB
IMG_6540.JPG	Sep 21, 2009 at 7:42 AM	2.8 MB
IMG_6541.JPG	Sep 21, 2009 at 7:42 AM	2.8 MB
IMG_6542.JPG	Sep 21, 2009 at 7:42 AM	2.5 MB
IMG_6543.JPG	Sep 21, 2009 at 7:42 AM	2.5 MB
IMG_6544.JPG	Sep 21, 2009 at 7:42 AM	2.2 MB
IMG_6545.JPG	Sep 21, 2009 at 7:42 AM	2.4 MB
IMG_6546.JPG	Sep 21, 2009 at 7:42 AM	2.3 MB
IMG_6547.JPG	Sep 21, 2009 at 7:42 AM	1.9 MB
IMG_6548.JPG	Sep 21, 2009 at 7:43 AM	2.4 MB
IMG_6549.JPG	Sep 21, 2009 at 7:43 AM	2.6 MB
IMG_6550.JPG	Sep 21, 2009 at 7:43 AM	2.6 MB
IMG_6551.JPG	Sep 21, 2009 at 7:43 AM	1.9 MB
IMG_6552.JPG	Sep 21, 2009 at 7:43 AM	3 MB
IMG_6553.JPG	Sep 21, 2009 at 7:43 AM	2.2 MB
IMG_6554.JPG	Sep 21, 2009 at 7:43 AM	3.3 MB
IMG_6555.JPG	Sep 21, 2009 at 7:44 AM	3.5 MB
IMG_6556.JPG	Sep 21, 2009 at 7:44 AM	3.5 MB
IMG_6557.JPG	Sep 21, 2009 at 7:44 AM	4 MB
IMG_6559.JPG	Sep 21, 2009 at 7:44 AM	2.5 MB
IMG_6561.JPG	Sep 21, 2009 at 7:45 AM	1.8 MB
IMG_6562.JPG	Sep 21, 2009 at 7:45 AM	1.8 MB
IMG_6563.JPG	Sep 21, 2009 at 7:45 AM	1.7 MB
IMG_6564.JPG	Sep 21, 2009 at 7:45 AM	1.7 MB
IMG_6565.JPG	Sep 21, 2009 at 7:45 AM	2.8 MB
IMG_6566.JPG	Sep 21, 2009 at 7:45 AM	2.4 MB
IMG_6567.JPG	Sep 21, 2009 at 7:45 AM	2.3 MB
IMG_6568.JPG	Sep 21, 2009 at 7:45 AM	2.4 MB
poster focus.JPG	Oct 21, 2010 at 8:17 AM	313 KB

```sh
#!/bin/sh

echo "Beginning photo sync..."

#if [ "$(hostname)"=="rpa.local" ]; then
#echo "$(hostname -s)"
if [ "$(hostname -s)" = "rpa" ]; then
  recipient_host="rpb.local"
  #recipient_host="10.0.0.49" #rpb
  #recipient_host="rpb"
  echo "Sending photos to "$recipient_host"..."
else
  recipient_host="rpa.local"
  #recipient_host="10.0.0.1" #rpa
  #recipient_host="rpa"
  echo "Sending photos to "$recipient_host"..."
fi

usb_drive_name="$(ls /media/pi/ | head -n 1)"
#usb_drive_name_escaped="(command printf '%q' $usb_drive_name)"
#usb_drive_name_escaped=${$usb_drive_name// /\ }
#usb_drive_name_escaped=${usb_drive_name// /_}

echo "Using USB drive:" $usb_drive_name

sender_path=/media/pi/$usb_drive_name/sending

recipient_path=/media/pi/$usb_drive_name/receiving

echo "Sending files in:" $sender_path
echo "Sending files to:" $recipient_host:$recipient_path

rsync --progress -a --recursive --ignore-times $sender_path/. pi@$recipient_host:$recipient_path

echo "Fin."
```

Personal Photographs

Cory Arcangel

Uncanny confusion, more than anything, was my reaction the first time I saw a superyacht IRL.
I spotted it in early spring, docked in the Port of Stavanger, located in the centre of the Norwegian city.
As a frequent cruise ship destination, Stavanger is not unfamiliar with massive ships jamming up its port, and the sighting, at first, wasn't extremely surprising.
But I knew something was off when I saw the ship's decks were lined underneath by soft LED lights that gave them the appearance of glowing in the dark.
Woah.
This I had never seen before.
Those lights were emitting the feeling of money, of pure excess, the way cruise ships (which are essentially floating Holiday Inns) never would.
This was not a cruise ship, but a private boat *the size of a cruise ship.*

The *Flying Fox* measures in at 136 metres, has an estimated 9,100 gross tonnage and can sleep up twenty-two passengers and a crew of fifty-four.
It features an aft pool on the main deck, a cinema, an elevator and two helipads that can accommodate an Airbus H155, the largest helicopter on the market, which is also housed on board.
The estimated value of the *Flying Fox* is USD 400 million and, according to the *Superyacht Times*, there are only thirteen bigger yachts in the world.
At its size and price, the *Flying Fox's* only superyacht peers are a handful of boats owned by the world's richest men:
Larry Ellison's *Rising Sun*, Sheikh Khalifa bin Zayed Al-Nahyan's *Azzam* and Roman Abramovich's *Eclipse* among them.

Of course, I'd seen pictures of these kinds of yachts before – most notably of mega art collector Dakis Joannou's yacht *Guilty*, camouflaged by Jeff Koons, which periodically clogs up my Instagram.
IRL, *Guilty* is thirty-five metres long, but on an iPhone screen – let's say, the iPhone 8 – it will have been flattened and reduced to about 138.3 x 67.3 mm (or approx. 14 x 7 cm).
Factoring in the border of the phone, its image on Instagram would be about 6 cm wide in portrait mode, not even the width of a credit card.
And considering that most images of *Guilty* are framed by water, the boat itself would be about 3 cm high. 3 cm!

Since those 3 cm proxies were my only previous experience
with superyachts, you can imagine how disorienting it was
to stumble upon the hotel-sized *Flying Fox*.

This type of shrinkage is typical of the "image world"
that both consumes us and fits so snugly into the palm of
our hands.
>   Where do the images in our "image world" come from,
>   you ask?
>   The cloud!
But what exactly is the cloud?
>   Technically speaking, the cloud is made of computer
>   servers dispersed around the globe; when I request
>   an image from the cloud, one of those servers sends
>   the image to my device.
>   Sounds simple, but the more granular you get,
>   the more complicated it becomes.
Take an image of Joannou's yacht
(https://www.instagram.com/p/ByInEQEDmjT/), for example.
>   A quick traceroute – a way to measure the route of an
>   internet request – from my location on the east side
>   of Stavanger reveals that ten (!) different servers
>   chime in to complete the request and send the image
>   to my computer.
>   These consist of two local servers in Stavanger,
>   one server in Sortland in the north of Norway,
>   and several servers at an unknown location from
>   my local telecom, Telia, as well as Facebook
>   servers in Ireland and another in Menlo Park,
>   California.
In between these international servers are routers and
other machinery and miles and miles of fibre-optic cable
running underneath the ocean.
>   And electricity – every aspect of this simple
>   interaction drinks electricity.

When you think of the cloud, and the ease and efficiency
with which it delivers us images and information, you
don't think of the physicality and the energy that's
involved.
>   Much of our consumer-facing technology, and the
>   language that we use to describe it, belies the
>   immense machinery working in real time to make our
>   digital interactions so instantaneous.
>   In Instagram's case, expediency is baked into
>   the platform's name.
And the term "the cloud" is one that connotes both the
ephemeral and the opaque, familiar enough to inspire a
kind of shrugging acceptance and mysterious enough to
obscure a true understanding of its make-up.

Both wealth and **data** [>p. 133] tend to amass invisibly.
>   As the US American actor Chris Rock puts it,
>   "If poor people knew how rich people are, there would
>   be riots in the streets!"

Put another way, until you're smacked in the face
with a 9,000-ton yacht at your hometown port,
it's hard to wrap your head around what being one of
the top 1 per cent that owns 50.1 per cent of the
world's wealth actually looks like in practice.
It's the same thing with data, which also gains
power through accumulation but often remains
unseen and abstruse.
It's not until digital technology manifests itself
physically that we can easily grasp its effect on our
society and the environment.
(On the latter point, in 2017, the US data centres
that host racks and racks of computers powering
our cloud used 40 per cent more energy than the
entire UK.)

As data and wealth are collected invisibility, the sheer
magnitude of kinetic power inherent in these stockpiles
forces ruptures, creating brief flashes of visibility.
Most likely the only reason the *Flying Fox* came into
the Port of Stavanger that night was because it was
avoiding German VAT - the yacht had just been built,
and it needed to enter a port outside of the EU
to be refunded the 19 per cent tax (in this case,
a refund of tens of millions of dollars).
Similarly, data also can't be hidden cleanly
forever.
This was thrown into sharp relief during the recent mass
shooting at Christchurch in New Zealand in which the shooter
filmed the massacre and streamed it live on Facebook.
The video wasn't flagged and immediately taken down
by Facebook because the platform's AI that's meant to
detect impermissible content hadn't been trained on
enough videos of the like to pick it up.
It had never encountered a live mass shooting
before.
"We are re-examining our reporting logic and experiences
for both live and recently live videos in order to expand
the categories that would get to accelerated review,"
the company said.

The *Flying Fox* is registered under a shell company in the
Cayman Islands; it's not publicly known who owns it,
although the Italian newspaper *L'Unione Sarda* guessed it
might belong to Jeff Bezos, the world's richest man.
I do know, though, the exact time and date I saw the
Flying Fox: 16 March 2019, at 20:51 at night.
This information is encoded in the JPEG my iPhone created
when it stored the image and simultaneously uploaded it to
my iCloud.
Apple relies on other companies to run its cloud,
and iCloud relies on S3, an Amazon web service.
Though it's widely known as the world's largest
e-retailer, Amazon is less well known as the
world's largest supplier of cloud services.

It would stand to reason that this is on purpose.
        The faster industry and infrastructure increases, the
        more distance there seems to be between the visible
        and the invisible, between the understood and the
        unknown.
                With efficiency comes distance.
Where did all the metal and components come from that
built the Macintosh computer I am typing on?
        I have no idea and, TBH, I'd be afraid to Google it.

Perhaps this is why there doesn't seem to be much demand
for accountability, or even visibility, of our data.
        When our personal photos float around the globe, our
        iPhones are minted in China or when Amazon sells us
        "more than ten million products available coast-to-
        coast with no minimum purchase", do we really
        understand the trade-offs?
                Can we grasp it in the abstract or do we need
                to see it for ourselves?

Cory Arcangel is a US American artist who makes work in a wide range
of media, including music, video, modified video games, performance and
the internet.

Portraits,
2006–2007

Portraits is an investigation into the construction of online identity through **avatars**[>p. 132], the **virtual**[>p. 138] characters that we create as our proxy personas in video games and on online platforms.

For their series of portraits, Eva & Franco Mattes invited members of the **Second Life**[>p. 137] **community**[>p. 136] to virtual photo shootings, thus transferring the traditional photographic processes of sets, light and poses to an **in-game**[>p. 135] environment.

Printed on large-format canvases, the **screenshot**[>p. 137] portraits are emotionally charged by the way their gazes address each other through the arrangement in the space. **Computer-generated**[>p. 133] and pixelated, these portraits manifest a somewhat dated digital aesthetic that is reflective of the mid-2000s, while emphasising technological imperfection in the pursuit of digital photorealism.

At the same time, they also speak to the ambivalence of their creators' hidden desires: the choice of avatar is both a projection and a retreat behind the digital facade. However, the women's faces, full-lipped and photographically frozen in extreme close-up, are trapped in stereotypical ideals of beauty – an expression of how the conventional gaze is perpetuated online and in virtual worlds, along with sexualised and sexist gender roles.

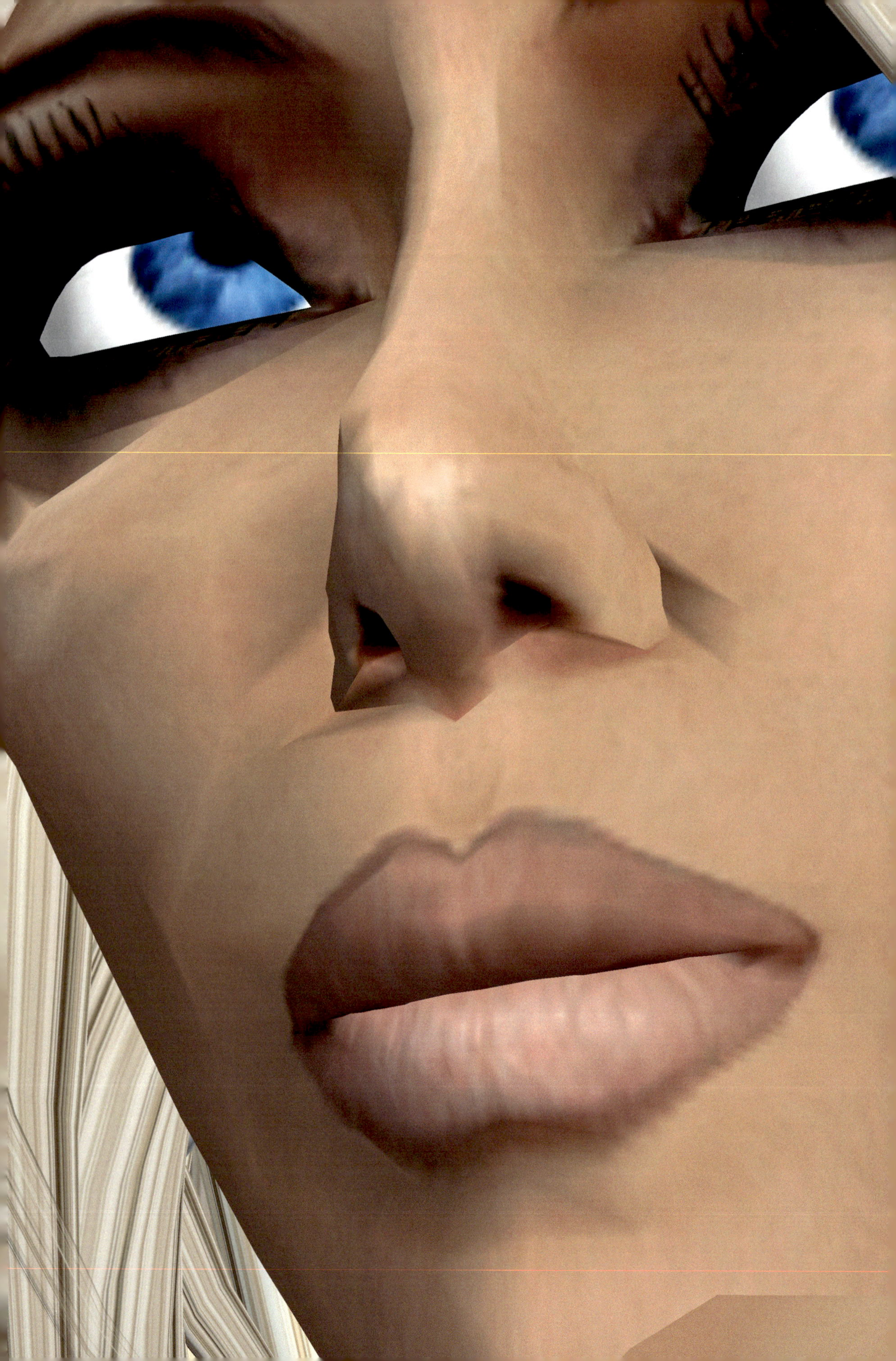

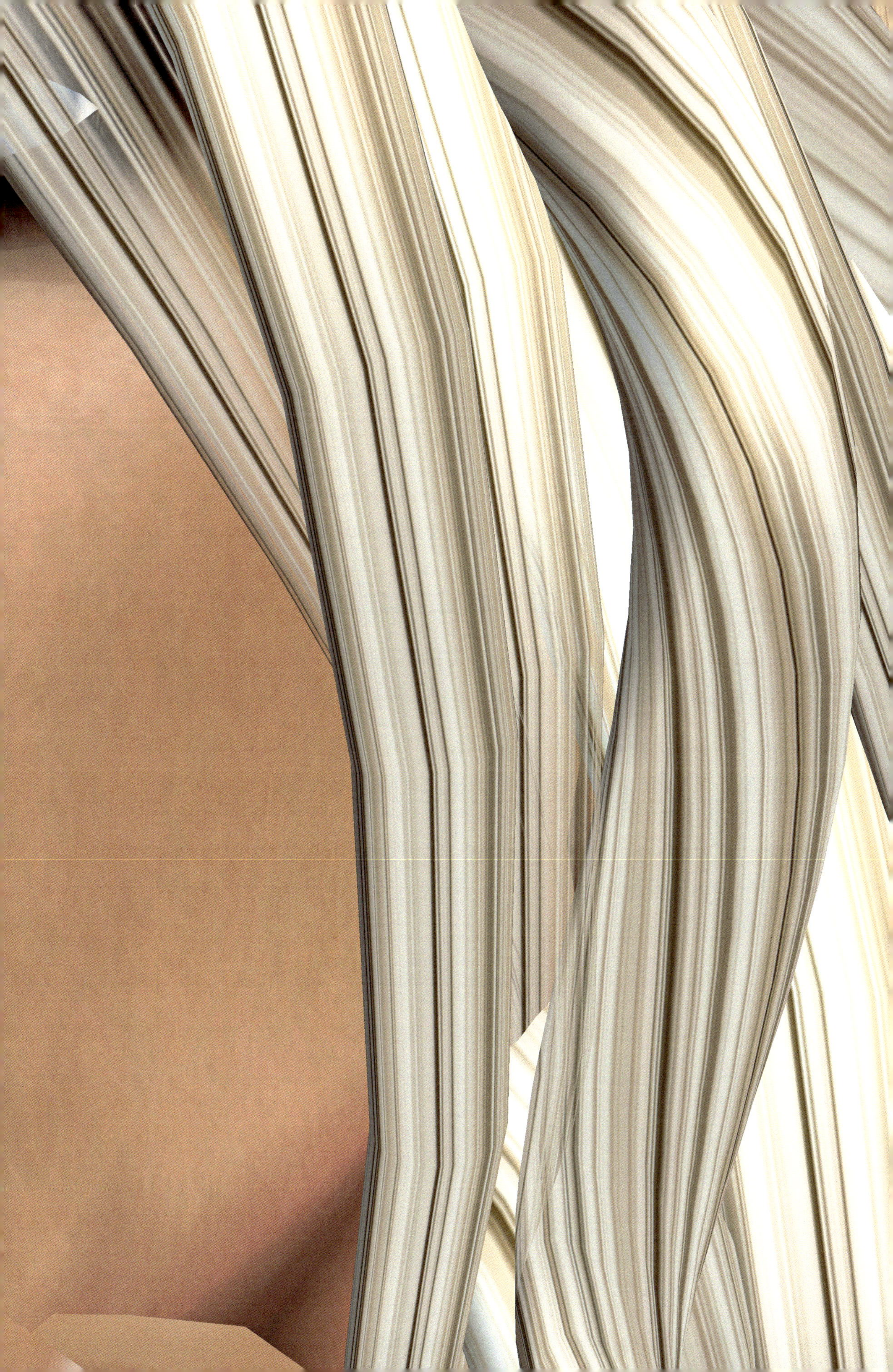

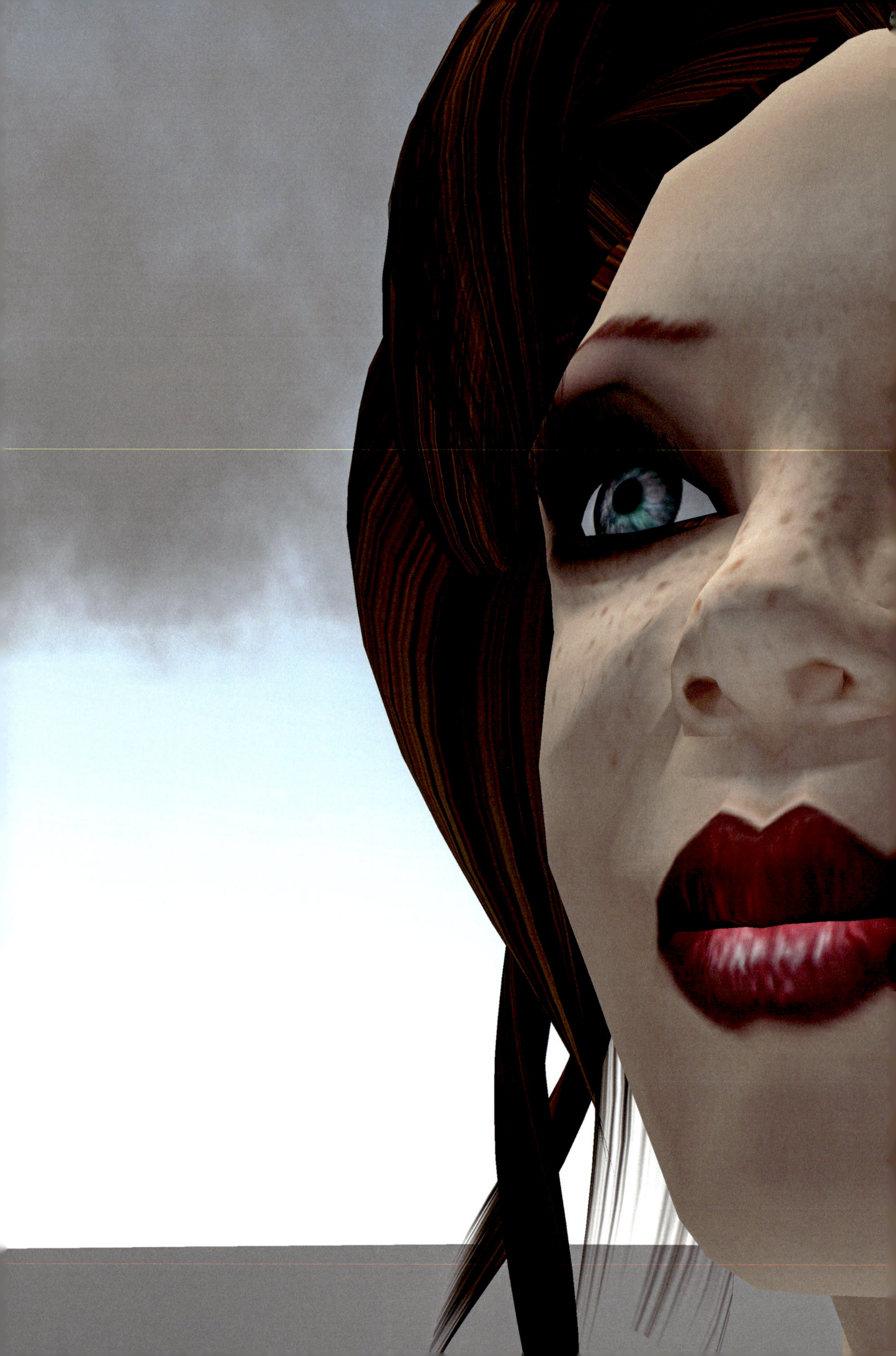

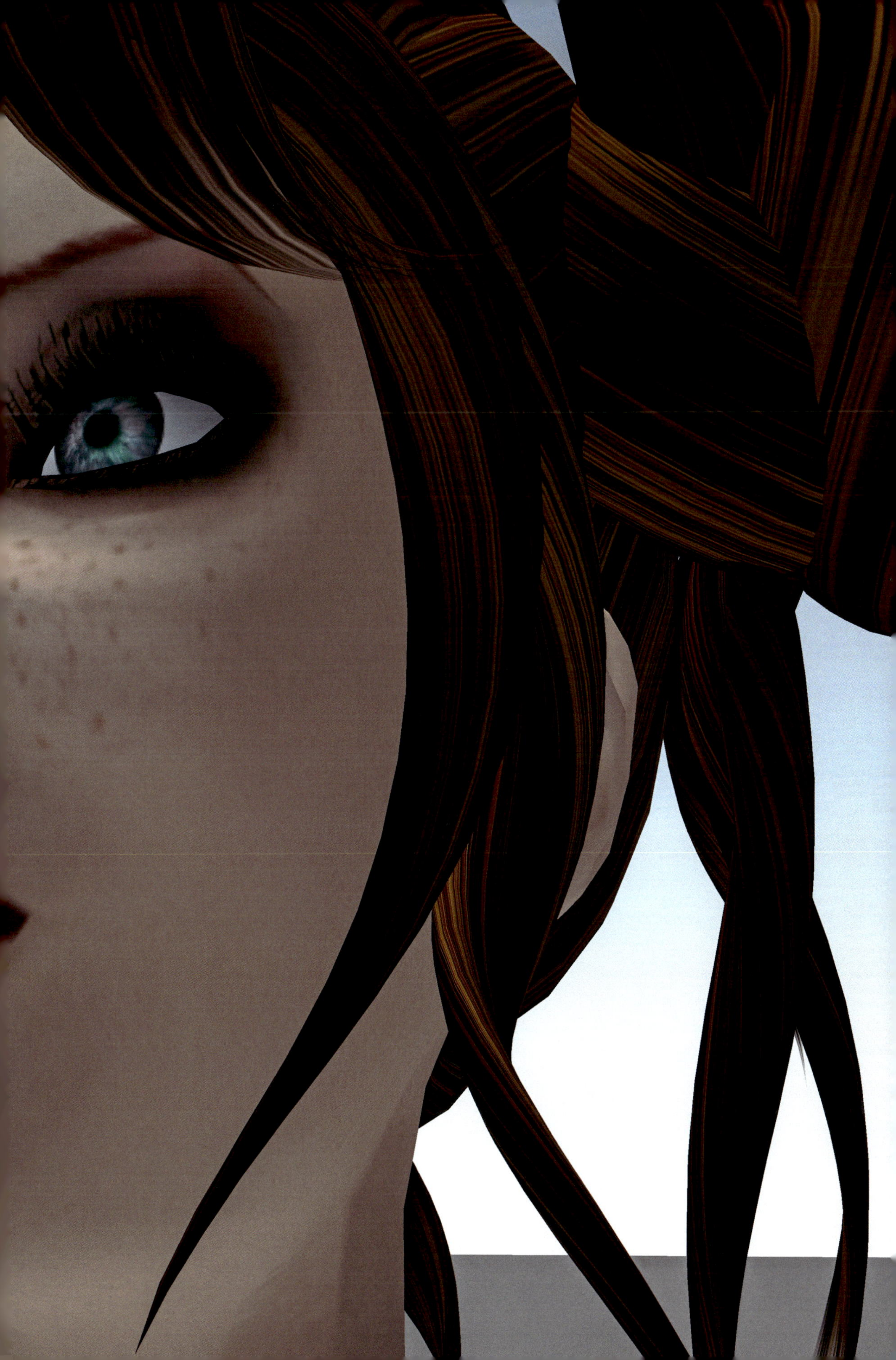

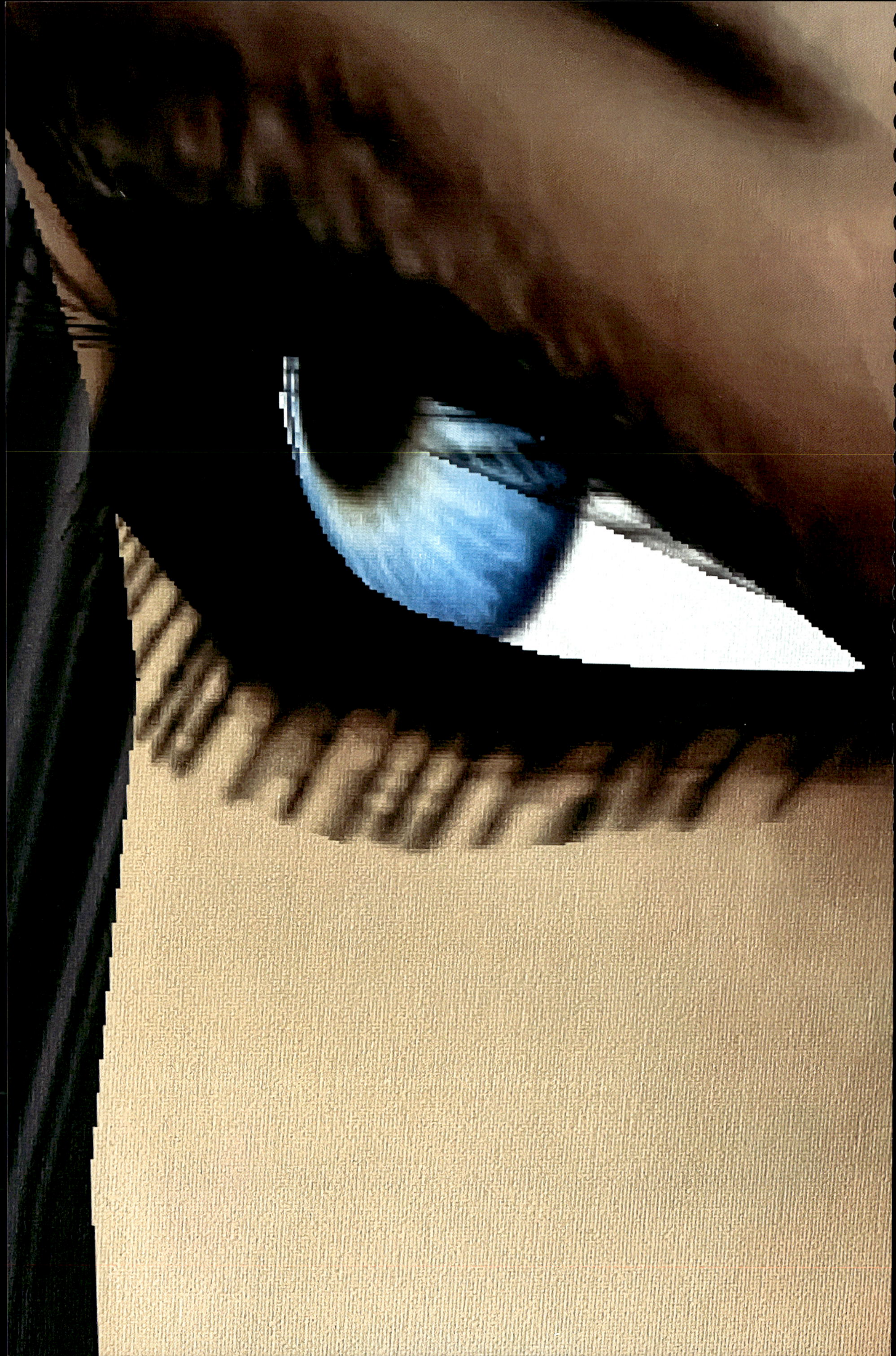

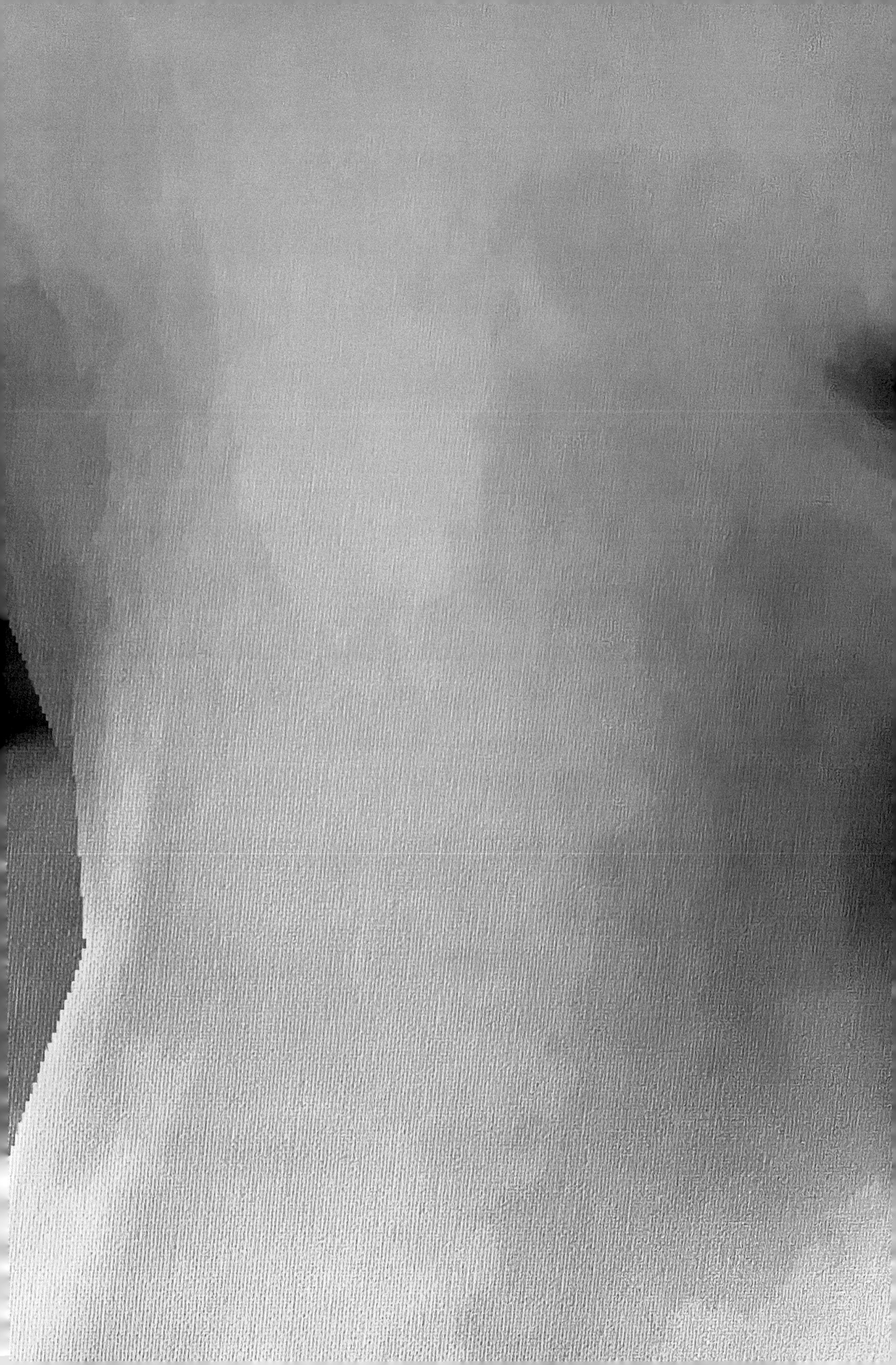

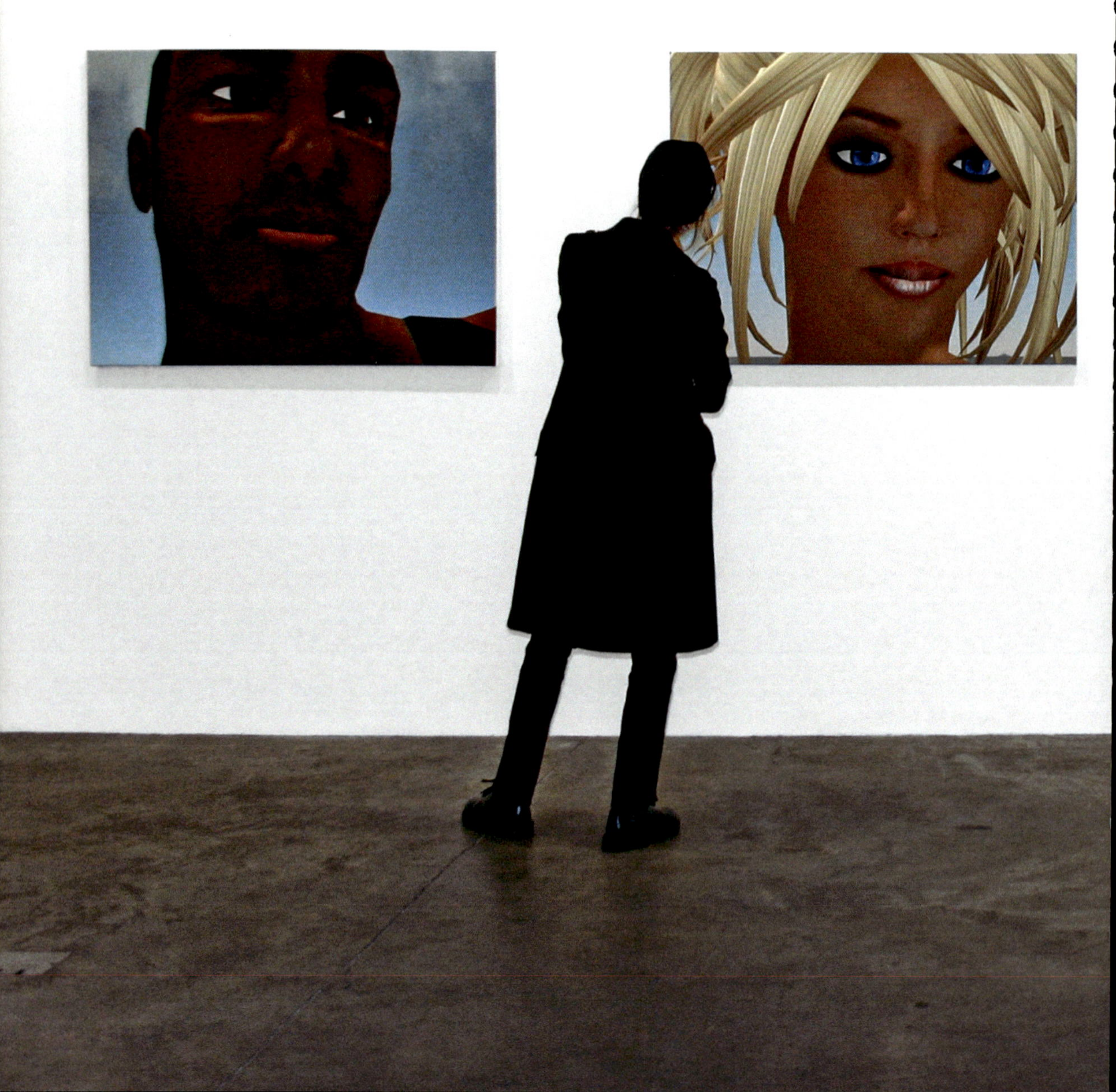

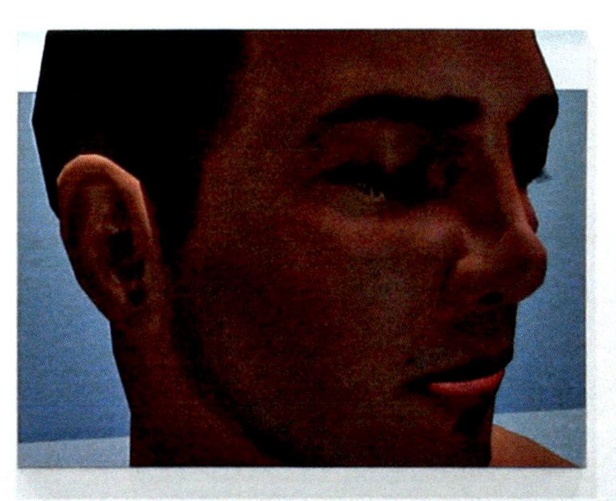 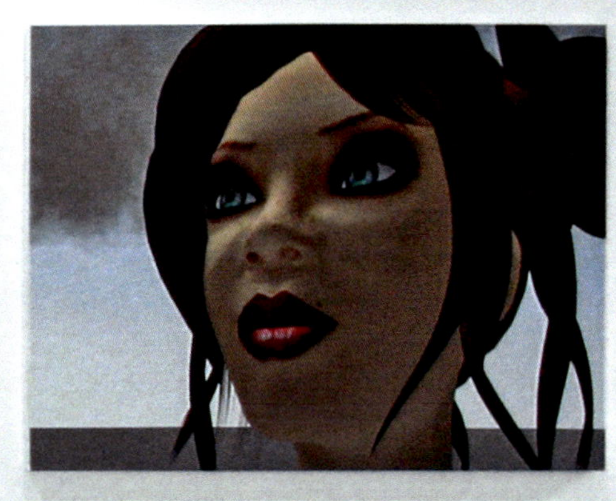

Fabio Paris

The opening of the Fabio Paris Art Gallery just happened to coincide with the dawn of the new millennium.

It was a turning point for the visual arts, anticipating what the turn of the century and millennium might bring, and the consequences of leaving the past behind – a mixture of social, political and personal experiences.

It was then that I decided to do what years of frequenting the art world had led up to and open a gallery.

It was inaugurated on 11 May 2000, in the spring of a new spring ...

I met and started working with Eva & Franco Mattes in 2003, when they went by the name of 0100101110101101.org.

They had been a duo since the mid-1990s and by that time they were among the leading exponents of Net Art.

I remember that back then I had also been intrigued by *Life Sharing* (2000-2003), a radical performance piece that presaged the death of privacy and envisaged a future of non-stop **sharing**^{>p. 137}.

But thinking back, our most interesting and creative conversations took place later, as both their practice and our relationship gradually matured.

We began to work together more regularly after the exhibition *Nike Ground* (2003).

For this project they created a fake Nike advertising campaign, which featured a website and a huge hi-tech container that was installed in Karlsplatz, a public square in Vienna.

The news quickly spread nationwide: Karlsplatz, one of Vienna's main squares, was about to be renamed Nikeplatz and a huge monument in the shape of Nike's famous Swoosh logo was going to be erected there.

The campaign sparked an outcry from the Viennese and Nike filed a lawsuit against the Mattes.

Against all odds, Eva & Franco won against the "giant".

As their fake communications campaign developed, it explored a series of issues such as the cultural hegemony of the US, the abuse of public space in European cities and, above all, the right to reuse the symbols that are forced onto us every which way and thus become part of the collective imagination (Nike being a prime example).

The performance lasted a month, was witnessed by thousands of people and was picked up by hundreds of newspapers, magazines and TV programmes across Europe.

In a review of the show, Bruce Sterling wrote,
      "So *Nike Ground* was a period effort.
      For all its mighty bulk, it was a thing as brief and
      glorious as a wheat-pasted Situationist poster during
      May '68.
            And it was ace.
      It was tops.
            There was simply nothing to match it.
                  It came screaming straight out of noone and
                  nowhere."[1]

The Vienna project was staged in the autumn of 2003 and
afterwards the works were exhibited in my gallery, from
8 January to 19 February 2005.

On 15 November 2006 Eva & Franco Mattes opened their first
exhibition of portraits of **avatars**[>p. 132] inhabiting the
virtual[>p. 138] world of **Second Life**[>p. 137].
      13 Most Beautiful Avatars was held at Ars Virtua
      Gallery, a contemporary art gallery based in
      Second Life, organised by Rhizome.org in
      collaboration with the New Museum of Contemporary Art
      in New York.
            This was followed up by a "real life" show at
            the Italian Academy in New York.
It was the first time that the tradition of portrait
painting had been used to depict digital beings, rather
than flesh and blood people.
      Roberta Smith commented,
            "What's remarkable is the eerie effectiveness
            of these works as paintings in the nonvirtual
            world. With their flat colors, slightly blocky
            features and assertive hair, these images of
            men and women exude a sexy artifice that is
            both seductive and a parody of seductiveness."[2]

The project went on for two years and led to the creation
of four series of portraits:
      13 Most Beautiful Avatars, *LOL*, *Portraits* and
      Annoying Japanese Child Dinosaur.
            I exhibited *LOL* in my gallery in January 2007.
The exhibition created a huge buzz, and I'll never forget
the Belgian collector who phoned an hour before the
opening to snap up the *Tory Innis* triptych. The show was a
success.

      Fabio Paris is an independent curator and former gallery owner from
      Brescia, Italy. He is co-curator of the show *Eva & Franco Mattes.
      Dear Imaginary Audience*, at Fotomuseum Winterthur.

---

1 Bruce Sterling, "Nike Ground", in *Eva and Franco Mattes: 0100101110101101.ORG* (Milan, New York: Charta, 2009), p. 92.
2 Roberta Smith, "Art in Review; Eva and Franco Mattes", *The New York Times,* 9 March 2007.

Hannah Uncut, 2021

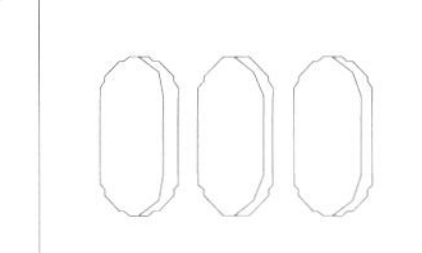

It's with our **smartphones**[>p. 137] that we capture our life in all its authenticity: all the **selfie**[>p. 137] attempts that didn't make it onto Instagram, the casual **screenshots**[>p. 137] that we save as mementos or the **meme**[>p. 136] we send around on **social media**[>p. 138].
It's the trial and error, the blurred shots and mis-framed angles that give a sense of our lives being lived.

For *Hannah Uncut*, a work commissioned by Fotomuseum Winterthur, Eva & Franco Mattes offered to pay USD 1,000 to anyone willing to sell their phone with all the pictures on it – thus making their private image archive accessible to the interpretation of strangers.
They selected Hannah from the UK, a woman in her late twenties whose life and personality unfolds through a slide show of images that accumulated over months – in chronological order and completely unedited.

The only artistic intervention is the rhythm of the images, emulating the pace at which we swipe through our phones.
Hannah's pictures show the evolution of photographic forms of communication and enactment associated with the mass diffusion of social media and smartphones.

Hannah, a child of **Generation Y**[>p. 134], uses screenshots as a matter of course, just as she applies **face filters**[>p. 134] to her selfies and plays with an expanded visual vocabulary that is geared towards **sharing**[>p. 137] her images online.
As such, Hannah's photo archive lays bare the construction and curation of the self – permeated by moments of authenticity and intimacy that unavoidably catapult us into the role of voyeurs.

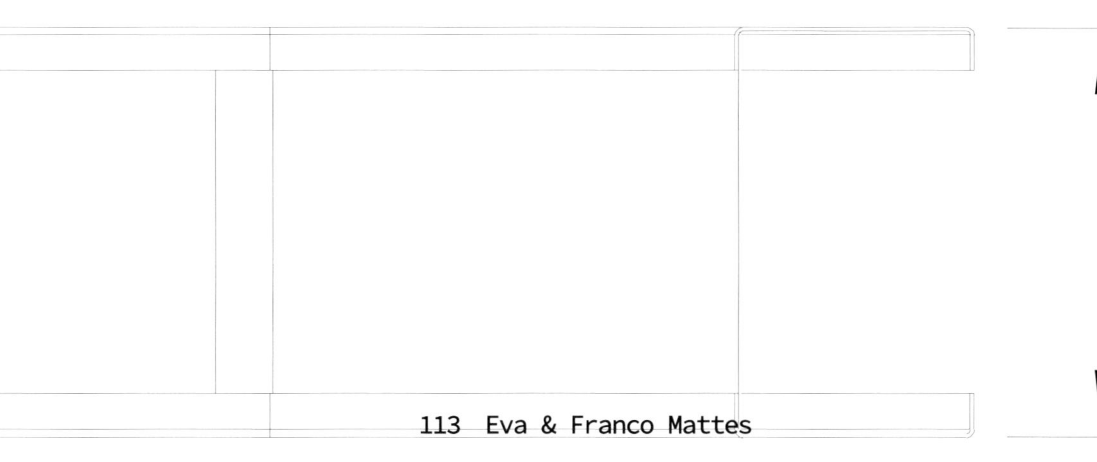

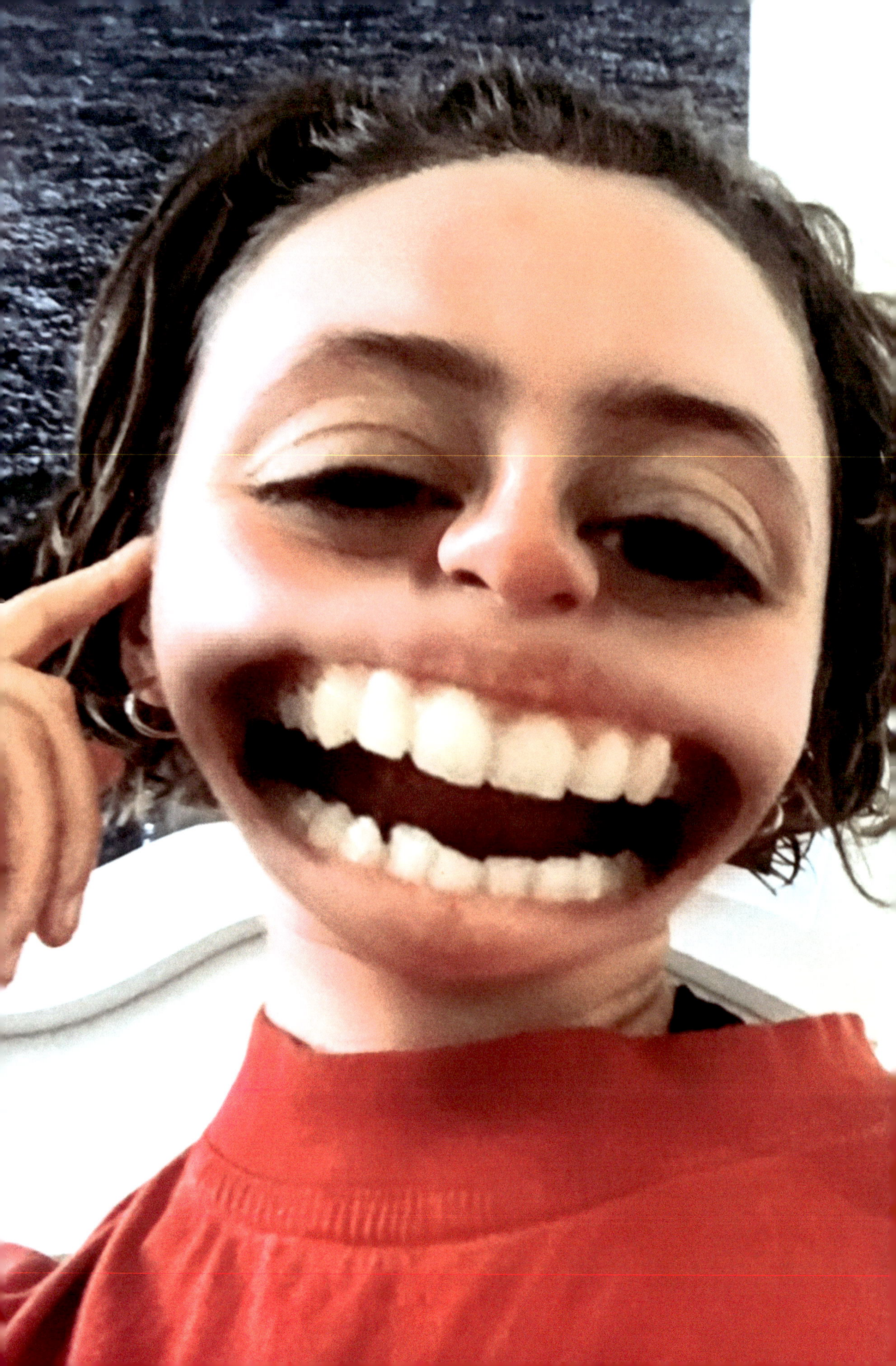

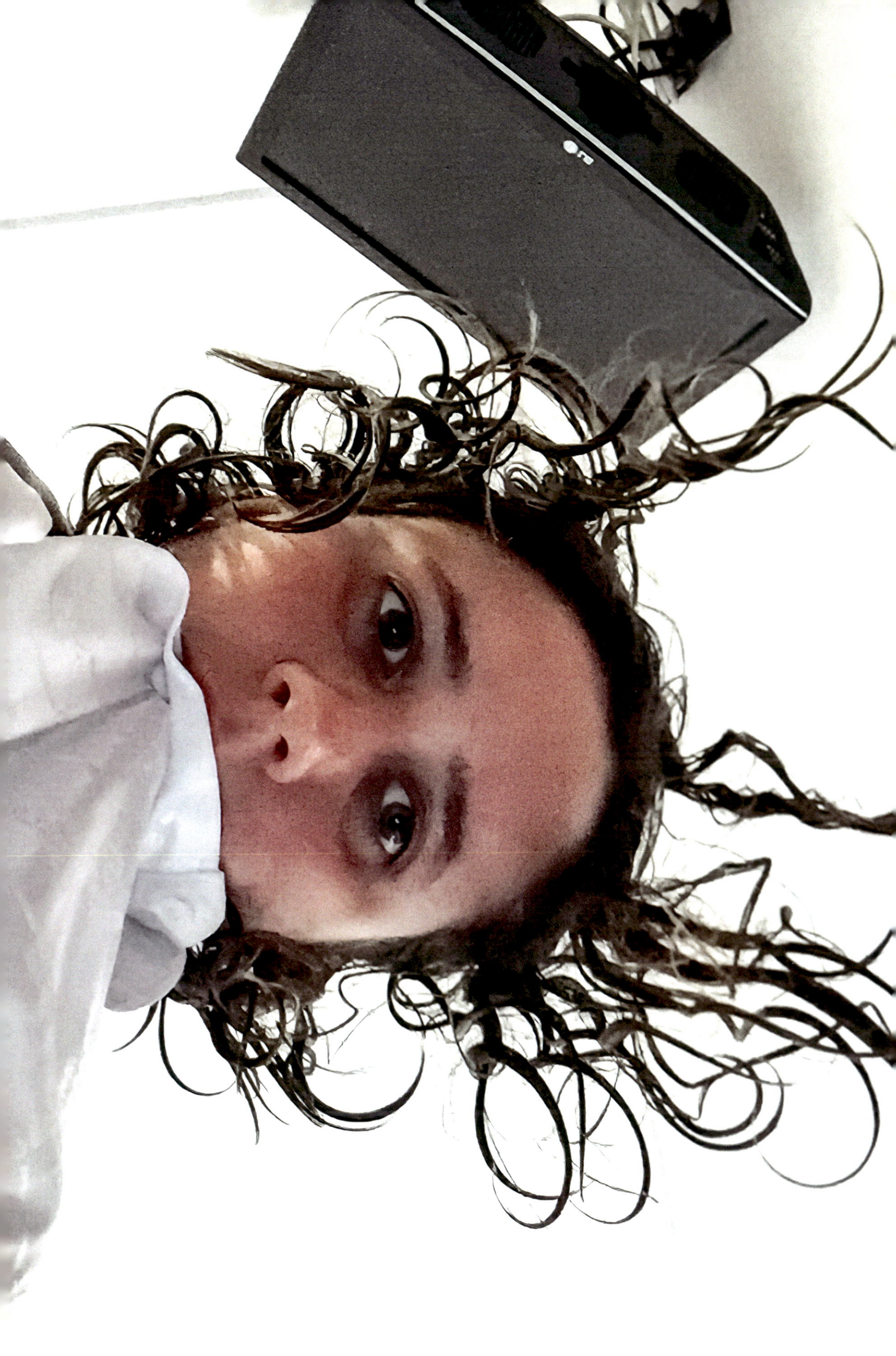

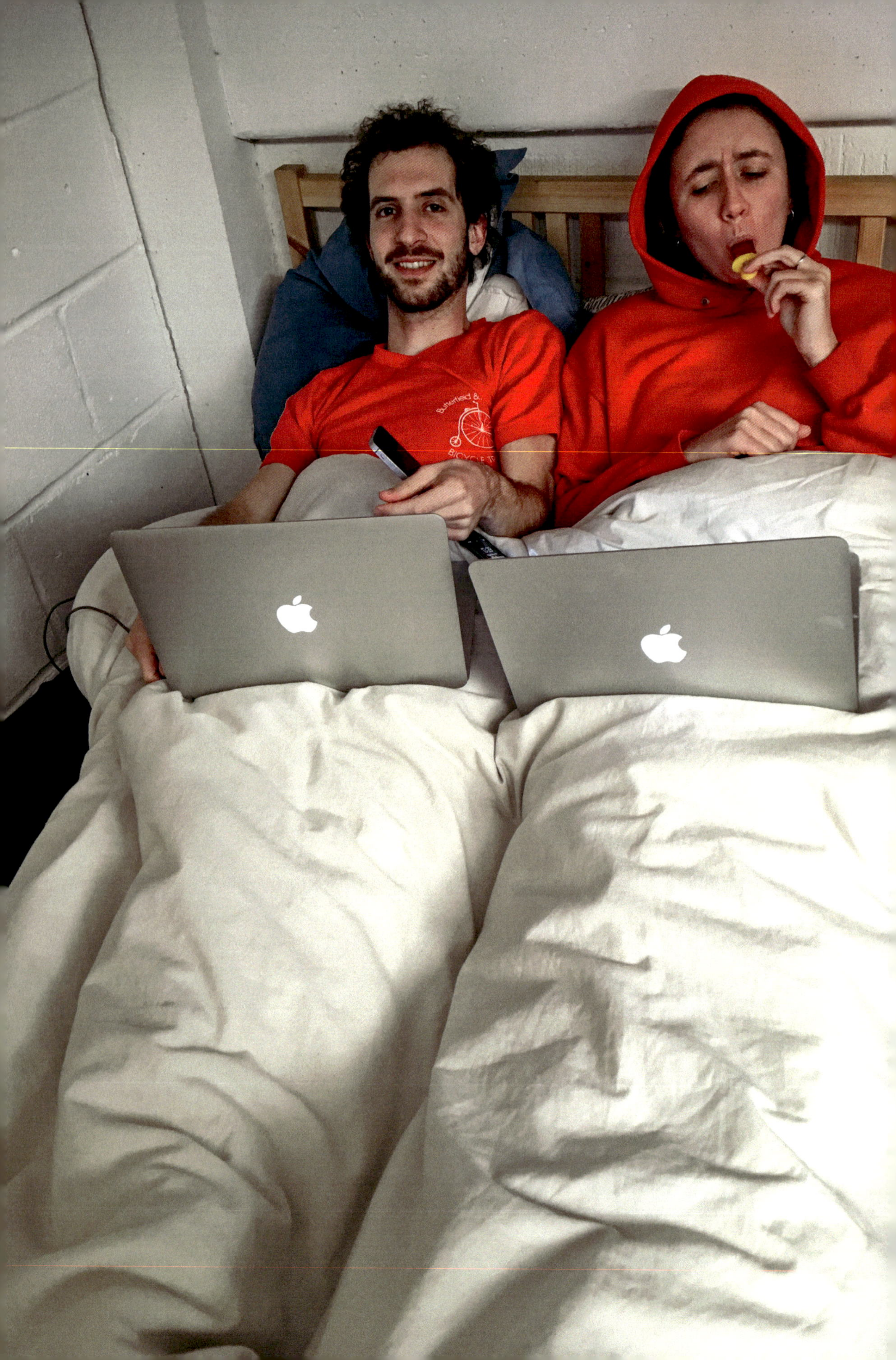

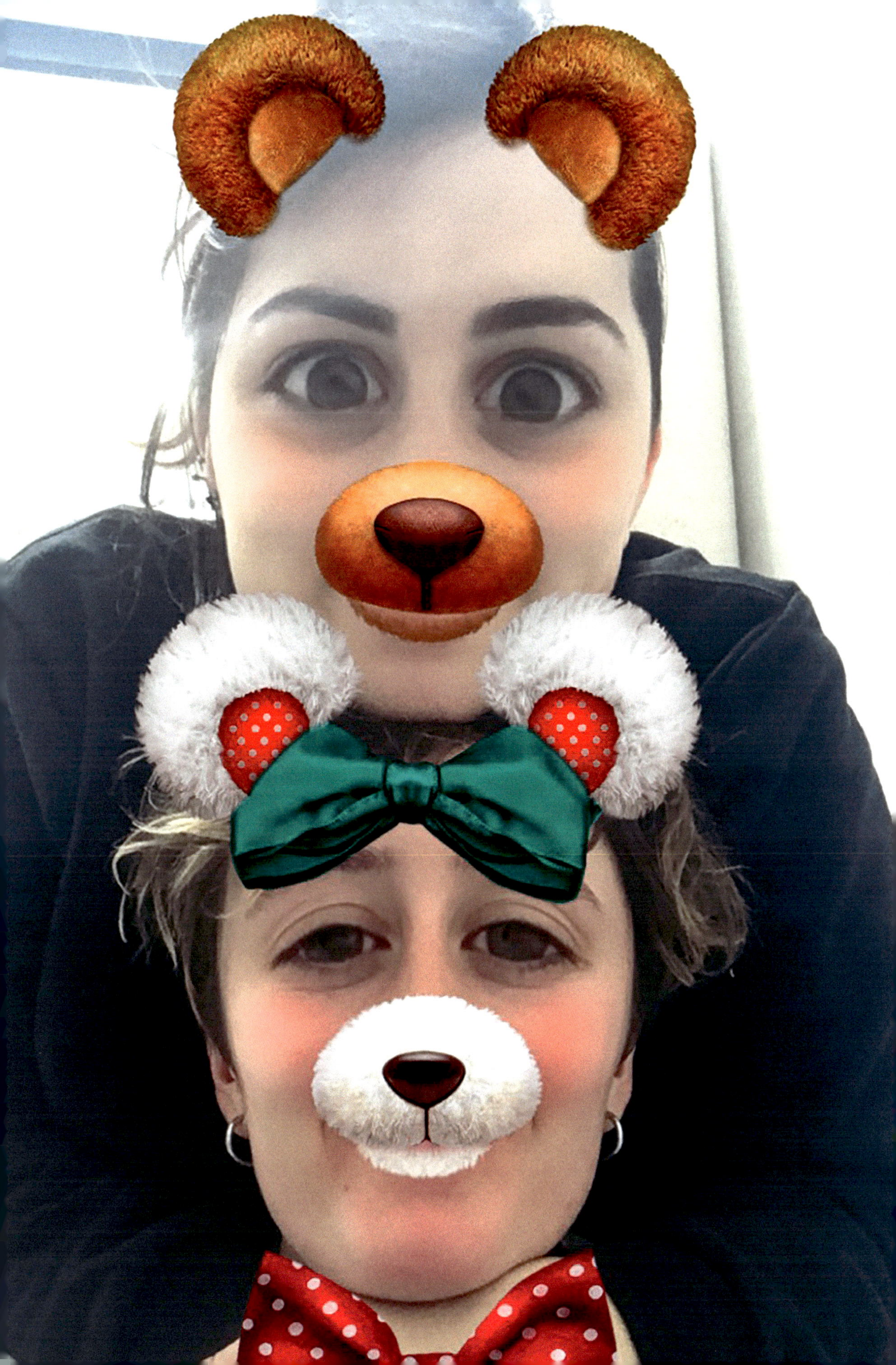

messian - birdsong

tried to map spore from bird flys from
tree to tree - dutch

list

Carsten Holler   proximity

Lygia clarke   closeness

Paul Macarthy   haptic

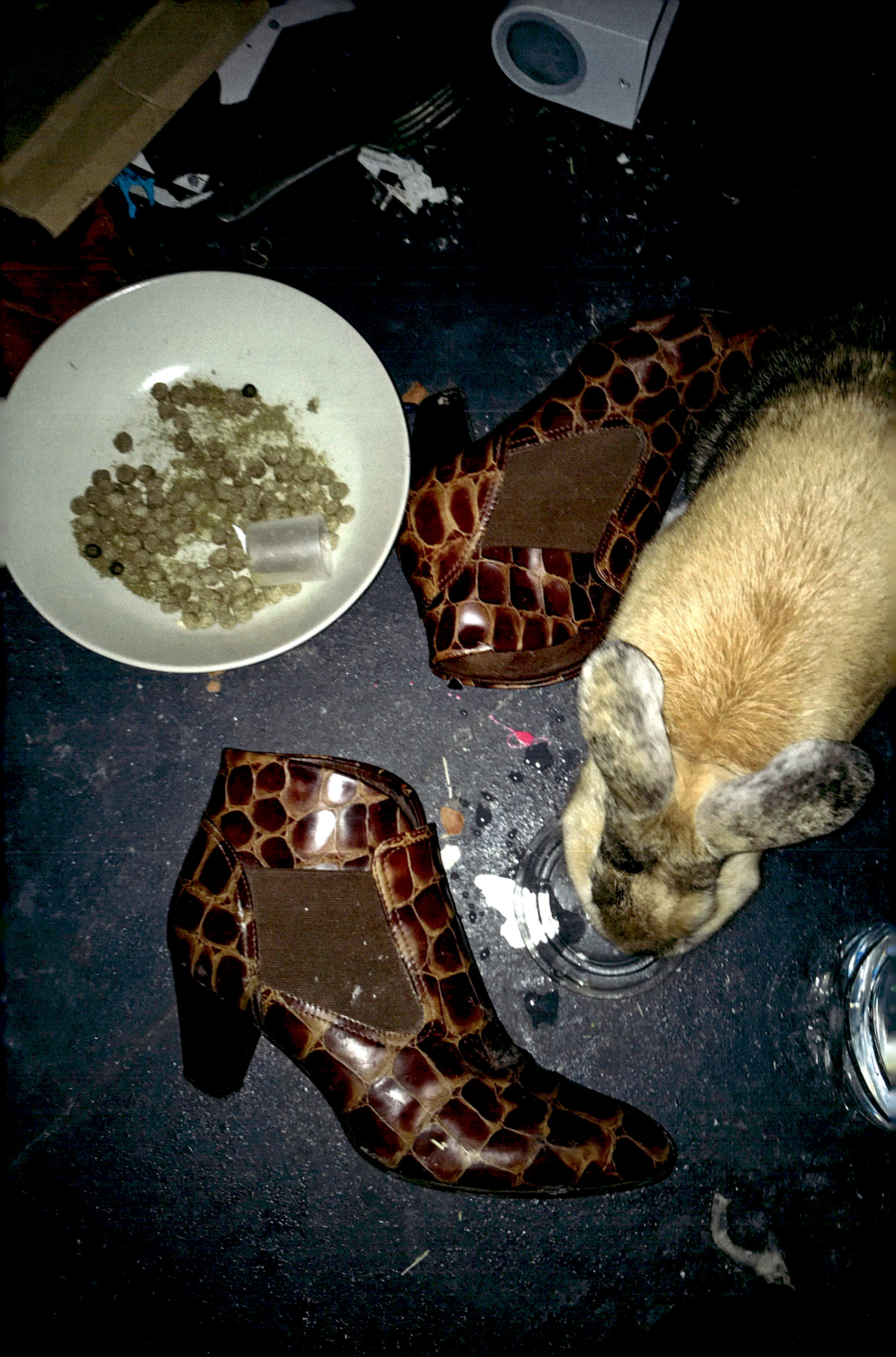

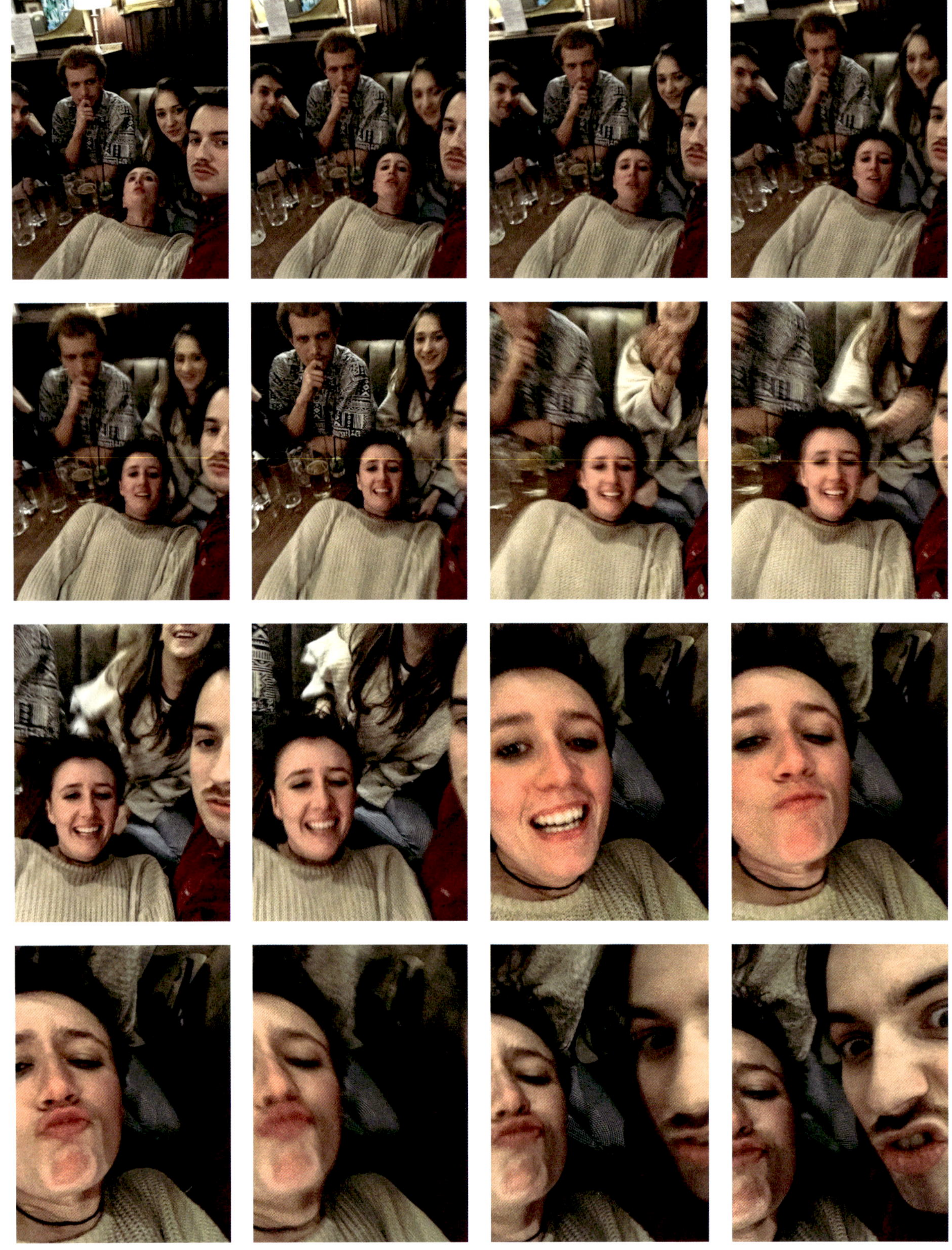

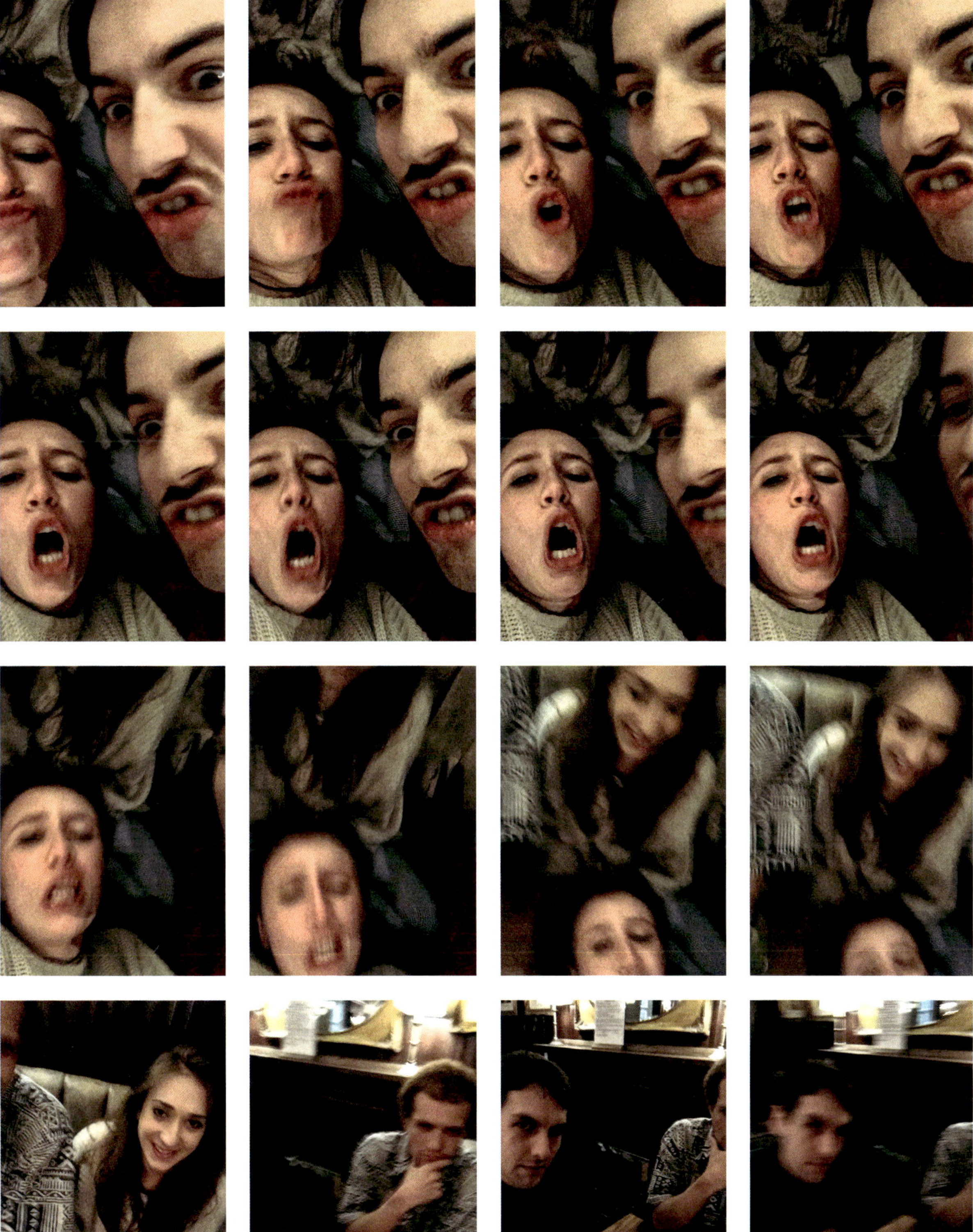

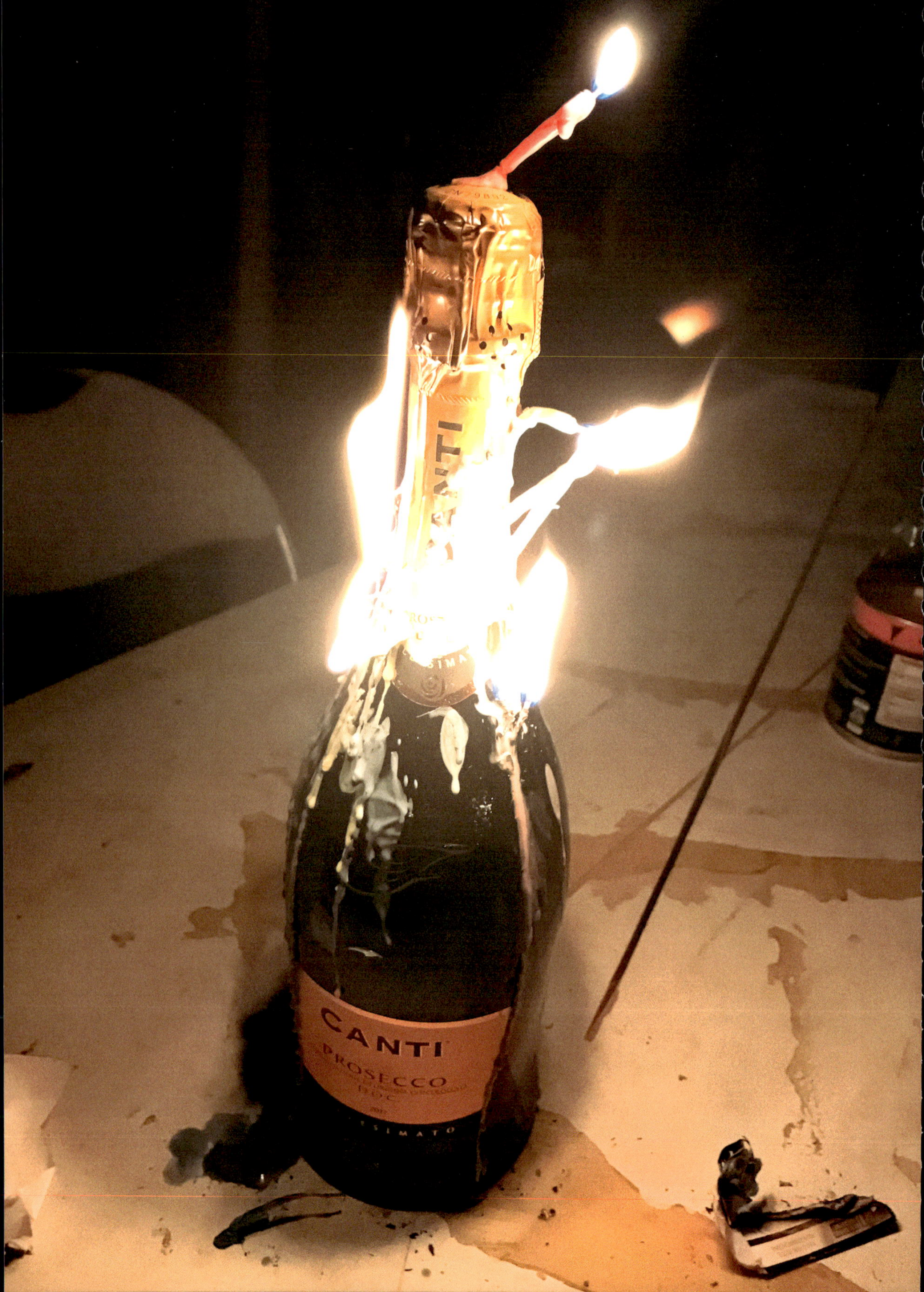
CANTI
PROSECCO
DOC
TSIMATO

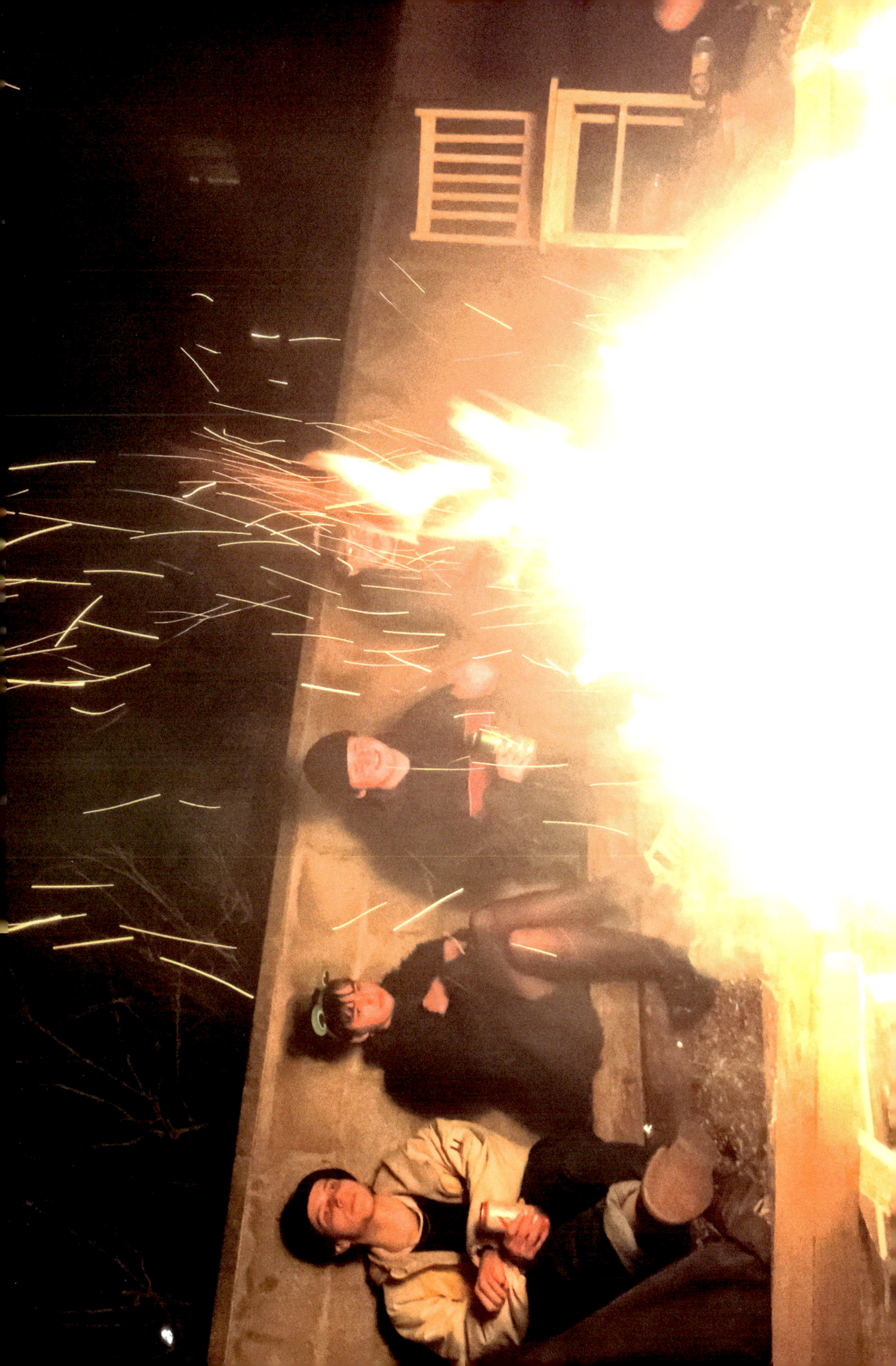

The Flight of the Networked Image: From Screen to Museum and Back Again

Katrina Sluis and Nadine Wietlisbach in Conversation

Nadine Wietlisbach: In 2021, Fotomuseum Winterthur is presenting the first solo exhibition by Eva & Franco Mattes to be shown in a museum context.
You were one of the first curators to present their works within the framework of a photo institution. How did that come about?

Katrina Sluis: I previously worked with Eva & Franco Mattes as part of *All I Know Is What's on the Internet*, an exhibition I curated at The Photographers' Gallery in 2018–2019.
The exhibition brought together eleven artists who were questioning the different forms of value, knowledge, meaning and labour that arise from the endless (re-)circulation of visual content online.
Included among works by Eva & Franco Mattes, Andrew Norman Wilson and Constant Dullaart was a commission by Jonas Lund, centred on a fictitious political consulting firm called *Operation Earnest Voice*, a kind of performative installation reversing Brexit in the wake of the Cambridge Analytica revelations.
These works hadn't really been shown in a photographic context, yet they have so much to say about how images are stockpiled, weaponised and distributed, and what happens at the interface between humans and machines.
These are really exciting practices to bring into the photo museum.

NW: Artistic practices like those of Eva & Franco Mattes are indeed tackling urgent questions about how our image-based practices are increasingly intertwined with the ethics and politics of our daily life – questions that might be even more pressing right now if we think of how the current pandemic has intensified our screen- and image-based behaviour.
Just like your exhibition at The Photographers' Gallery, doing the solo show *Dear Imaginary Audience,* with Eva & Franco is an institutional statement by Fotomuseum Winterthur:

we want to stress that the **networked image**[>p. 136] represents
a significant shift in the evolution of photography and
its modes of usage.

    This shift, which affects the production, circulation
and consumption of images, is so ingrained in our
everyday habits that it remains largely invisible
and unquestioned: we take **screenshots**[>p. 137] to remember
a recipe or send personal photographs to our family
chat but we barely give a moment's thought to what
this actually means in terms of how it restructures
our lives and relationships.

Image practices are inextricably linked to representation,
economies and politics – they are all dominated by the way
images are shared and circulated within our networked society.

KS: Just the other day I found myself browsing
Life Sharing (2000–2003), an early work by Eva & Franco,
preserved by Rhizome's excellent *Net Art Anthology*, in
which they made the entire contents of their personal
computer publicly available.

    While voyeuristically browsing the email archive of
these misfit European artists, I was surprised to
read a twenty-year-old email correspondence between
them and a mutual acquaintance I'd had coffee with
that morning in suburban Canberra!

    It struck me how the liberating potential of
limitless digital storage has dramatically
shifted over this period – archiving one's life
comes with the perpetual risk of potential exposure.

With so many bits of ourselves floating around the web,
these **data**[>p. 133] shadows resemble threatening zombies that
can come to haunt us in unexpected ways.

    For cultural institutions wanting to collect,
preserve or exhibit **social media**[>p. 138] content, this
can have unintended consequences.

    When The Photographers' Gallery presented *One
Terabyte of Kilobyte Age* by Olia Lialina and
Dragan Espenschied, it involved exhibiting ten
thousand web pages from GeoCities, in the order
in which they were last updated.

I was surprised to walk in one morning to see the antique
web page of someone I used to work with in Sydney twenty
years ago.

    When I told him about it, he was quite traumatised and
immediately asked me to erase it from the web
completely.

    The distance between innocently **sharing**[>p. 137]
pictures of one's cat and one's online self
being publicly exposed is something that the
show at Fotomuseum Winterthur traverses.

For example, in the new work that you've commissioned,
Hannah Uncut (2021), Eva & Franco confront us with the
possibility that everything in your camera roll could
potentially be harvested as material
for art.

What does it mean to be "uncut" now at a time when we're so heavily invested in curating our identities online?

NW: *Hannah Uncut* really shows how our habitual ways of using photography have changed and evolved over the last decade, and especially how networked images are being made for a kind of **imaginary audience**[>p. 135] – mainly because we know they're going to be shared online eventually.
The only – albeit incredibly important – modification carried out by the artists is to work with the pace and the rhythm of how the images are presented.
It's all about this experience of sitting through the photographic lifespan of a person, which is transformed through this very minor artistic intervention.

KS: There is also something incredibly moving and strange about sitting through thousands of images of someone's unedited, un-Photoshopped, un-Instagram-**filtered**[>p. 134] life.
What does it mean to spend an hour immersed in months or even years of a single person's photo feed?
There's something unique and almost blasphemous about experiencing this in the gallery space.
Yet if we compare it to their earlier work *Personal Photographs* (2019–) and imagine the many images without viewers that circulate on these networks, you can also see a shift in how Eva & Franco approach their material.
When they started off in the late 1990s, they focused on the politics of the web's interface:
in *Vaticano.org* (1998), they made a copy of the official website of the Vatican, relying on its visual authority to trick the viewer into exploring the bastardised surrogate they had created.
Over time, Eva & Franco have turned their attention to the human and non-human infrastructures that lie beyond the web's interface.
So, in *Life Sharing*, they start to give people access to their actual hard drive.
In recent works like *Dark Content* (2015), they draw our attention to the human filters who clean up our social media feeds.
They humanise these abstract systems and make them intelligible, suggesting that the most political aspects of the photographic image are now happening, perhaps, outside the pictorial frame.

NW: An important aspect of the show is definitely making the invisible visible.
When it comes to the networked image, one of the main issues is not being able to grasp how many things are actually taking place below the surface level, not only as photographers but also as consumers and as image sharers. How, for example, are images economically entangled with multi-billion-dollar

industries and their interests, which are based on exploitation and the psychological strain of cheap labour?
I think a lot of Eva & Franco's works, even the older pieces, are about these hidden infrastructures, as you point out.
These layers are hard to transfer into a physical space, unless you create work that adds one aspect or the other to a bodily experience you might have in an exhibition space – as Eva & Franco do most strikingly in *BEFNOED* (2014–), where the viewers really have to physically engage with the screens.
Artists like Eva & Franco are able to transfer and, as it were, translate many of those ambivalent questions into a form which creates a spatial experience that is representative of online culture, yet also approachable.
It's torture and fun at the same time.
For me, I believe that this is very much one of the roles of an institution that focuses on a medium like photography: to critically question the medium it gives a home to. Photography has been sheltered within institutions for a long time, its elusiveness hidden behind the false claim of authenticity as the be-all and end-all.

KS: I agree. Eva & Franco are very good at what might be called "representing representation".
They also offer novel answers to questions that have haunted me personally as a digital curator, such as:
What is the visual language of the networked image on screen? How do you curate post-photographic culture?
We have seen in some institutions a tendency to print images off the internet and exhibit them on the wall.
But through this gesture, the richness of the surrounding interface is stripped away:
Where does the networked image begin and end?
Certainly, there is a need for new methods for and approaches to exhibiting digital visual culture in all its complex materiality and slipperiness.
I think many artists are taking up this challenge in their own practice, and Eva & Franco are committed to finding ways of staging or materialising these tensions for a gallery audience.
In the museum space we are prompted not to scroll past, moving ever onwards to the next seductive image, but to look again and critically question the horrifying, funny, sick, banal and strange image cultures that find their home online.

NW: I think that what you are referring to is made very visible in the taxidermic cat sculptures *Ceiling Cat* (2016) and *Half Cat* (2020).

In a clever and playful way, Eva & Franco transfer
the mainstream practice of lolcat **memes**[>p. 136] into the
exhibition space and thus act as a sort of mediator
to a more classically trained museum audience.
They have not only humorously turned the meme –
an image that is endlessly reproduced and
altered online – into a work of art but also
recirculated it online by uploading an image of
Ceiling Cat from the SFMOMA show onto Wikipedia.
When we think of the ubiquity of the image in an
institutional context, we see how this is in stark
contrast to the framed photograph on the wall, the
"original", which has determined how general knowledge
about photography constitutes itself – for a very long
time it was all about the notion of originality and
authorship.

KS: Yes, it's exciting how their cat-meme sculptures turn
established photographic culture on its head, ignoring
technical mastery and modernist authorship in order to
celebrate the aesthetic brilliance produced by networks of
misfit **users**[>p. 138].
I very much enjoy how Eva & Franco emphasise
photography's agency not as a technology of
representation but as a technology of viral
reproduction.
I share their fascination with the way images
escape from 4chan into Facebook into the gallery
and back again, generating new forms of economic
and cultural value.
In 2012 I developed a cat photography show at The
Photographers' Gallery, which was a way for me to traumatise
my colleagues by taking this cultural form seriously.
Joking aside, it allowed us to have an extended
conversation about the affective and economic
infrastructures of what we might term the
"cat-photography-industrial-complex".
The press responded to this gesture by publishing
opinion pieces about whether cat photography is
now "art", which of course misses the point.
Working with such material allows institutions to trace
the increasing flight of expertise from the museum
to the **online communities**[>p. 136] who congregate around the
networked image.

NW: This changing of currencies is also interesting when
you think about how the **attention economies**[>p. 136] have changed
over time in relation to the networked image.
Works like *Dark Content* or the more recent *The Bots*
(2020) are a clever comment on the way the economical
strings are being pulled in the background and how
internet giants rely on the exploitation of labour.
One aspect I really love about the new work
The Bots is that on the surface the videos look
fun and light because they are disguised as
make-up tutorials[>p. 135].

The content, however, is deeply disturbing.
This seems to me to be a comment on internet culture per se.
Think, for example, of all the influencers and
their perfect surface appearance, which hides
the amount of pressure they are under to
constantly perform for audiences and the camera.

KS: What kinds of subjectivities and collectivities are
being produced here? The show's brilliant title –
Dear Imaginary Audience, – really speaks to Eva & Franco's
concern with spectatorship and complicity, underlined in
works such as *Emily's Video* (2012) or *BEFNOED*.
I'm still haunted by *Freedom* (2011), in which Eva
enters the game environment of *Counter-Strike* and
pleads with the players not to kill her, because
she's "making an art performance". She inevitably
fails to convince them and we witness her die over
and over again.
By confronting us with morally dubious online behaviours,
I think Eva & Franco ask us to face the possibility that
maybe photography is not something to be celebrated but a
practice that we should be suspicious of.
Photography wants more and more of your time.
It wants more of your attention.
It's a lure, a subversive engine for generating new
economies of data which you are unlikely to profit from.
In this respect, *Dear Imaginary Audience,* offers a
compelling argument about how the politics of the image
has radically mutated in **computational**[>p. 133] culture.

NW: In Jodi Dean's piece in this publication, one of the
points she addresses relating to networked images is this:
"When we look for something new and it finds us, who
is to blame?"[>p. 35]
This questioning of responsibilities on a
personal, social and institutional level seems
to me to be also implied in the title
Dear Imaginary Audience,.
What are we looking at, and what is our role and responsibility?
Where can we still claim innocence in our use of
images and the way we participate within a networked
context?

KS: We can even direct this question of complicity to
today's cultural institutions, where beacons are
increasingly used to track audiences and heat-map where
they congregate, turning the museum into a space of
surveillance in the name of data-driven decision-making.
Institutions are certainly guilty of approaching
technology as shiny tools for innovation and
underestimating their cultural and ideological power.
I'm also thinking here about the current hype
around artificial intelligence (AI), which is
allegedly positioned to help museums revive their
collections and understand their audiences better.

I would argue that this is particularly provocative for our respective institutions, given that AI is a fundamentally photographic project.

What would it mean to dismantle this rhetoric and instead think about the computer scientist as a photographer or as a generator of images who profoundly interferes with culture?

Why isn't ImageNet, the premier data set most AI **applications**[>p. 132] are trained on, part of our institutional collections of photography?

I firmly believe that the continued fetishisation of a narrow canon of photographers is damaging our ability to talk about what's actually happening beyond art in the realm of visual culture.

Our screens and apps offer a simulation of analogue culture – and its power as a cultural form continues to be exploited by social platforms.

I'm beginning to wonder if it might be more productive to "forget photography" – which is the provocation behind a new book by Andrew Dewdney.

NW: I would definitely agree that at present any kind of framework we are familiar with, be it the image frame or the screen, is limiting our ability to really think about visual literacy and the way we tackle the changing nature of photography in the twenty-first century.

I strongly believe that the lens of art history was very restrictive when it came to understanding photographic practices, and that photography always requires an interdisciplinary approach, which needs to expand even more now that photography is computational, networked and **algorithmic**[>p. 132].

It's important to think outside this classical idea of the frame, the screen and the exhibition space – and yet bring the reflections back to these spaces to confront us, as Eva & Franco are doing.

Katrina Sluis is Head of Photography & Media Arts at the Australian National University, Canberra, and Adjunct Research Curator at The Photographers' Gallery, London.

Nadine Wietlisbach is Director of Fotomuseum Winterthur.

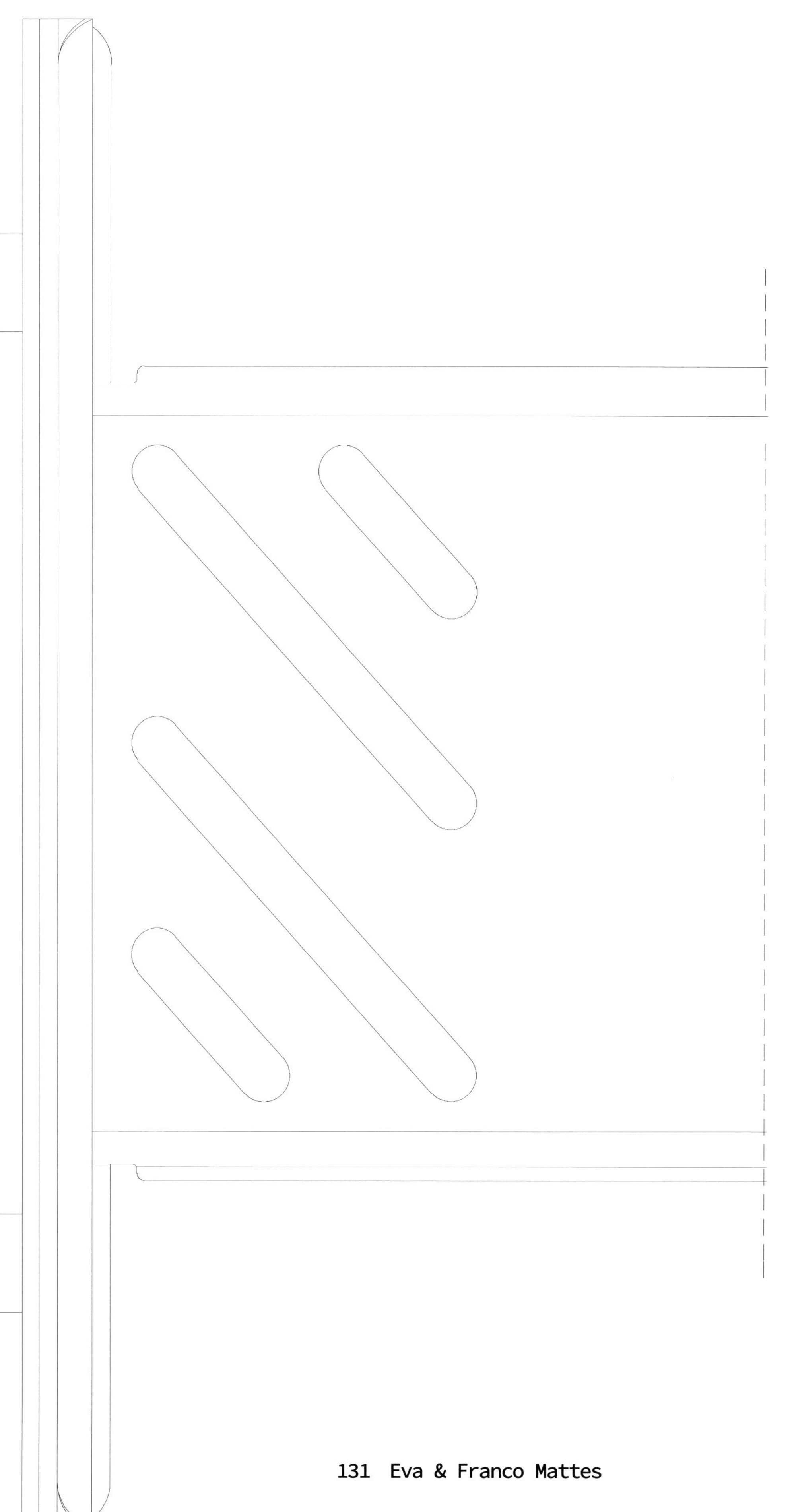

Glossary A–Z

Algorithm

An algorithm is a set of instructions that define the exact steps by which a computer program or a piece of software executes tasks.

Algorithms determine what you see on the internet: for example, when you do an online search for a computer game, the ordering of the web pages that are displayed is specified by an algorithm.

App(lication)

A computer program that is already installed on a device (especially on mobile devices like smartphones and tablets) or can be downloaded as an add-on feature.

Apps include image-editing software, computer games, email programs, etc.

Avatar

Avatars are graphical representations, animations and caricatures that users can choose and create online, in video games, on community websites like Second Life, in internet forums or on social media, in the form of virtual game characters and action figures or online personalities.

The term was originally coined by US American author Neal Stephenson in his science-fiction novel *Snow Crash* (1992), with its depictions of proxy graphical characters in the metaverse, a fictional virtual world on the internet.

Avatars can often be fully configured and edited – they range from humanoid figures to animals and fantasy creatures. While some are only deployed as 2D images, others can be run as 3D models (CGI) in virtual worlds, where they can communicate, act and interact in real time. Even though avatars can operate as virtual proxies, they allow users to conceal their true identity by retreating behind an anonymous persona and fantasy projections.

Big Brother

In the context of today's online culture, the term Big Brother stands for a totalitarian surveillance apparatus (state or private) that is able to access all our public and private information by monitoring, collecting and analysing the data we leave behind online with every Google search, every bank transaction and every "like" on social media.

The term was first coined by George Orwell in his dystopian novel *1984*, a fictional account of a surveillance system that is ever-present yet remains invisible – an idea inspired by the figure of the Soviet dictator Stalin.

The expression was popularised by the reality TV show *Big Brother*, in which a group of people living together under the constant eye of video cameras enact their day-to-day lives as a form of extrovert exhibitionism that caters to the voyeuristic gaze of an international TV audience.

Bot

A bot – the word is derived from robot – is an automated computer program that can carry out repetitive tasks on its own.

In recent years, the "social bots" that are used on social media platforms like Facebook and Twitter have made headlines.

Taking the form of human actors and disguised behind fake profiles, social bots are programmed to respond automatically to particular keywords by liking, commenting on and sharing posts or even publishing content themselves.

They are increasingly being used as part of election campaigns and to spread misinformation.

"Chat bots", meanwhile, are designed to communicate interactively with users by means of a text-based dialogue system, and search engine bots, or "web crawlers", automatically trawl the internet looking for websites that they can then index and make findable via the Google search function. Bots thus encroach significantly on our everyday lives and play a major part in how information circulates online.

Computer-generated imagery (CGI)

Computer-generated imagery, or CGI for short, is a term drawn from the world of film production. CGI is not recorded with a (film or photo) camera but computer-generated as two- or three-dimensional graphic images (computer graphics) and set in motion (computer animation). CGI is used in films, video games, art and advertising - it is also deployed in other areas, such as medical imaging, simulations or 3D-architectural models. The first developments in photorealistic CGI - and thus the computer's evolution as a visual medium modelled on photography - date back to advances made in the 1970s that were largely driven by the film industry, especially in the area of special effects.

Computational photography

Computational imaging systems, based on software and algorithms, have become an important part of today's digital and smartphone cameras. One simple example is the common panorama function available on smartphone apps and digital cameras, where an algorithm calculates and puts together multiple images into a seamless continuous picture. More complex use of computation in photography can be found in so-called machine vision and machine learning algorithms. These are programs that analyse the image data and draw out specific information. Think of current software that recognises faces or detects objects, auto-editing tools or (face) filters that modify the live camera feed of one's smartphone on apps like Snapchat and Instagram. Augmented Reality, Virtual Reality and computer-generated images are all examples of how computation and software extend and transform photography and our understanding of it.

Content moderation

Every day millions of photos are uploaded to social media. This includes material that is violent, pornographic and offensive. To filter this out as quickly as possible, internet giants like Facebook, YouTube, Google or Twitter employ people - so-called content moderators - to click through the content and clean up the visible interface by removing images of violence, torture, suicide, terrorism, rape or child pornography. These moderators need to decide in a matter of seconds what kind of material they are dealing with and whether it violates guidelines. Often contracted via external companies and working from developing and emerging economies, workers need to sign a non-disclosure agreement and receive low wages. Due to the lack of psychological support and their exposure to deeply disturbing images, they are prone to post-traumatic stress disorder.

Darknet

The darknet is often characterised as the "shady side of the internet". Unlike the internet we use on a day-to-day basis, which is available to anyone with a standard browser and whose content is findable using search engines like Google, the darknet can only be accessed with the help of special software. The so-called Tor browser, which enables access, ensures that the data traffic is fully encrypted. This means that all activities can be carried out anonymously and are untraceable, which is why the darknet regularly makes the headlines owing to its association with criminal activities such as drug trafficking and arms dealing, pirate copying and offensive content. The anonymity and invisibility it affords also benefit activists, whistle-blowers and journalists. Finally the darknet is used by some artists as a material repository or even as an exhibition space.

Data images

A photographic image shot with a smartphone or a modern-day camera or captured as a screenshot is digital. It consists of electronic data stored in the form of a binary code made up of zeros and ones, which appear on the screen as a photograph thanks to algorithms - precisely defined series of instructions on the basis of which a computer program will carry out specific tasks step by step.

An image file also stores additional data that is invisible to the eye, so-called metadata.
Metadata provides information, for example, about the date and time a photograph was taken and the geographical coordinates of where it was shot.
This means that when we circulate images, we give away more information about ourselves than we are usually aware of.
It is common for massive amounts of image data to accumulate on our digital devices over a period of decades.
Although this may seem immaterial, the storage depends on space and material objects like hardware and infrastructure, in turn having a major ecological impact on the environment.

Face filters/ Augmented Reality

Face filters like the ones provided by Snapchat are Augmented Reality (AR) applications that allow us to insert virtual filters onto our face in real time when taking a selfie.
AR is a technology that enables users to visually connect the real world with virtual objects, either by superimposing computer-generated objects on a real space or conflating the two in a process of fusion. For this reason, AR is also known as Enhanced Reality or Mixed Reality.
The hybrid nature of AR distinguishes it from Virtual Reality (VR). While AR supplements reality, VR is a complete simulation of the visible environment, immersing users in the feeling of being in another world.
AR has become a familiar feature of modern life in the form of the Nintendo mobile game *Pokémon Go*, which became a global craze in 2016, or smart glasses such as Google Glass, a product that was released on the US market as a beta version in 2014.
AR is also used in engineering, medicine, advertising, art and entertainment as well as in the military industry.

Generation Y (Millennials) and Generation Z

Generation Y (Gen Y, for short) or Millennials are people born between the early 1980s and late 1990s.
On the one hand, this group is regarded as having a tendency to question (the letter Y standing metaphorically for Why?), while, on the other, they are also considered to be "digital natives" who grew up in the internet age and are characterised by an affinity for technology.
Most of them got to know the World Wide Web, MP3 players, SMS messaging, mobile phones, smartphones and tablet PCs in their late teens.
The defining historical events for this generation are the Columbine High School shootings (1999), the terrorist attacks of 11 September 2001, the war in Afghanistan (from 2001 on), the introduction of the euro (2002), the Iraq War (2003), the tsunami disaster (2004) and various financial crises.
Generation Z (Gen Z, for short), which is assigned to the period from 2000 onwards, usually have an intuitive edge over older generations in terms of digital technologies and platforms, as they were born into pre-existing digital infrastructures – smartphones, Web 2.0 – and grew up using them and seeing them evolving. Gen Z is also seen as becoming increasingly politicised, especially in relation to issues like climate change activism and the #BlackLivesMatter movement.

GIF

The Graphics Interchange Format, or GIF for short, is an image file that is compressed in size and can thus be distributed more quickly.
In the first years of the internet around 1990, GIFs became the standard format for colour images. While the JPEG format took over in 1993 and is more commonly used today, the advantage of the GIF was that several individual images, overlaid on one another, could be stored in a single file and displayed in web browsers as animations.
Thus, they were often used in static websites as moving images.
This helped GIFs make a comeback in the 2010s. Similar to memes, animated GIFs first gained currency on image-sharing platforms and internet forums, before spreading to social media as a means of communication and later shared through instant messaging systems like WhatsApp from the late 2010s on.

GIFs are sent as comments, emotional reactions, quotes or purely for entertainment, often making reference to current events or showing people from popular culture.

Gig economy/ Crowdsourcing

The gig economy is the outsourcing of minor, short-term jobs to independent self-employed contractors, freelancers or those in marginal employment. Online platforms are often used to make it easier for companies to contact contract workers. Some prominent examples here are private transport services like Uber or food delivery couriers such as Deliveroo and Foodora. The people operating these platforms often take a commission, while the workers have to provide their own resources up front, such as mobile phones and vehicles, in order to do the job. Services of all kinds are offered via the gig economy - from social media marketing to financial accounting and logo design. Through crowdsourcing, companies often outsource certain tasks to a distributed group of users. Although gig working is a simple and flexible way of making extra money, it comes under fire for the poor conditions that people must often work in and the lack of any benefits like health, unemployment or pension insurance.

Hardware

Hardware, as distinct from software, refers to all the components in a computer that manifest physically, i.e. all the material components - both mechanical and electronic - of a desktop PC or laptop, including the screen, keyboard, hard disk, graphics card and power cable.

Imaginary audience

The term describes a psychological state in which a person imagines and is convinced that their every action is being watched by an audience. The condition was first described in 1967 by child psychologist David Elkind, who observed how some people, especially teenagers, are unable to properly distinguish between their own ego and the outside world and thus transfer the formation of their thoughts and sense of self-worth onto external figures. The conjuring up of an imaginary audience, which can happen to people of all ages, has become reality to some degree for all users of social media and online communities: the content that we share on these platforms is directed at an audience whose actual composition and reach we do not know - we thus increasingly internalise the view and opinions of an imaginary audience and define our self-image (and self-esteem) on the basis of external reactions.

In-game photography

The term in-game photography refers to screenshots taken while playing a video game, which has become an art genre in its own right. Video games as entertainment and experiential spaces often develop in association with the film industry, therefore spawning image worlds that strive towards photorealism. Numerous players roam these digital game worlds not to follow the actual game instructions but rather focusing entirely on landscapes, portraits or architectures, very much in the mould of traditional photography. Meanwhile, many games, and even the controllers, have a built-in photo mode that allows people to take screenshots and share them online. For example, at the touch of a button, Spiderman can take a selfie on PlayStation 4 that can be stored and viewed in a digital album. This transforms the characters adopted by the gamers, also known as avatars, into virtual photographers.

Instant messaging

As the name suggests, instant messaging involves the quick dispatch of pictures and short text and voice messages via apps like WhatsApp. It has now largely superseded SMS and MMS.

Make-up tutorials

Social media is used to circulate short user-generated videos that serve as tutorials providing a step-by-step explanation of a particular topic or operation. Make-up tutorials represent a popular format for introducing cosmetic products and techniques and have now established themselves as a discrete genre with a specific community on a wide range of platforms. Owing to its uncontroversial, nondescript content, this popular online format is increasingly being used to put out veiled political messages whose content would otherwise become subject to censorship and be deleted.

The users thus provide information not only about lip gloss and eyeshadow but also about government abuses and political impropriety: an example here is a make-up tutorial in summer 2020 by US Congresswoman Alexandria Ocasio-Cortez that was distributed by *Vogue* and contained a feminist, political message.

Memes

Memes are mostly humorous images and videos that are shared and edited by users of social media.

In most cases, they are humorous, ironic or caustic comments on social, political and cultural issues or current affairs. They can be made with the help of a meme generator, which can crop the images (mostly sourced from the internet) into a rectangular form and overlay them with a short text, usually written in the Impact typeface. The most popular animal used for memes is the cat. The furry feline appears, for example, as *lolcat* (derived from the abbreviation LOL, or "laugh out loud", and the word cat) or as *ceiling cat.*

The term meme is derived from the Greek word *mimēma* ("imitate") and was coined by the evolutionary biologist Richard Dawkins in *The Selfish Gene* in 1976. In the wake of digitisation, this definition was eventually used to describe the viral internet phenomena of image-text creations.

Networked image

The networked image represents a significant shift in the evolution of photography and its modes of usage. While its analogue predecessor was mostly distributed in printed form - as a print on paper, glass or metal, or a copy in newspapers, magazines and books or on posters - the networked image is a photograph recorded with a digital camera, a smartphone, drones, scans or surveillance cameras - or, in the case of memes, GIFs and computer-generated images (CGI), created entirely digitally and circulated online on social media.

The technical precondition is the combination of camera and image processing with the internet, allowing photos to be disseminated via digital networks and platforms immediately or just after they have been taken.

Capturing a moment in time is no longer the primary reason for taking a photo; rather, it is more about communicating and sharing, which is why the networked image is also called the "distributed image" or "conversational image".

Online community

An online community is an organised group of people who communicate and interact with each other in virtual spaces online. They organise themselves via social media, photo-sharing platforms, internet forums, and through avatars on websites and in video games.

Reaction video/ Attention economy

A reaction video is typically posted online on social media. Instead of showing the actual event, it consists of a series of different people reacting to what has been filmed. While these videos have their origins in the Japanese TV shows of the 1970s, they mainly circulate today on the popular video platform YouTube.

The emotions of the people on camera, which may range from laughter to disgust, pity and fear, are relayed to the viewers, making the videos part of the attention economy and an apt expression of it, as attention is turned into a good that can be exploited within a value-added chain. Converted into a lucrative resource, an economic asset and form of social currency, spectatorship is thus integrated more strongly than ever into capitalist cycles.

Our likes, clicks and shares fuel this system and ultimately make us complicit in it.

Screenshot

The screenshot, a snapshot of a screen, freezes a moment at the touch of a button or the push of a key just like a digital or analogue camera and is therefore considered a photographic medium.
The screenshot function is written into the software and can be recorded by almost any screen-based electronic device – be it a computer, smartphone or game console.
It can be saved as a file, copied to the clipboard, printed directly or immediately shared online.
We are often unaware of the degree to which screenshots determine and organise our everyday lives. Whether as a reminder of recipe ingredients for a trip to the shops, the next train connection, the description of a route on a journey where there is no mobile data access or a snapshot from our last video phone call, screenshots are an integral part of our networked culture today.

Second Life

The virtual online world Second Life was released by Linden Lab in 2003. It gives users the opportunity to design their own 3D environments and to inhabit them as avatars, i.e. virtual alter egos.
Users can communicate and interact with one another via their avatars and even offer services and goods that can be traded with a specially created currency.
They can also team up to design their environment and individual look.
This provides anonymity, while also enabling virtual interest groups to come together, particularly in the area of role play.
Second Life's international reach and unrestricted scope for creativity mean that it has also been discovered by artists and is widely used in the art world. Once one of the largest online communities, Second Life has, however, seen its number of active users and media presence diminish significantly in recent years.

Selfie

Derived from the word "self", the selfie is a picture that shows the face of the photographer, who has typically taken the photo themselves using a smartphone held at arm's length.
People upload and send selfies via apps like Instagram or WhatsApp, a phenomenon that took off with the emergence of social media in the 2010s.
The selfie is not to be confused with the traditional photographic self-portrait but should rather be seen in the context of the networked image and as a contemporary means of communication.
It forms part of a larger social or even economic network that generates its own iconography and practices.
For this reason, the US American political scientist Jodi Dean also describes the selfie as the "imitation of others and our imitation of each other".
In this way, selfies (re-)produce ideas of culture, social class or gender in the digital realm.

Sharing

Sharing is a popular practice in the internet era. Networked images are often produced and post-processed with the aim of sharing them with friends, specific communities or an anonymous audience.
This content is disseminated – uploaded, liked and shared – via photo-sharing platforms like Flickr (2004), photoblogs (e.g. WordPress, 2005), social media networks like Facebook (2004), Twitter (2006), Instagram (2010) and TikTok (2016) or instant messaging apps like WhatsApp (2009) and Snapchat (2011).
Photosharing came out of what was called Web 2.0 (2004), which made it possible to actively share content on the World Wide Web.
As a result, much of what was once shared only in the private sphere has shifted to a (semi-)public space – sometimes without there being any kind of conscious decision behind it.

Smartphone photography

There is scarcely any other medium that is as firmly anchored in our everyday lives as smartphone photography.

We use it to store information and capture important moments in our lives, sharing quickly and effortlessly the pictures we take with our family, friends and online contacts. Developments over the past thirty years have made this possible, from Toshiba's first mobile phone in 1999 with a built-in low-resolution camera, to the image-based MMS (Multimedia Messaging Service) which evolved from the SMS (Short Message Service) at the end of the 2000s, to the emergence of the web-enabled smartphone with Apple's first iPhone in 2007 that had a built-in 2 megapixel digital camera. This combination of mobile cameras and social media apps or instant messaging systems like WhatsApp, which allow direct access to online distribution channels, has led to an unprecedented degree of circulation of photographic images.

Social Media

Social media are digital platforms that make it possible for users to have contact with each other virtually and to create and distribute their own content (images, texts, videos, etc.), so-called "user-generated content".
Social media platforms include Facebook, Instagram, Snapchat, TikTok, Twitter and YouTube. By virtue of these platforms, photographs and videos have had a decisive impact on our lives and our society: they have made it possible for us to involve family and friends in our everyday lives, independent of time and place, quickly, easily and more or less in real time. Networked images put us in a new position, whereby we are simultaneously producers, consumers and distributors, while they spawn new forms of visual communication, such as memes, selfies and GIFs. Our social exchange is increasingly conducted via photographic content that is posted, liked, shared, screenshotted, downloaded, reprocessed and circulated.

Software

Software refers to all the programs on a computer. It controls the computer and issues commands. Common examples are the Microsoft Office software package, including Word, Excel and PowerPoint, or the Adobe image- and video-editing software.

User

The term user not only refers to people operating networked devices like computers, laptops, tablets and smartphones but also anyone making use of digital apps, online communities and social media. Since users can take on different roles – as passive followers (following people, institutions and companies on social media), as gamers or as bloggers or vloggers (active authors and editors of text and video posts), their online activity can assume a variety of different forms.

Virtual

The term virtual denotes images and worlds – Second Life, for example – that are generated in the computer and either simulate reality in photorealistic terms or, depending on the technical options available, can be designed as desired to suit the promptings of one's fantasy and imagination.

Web 2.0

Web 2.0 – often referred to as the "Participative Web" or "Social Web" – was first popularised in the mid-2000s: it opened the door to user-generated content and allowed people to exchange ideas with an online community within the context of social media. In terms of internet usage, this constituted a significant modification of the first-generation internet, the Web 1.0 era, in which users were initially restricted to passively viewing content offered by website operators. Examples of Web 2.0 features include social media platforms like Facebook, Twitter and Instagram, collaboratively created online encyclopaedias such as Wikipedia, tagging systems – which index keywords on websites and in links –, video-sharing sites like YouTube, image-sharing sites like Flickr and participative web applications.

Further terms relating to contemporary forms of photography and its history can be found as a timeline and glossary at www.photographic-flux.com, a project by Fotomuseum Winterthur.

Images / Credits

Book covers
    Front: *Half Cat*, 2020. Photo: Delfino Sisto Legnani
    Back: *My Generation*, 2010, installation view Fotomuseum Winterthur, 2017.
        Photo: Christian Schwager

Half Cat, 2020, taxidermy cat, 42 x 15 x 24 cm
    p. 12 "Half Cat" meme, anonymous
    p. 13 "Half Cat" original photograph, anonymous
    p. 14 Photo: Delfino Sisto Legnani

Ceiling Cat, 2016, taxidermy cat, 56 x 13 x 20 cm, custom-made hole, 13 x 13 cm
Collection of the San Francisco Museum of Modern Art (SFMOMA)
    p. 22 Photo: Katherine Du Tiel
    p. 23 "Ceiling Cat" meme, anonymous
    p. 24 Installation view Team Gallery, Los Angeles, 2019. Photo: Jeff McLane
    p. 25 Google image search for "Ceiling Cat"
    p. 26-27 Installation view Open Data Institute, London, 2018.
        Photo: Theo McInnes

The Bots, 2020, customized OKA desks, monitors, videos, headphones,
various cables
    p. 30-31, 40 Screenshots from *The Bots (Greek)*, featuring Bobbi Salvör Menuez
    p. 32, 42-43 Screenshots from *The Bots (Italian)*, featuring Ruby McCollister
    p. 33, 39 Screenshots from *The Bots (Arab)*, featuring Jake Levy

Dark Content, 2015, customized IKEA desks, monitors, videos, headphones,
various cables
    p. 41 YouTube screenshot
    p. 44-45 Installation views Carroll/Fletcher Gallery, London, 2016.
        Photo: Julian Abrams
    p. 46-47 Installation views BAK, Utrecht, 2018. Photo: Tom Janssen

Abuse Standards Violations, 2016-, UV prints on plexiglass,
100 x 100 cm and 100 x 150 cm each, various insulation materials, spacers, screws
    p. 50, 58-59 Installation views PHI Foundation for Contemporary Art,
        Montréal, 2019. Photo: Melania Dalle Grave for DSL Studio
    p. 51, 60 Installation views Carroll/Fletcher, London, 2016. Photo: Julian Abrams
    p. 52-57 Details from panels
    p. 61 Installation view Biennale für aktuelle Fotografie, Mannheim, 2017.
        Photo: Toni Montana

BEFNOED, 2014-, videos, monitors, custom wall brackets, various cables,
dimensions variable
    p. 64-65 Screenshots from *Balaclava Snacks*, 4:04 min.
    p. 66-67 Screenshots from *Covered Blanket*, 2:48 min.
    p. 68-69 Screenshots from *Licking Rim*, 2:22 min.
    p. 70-71, 73-75 Installation views Carroll/Fletcher, London, 2016.
        Photo: Julian Abrams
    p. 72 Installation view PNCA's Feldman Gallery, Portland, 2014.

Emily's Video, 2012, video, 15:52 min., dimensions variable
    p. 78-83 Screenshots from video
    p. 84-85 Installation view PHI Foundation for Contemporary Art, Montréal, 2019.
        Photo: Melania Dalle Grave for DSL Studio

Personal Photographs, 2019-, cable tray, ethernet cables, digital images,
Raspberry Pi single-board computers, micro SD cards, USB flash drives,
custom software, dimensions variable
    p. 88-89 Installation views Careof, Milan, 2019.
        Photo: Delfino Sisto Legnani & Melania Dalle Grave for DSL Studio
    p. 90-92 Installation views PHI Foundation for Contemporary Art,
        Montréal, 2019. Photo: Melania Dalle Grave for DSL Studio
    p. 93 Installation view Team Gallery, Los Angeles, 2019. Photo: Jeff McLane
    p. 94 142 image files from September 2009, screenshot
    p. 95 Imagesync.sh software, screenshot

Portraits, 2006–2007, prints on canvas
    p. 102–103 *Jeanne Varun*, 91 x 122 cm
    p. 104–105 *Nyla Cheeky*, 91 x 122 cm
    p. 106–107 *Taba Asturias* (detail), 87 x 114 cm
    p. 108–109 *13 Most Beautiful Avatars*, installation view Postmasters Gallery,
        New York, 2006.

Hannah Uncut, 2021, video, dimensions variable,
Collection Fotomuseum Winterthur
    p. 114–123 Screenshots from video

Fotomuseum Winterthur

Director: Nadine Wietlisbach
Managing Director: Remo Longhi
Exhibition Curators: Doris Gassert, Fabio Paris
Exhibition Assistant: Mona Schubert
Exhibition Organisation: Therese Seeholzer
Research Curator: Doris Gassert
Digital Curator: Marco De Mutiis
Assistant Curator: Mona Schubert
Art Handling, Registrars: Andrea Hadem, Herbert Weber
Communication: Julia Sumi
Creative Technologist: Fernando Obieta
Partnerships/Memberships: Corinna Köhler
Fundraising: Sabine Otto
Administration: Brigitte Boateng-Knapp (Head), Nadine Kaiser
Accounting/Personnel Administration: Monique Ursprung
Front-of-House Coordination: Rita Capaul, Deliah Keller
Museum Shop: Evelyn Huber
Museum Technicians: Maurus Ambühl, Helene Rüegger
Installation Team: Ueli Alder, Bea Dörig, Christian Eberhard, Andrea Hadem,
    Flavio Hodel, Benedikt Redmann (Exhibition Technician), Elio Ricca,
    Andrea Züllig, Herbert Weber (Head of Installations)
Interns: Lucinda Grange, Laura Kneisel, Neve Regli
Art Education: Carol Baumgartner (Head of Digital Art Education),
    Luisa Baselgia, Madleina Deplazes, Saada Elabed, Catharina Hanreich,
    Janis Huber (Project Leader/Communication *From Print to Pixel*), Vicky Kiefer
    (Research Associate Art Education), Annina Oliveri, Katharina Rippstein,
    Christina Schmidt (Head of Art Education)
Library: Céline Brunko, Matthias Gabi (Head)

Acknowledgment

Eva & Franco Mattes would like to thank Doris Gassert, Fabio Paris,
Nadine Wietlisbach, Mona Schubert and all the Fotomuseum Winterthur staff,
Cory Arcangel, Clément Chéroux, Jodi Dean, Katrina Sluis,
Studio Achermann (Beda Achermann, Yves Gerteis), Vanessa Thill, Matteo Cremonesi,
Postmasters Gallery, New York (Magdalena Sawon, Tamas Banovich),
Team Gallery, Los Angeles (José Freire, Nico Dregni), Todd Von Ammon,
Jonathon Carroll, Steve Fletcher, Matt Nightingale, Jean-Yves Noblet,
Delfino Sisto Legnani, Melania Dalle Grave, Adrian Chen, Callum Leo Hughes, DIS,
Jake Levy, Ruby McCollister, Bobbi Salvör Menuez, Alain Servais, Carlo Clerici,
Andrea Lancini, Matteo Ghidoni, Tonki, Marco Fogliata, Sandino Scheidegger,
Tina Rivers Ryan, Rika Fujiki, Martina Angelotti, Stefano Raimondi, Erandy Vergara,
Cheryl Sim, Kendra Jayne Patrick, Matteo Lucchetti, Fabian Knierim,
Mack McFarland, Alana Kushnir, David Huerta, Christiane Paul, Omar Kholeif,
David Horvitz, Kai&Ian.

This book is published to coincide with the exhibition
Eva & Franco Mattes. Dear Imaginary Audience,
at Fotomuseum Winterthur, 23 January – 24 May 2021.

Eva & Franco Mattes. Dear Imaginary Audience,
was kindly supported by Ernst and Olga Gubler-Hablützel Stiftung
and the Friends' Association Fotomuseum Winterthur.

Colophon

Editors: Doris Gassert, Fabio Paris, Mona Schubert, Fotomuseum Winterthur
Editorial Team: Doris Gassert, Mona Schubert
Concept Design: Studio Achermann, Zurich
Design: Studio Achermann, Zurich (Yves Gerteis, Carolina Sanches)
Authors: Cory Arcangel, Clément Chéroux, Jodi Dean, Doris Gassert, Fabio Paris,
    Mona Schubert, Katrina Sluis, Nadine Wietlisbach
Translations: Simon Cowper (from German), Angela Kent (from French),
    Anne Carruthers (from Italian)
Copyediting and proofreading: Simon Cowper, Doris Gassert, Mona Schubert,
    Therese Seeholzer, Vanessa Thill
Printing: Offsetdruckerei Karl Grammlich GmbH

The book was conceived in close collaboration with Eva & Franco Mattes.

Fotomuseum Winterthur
Grüzenstrasse 44+45
CH-8400 Winterthur
www.fotomuseum.ch

Spector Books
Harkortstrasse 10, D-04107 Leipzig
www.spectorbooks.com

Distribution
Germany, Austria: GVA, Gemeinsame Verlagsauslieferung Gottingen GmbH & Co. KG,
www.gva-verlage.de; Switzerland: AVA Verlagsauslieferung AG, www.ava.ch;
France, Belgium: Interart Paris, www.interart.fr; UK: Central Books Ltd,
www.centralbooks.com; USA, Canada, Central and South America, Africa, Asia:
ARTBOOK/D.A.P., www.artbooks.com; Australia, New Zealand: Perimeter Distribution,
www.perimeter-distribution.com

The German edition of this book was also published by Spector Books
under the following ISBN: 978-3-95905-472-0

First edition
Printed in Germany
ISBN 978-3-95905-477-5